REINVENTING THE WORKPLACE

REINVENTING THE WORKPLACE
Second Edition

Edited by John Worthington
DEGW PLC
Porters North, 8 Crinan Street,
London N1 9SQ

AMSTERDAM • BOSTON • HEIDELBERG • LONDON • NEW YORK • OXFORD
PARIS • SAN DIEGO • SAN FRANCISCO • SINGAPORE • SYDNEY • TOKYO

Architectural Press is an imprint of Elsevier

ELSEVIER

Architectural
Press

Architectural Press is an imprint of Elsevier
Linacre House, Jordan Hill, Oxford OX2 8DP
30 Corporate Drive, Suite 400, Burlington, MA 01803

First published 1997
Reprinted 1998
Transferred to digital printing 2003
Second edition 2006

Permissions may be sought directly from Elsevier's Science & Technology Rights Department in Oxford,
UK: phone: (+44) 1865 843830, fax: (+44) 1865 853333, e-mail: permissions@elsevier.co.uk. You may also
complete your request on-line via the Elsevier homepage (http://www.elsevier.com), by selecting
'Customer Support' and then 'Obtaining Permissions'

British Library Cataloguing in Publication Data
A catalogue record for this book is available from the British Library

Library of Congress Cataloguing in Publication Data
A catalogue record for this book is available from the Library of Congress

ISBN-13: 978-0-7506-6175-1
ISBN-10: 0-7506-6175-5

For information on all Architectural Press publications
visit our website at www.architecturalpress.com

Printed and bound in Great Britain

05 06 07 08 09 10   10 9 8 7 6 5 4 3 2 1

CONTENTS

FOREWORD

FRANCIS DUFFY
DEGW Founder

09 May 2005

The first edition of John Worthington's prescient collection of papers — it is hard to believe that they were published as long as ten years ago — brought into focus a series of penetrating insights into the changing nature of the physical landscape of office work, the outline of which was beginning to emerge at that time. In this second and completely reorganised and rewritten edition, a mixture of new and revised papers captures the same high level of acuity and excitement. However, the developments described in these pages bring to the current lively debate on the new workplace an entirely new layer of maturity, reflection and study, based firmly on a wide variety of global, first-hand experiences. These essays are a robust corroboration of what may soon be generally seen as the most important step change in the nature of work since the Industrial Revolution. This new revolution will affect not just workplace design but, much more importantly, will transform our understanding of the relationship between work and life.

The great agent of change which makes new ways of working inevitable is, of course, information technology, the power, reliability and robustness of which are already evident in their impact not only on work processes within the office but on every train, in every airport lounge, at every street corner, and in every classroom, library and café. Office work, no longer confined to office buildings, is everywhere.

The practical implications are huge. In the spatial realm, at the micro-level of the workplace, the longstanding assumption of permanent, individual ownership of workstations by office workers is being replaced by the appropriation by increasingly mobile office workers of a whole series of settings, inside and outside the office. Each of these multiple settings has specific environmental qualities appropriate to different facets of office work but all of them are bound together by an invisible network of communications. It is interesting that at the scale of the city, increasing mobility does not appear to be challenging the centripetal strength of densely networked urban centres. In fact, new ways of working are probably making such centres more attractive than they have ever been.

Nevertheless, as the industrial era's twin imperatives of co-location and synchrony are eroded, the peaking phenomenon at both ends of the working day is becoming less necessary. Rush hours have shaped the cities of the twentieth century, not to mention the lives of countless millions of commuters, through centralised and inherently inefficient urban transportation systems.

But it is not the planning of physical space in cities and offices that will be most affected by the technologically stimulated revolution described in the fascinating series of essays in this book. The real challenge is that the huge potential that is making new ways of working so attractive in so many ways to so many people could be equally abused by both employers and employees. The same technology that allows people unprecedented freedom to choose their time and place of work also opens them up to unprecedented accessibility, twenty-four hours a day, seven days a week. The ubiquitous PDA has an equal chance of becoming a symbol of freedom or of oppression.

When farm workers came down from the hills into the cobbled streets of smoky mill towns at the beginning of the nineteenth century, they were forced to abandon an ancient agricultural calendar based on the organic rhythm of climate, crops, livestock, seasons and saints' days. In exchange, they suffered a daily and weekly timetable based on the imperatives of machines which demanded from those who tended them the twin disciplines of synchrony and co-location. One temporal convention was forcibly exchanged for another. The distorted shape of our cities bears witness to the consequences. Today, at the real beginning of the Knowledge Economy, the greater challenge that faces us is not the design of the use of space, difficult as that will be both at the scale of the workplace or the city, but rather the necessity of inventing new temporal conventions that will allow us to control our new and wonderful but potentially fearsome electronic technology so that we can enjoy our newly won autonomy in creative, civilised and non-self-destructive ways.

ACKNOWLEDGEMENTS

The inspiration for the first edition of this book, published in 1997, originated with a workshop held in the summer of 1995 at the Institute of Advanced Architectural Studies, University of York. Participants included colleagues from DEGW and representatives from leading corporations, property investors, and suppliers, from as far afield as Japan.

The workshop recognised that the function of the office was in flux and that this was reflected in new work settings. In North America, Michael Joroff of MIT and Frank Becker, Professor of Facilities Management at Cornell University, had undertaken a major study for the International Development Research Council (IDRC), entitled 'Corporate Real Estate 2000: Reinventing the Workplace'. In Europe similar themes were being explored by both Workplace Forum, a knowledge sharing club co-ordinated by DEGW and the British Council of Offices (BCO).

The contributions from the workshop formed the core of the original publication with additional authors drawn from participants at Workplace Forum. To update the second edition new authors have been drawn from my colleagues at DEGW who have provided an international dimension.

Most of the chapters in the first edition have stood up well to the test of time. The greatest changes have not surprisingly, been the sections on information technology, management and procurement, and working solutions. Contributions from the first edition have been reviewed by the original authors and updated, whilst Sections 3–5 are, for the most part, entirely new contributions.

As editor, I owe a debt of gratitude to both the original and new contributors, and to my colleagues in continental Europe and North America who have been rethinking the workplace: Bill Simms and Frank Becker at Cornell University, Michael Joroff at MIT and Volker Hartkoff at Carnegie Mellon. Nearer home, Karen Mosbeck from the Danish Government Property department (SES) has energetically applied the principles of new ways of working, and Jan Ake Granath and Bo Ostrom, with their colleagues at Chalmers University of Technology, have built on the concepts of strategic briefing, space planning and change management at both the building and city scale. In The Netherlands, Hans de Jonge and

Geert Dewulf, now at the Department of Project Management and Real Estate of the Technical University Delft, established an academic curriculum and body of research that has given substance to an emerging discipline.

This collection of essays would not have been possible without the insights and energy of Frank Duffy, my co founder at DEGW, who has been the inspiration for rethinking the world of work and how it is housed and managed. This second edition, with over half the contributions from DEGW, is a testament to the practice's concern to combine reflection and action through a programme of enquiry, innovation and communication.

From the first edition, the contributions of Mick Bedford, Sam Cassels, and David Jenkins (past colleagues from DEGW) provided valuable foundations for the thinking that has continued to flourish in the practice. In the field of communications technology, Bill Southwood of Arup Communications has been an inspirational collaborator in unravelling the relation between technology, buildings and the businesses they serve. John Connor in the first edition provided a telling contribution from the viewpoint of a commentator who began his career in IBM, then moved out as an outsourced service provider at Procord and most recently has moved back to corporate real estate at Price Waterhouse Coopers (now within IBM). Finally, Steen Andersen has continued to be an advocate for the new workplace both in Denmark and outwards into the expanded European Community.

This second edition would not have been possible without the commitment and tenacity of Douglas Brown, Managing Director DEGW, and the coordination, chivvying and cheerful support of Rosemary Croal who provided the continuity for the project. Finally, Tony Flower provided speedy and effective sub-editing to meet tight deadlines and give consistency to a wide range of differing contributions.

John Worthington
Co-Founder DEGW
Graham Willis Professorship, School of Architecture, University of Sheffield

SPONSORS

DEGW is a leading strategy and design consultancy operating from twelve offices worldwide. Our international experience enables us to work with clients to develop appropriate local solutions that achieve business objectives. Our unique mix of professional skills enables us to address a wide range of design issues, from long-term real estate strategy to the practical implementation of design concepts. Our projects accommodate the implications of the changing nature of work at all scales from the workplace to the city. We use our knowledge to help our clients use space more productively, to enhance organisational performance, and to develop solutions which are flexible over time. Whether working with corporate clients, government, city planners or developers, our focus is always *design for change*.

Workplace Forum aims to advance the understanding and practice of the relationship between the built environment and organisational performance. Established in 1992, the forum provides a research and learning network focused on global best practice in workplace design, technology, and management, encourages knowledge sharing amongst senior professionals from real estate and property, IT, and HR, and develops knowledge and intelligence through research to inform better decision making.

www.degw.com

Deloitte

Most of us in business spend between 25 and 40 per cent of our time in a workplace of some description or another. We create and break important relationships, we carryout key processes, and we broker important deals. At Deloitte, we think that our activities and those of our clients in the workplace are so important that it is not only worth getting the workplace right, it is essential.

At Deloitte, we advise from experience and the advice we give our clients in creating tangible value from the workplace is no exception to this. We have to practice what we preach and in doing so, receive the benefits of productive people, high-quality work and satisfied clients. Deloitte is both a virtual organisation, able to work in any place at any time but also a real organisation catering for a diverse workforce who sometimes needs to work creatively, sometimes needs to concentrate, but always needs to deliver. We understand the value of working with professionals such as DEGW to tailor our workspace to our processes and we understand the place workplace has in any company strategy including our own.

The Real Estate Solutions Group within Deloitte works for corporate occupiers. We bring specialist property, consulting, tax and financial expertise together to assist our clients in understanding the importance of the workplace in meeting their business needs. We do not design the workplace; we leave that to the experts, what we do is help businesses to analyse their requirements for all aspects of property both their physical needs in terms of space and process and their financial needs, identifying clearly the benefits to the bottom line. Working with colleagues such as DEGW, we also plan and implement our recommendations resulting in improved and exciting workplaces for our clients. Life is short (and time in the office can be long) — why not use the workplace to help get the most out of it.

www.deloitte.com

GSK – real estate supporting effectiveness, people and culture

Since the merger four years ago, GlaxoSmithKline, one of the world's leading research-based pharmaceutical and healthcare companies, has been committed to embracing change, turning challenges into opportunities and new thinking into new ways of working to deliver its competitive advantage.

Post-merger GSK needed a global model for its estate. One that would support its new culture, express the GSK Spirit and be effective in contributing to business performance. It was with this background that GSK's Space Programme was written — a set of guiding principles for acquiring and reconfiguring space based on researching the needs and habits of GSK people themselves and how they use their workspace.

GSK are applying Space Programme on an opportunity basis globally. Consistent global principles are locally interpreted. Space Programme projects are tested with results feedback to inform the evolution of the guidelines. Treating real estate as an actively managed business resource, there to support the effectiveness of people and systematically measured for constant improvement and learning is central to GSK's philosophy towards their real estate.

www.gsk.com

Haworth

Haworth, Inc. is a world-leading designer, manufacturer and marketer of office furniture. Based in Michigan (USA), we operate in 120 countries, with over 27 manufacturing plants and more than 7600 members. To better understand the important distinctions around the world, Haworth conducts thorough market research within each of its regions, focusing upon unique customer needs and characteristics. The result is a product portfolio and service capabilities that leverage our global platform and is in alignment with market needs.

With the widest range of product solutions, Haworth is an integrator for adaptable workplaces. From floors and infrastructure to systems furniture to freestanding furniture, we can address an entire interior solution. The goal of such adaptability is to transform client's furniture from inflexible assets into strategic business tools.

As a market leader and innovator within the furniture industry, Haworth invests heavily in research and development. From extensive ergonomics research and testing to cognitive psychology, we study how furniture solutions can most enhance people's effectiveness in the workplace. It is not enough, though, to simply provide great furniture products. Cultural and workstyle distinctions also play a major role in designing the ideal office. It is necessary to align the right furniture solution to a unique set of cultural and functional needs. To address this, Haworth supports its clients with tools and services that are based upon the latest research information. And with both regionally focused design centers and branches of Haworth's Ideation Group established in various geographies, we are able to conduct localised research and product development while leveraging our global knowledge base.

www.haworth.com

CONTRIBUTORS

Adryan Bell
DEGW plc
www.degw.com

Director of DEGW, with global responsibilities for its workplace change management services and Government projects. Prior to joining DEGW in 1998, Adryan was head of internal communications and a member of the strategic change team at Scottish Enterprise and was responsible for creating its award-winning *Workplace for the Future* project.

George Cairns
University of Essex
www.essex.ac.uk

Professor of Management at Essex Management Centre, University of Essex, UK. George Cairns is an architect and has developed his research interest in the workplace to embrace the separate but related organisational, technological, physical and social environments of work.

James Calder
DEGW plc
www.degw.com

Managing Director of DEGW Asia-Pacific, James joined DEGW in London in 1991 where he worked on a wide variety of research and consultancy projects for clients such as British Telecom, Goldman Sachs and Heathrow Airports. Since returning to Australia to establish DEGW Asia-Pacific in 1996, he has been responsible for strategic briefing, building appraisal and user-led research studies as well as managing the business in the region.

Nicolla M. Gillen
DEGW plc
www.degw.com

Associate Director, DEGW, working in workplace strategy with a great interest in research environments. Nicolas joined DEGW in 1998 and works across the business in workplace strategy, urban planning and design. She is the account manager for GlaxoSmithKline, which encompasses a wide range of activities from Workplace Guidelines, to research environments to change management.

Rob Harris
Ramidus Consulting Limited
robharris@ramidus.co.uk

Dr Rob Harris specialises in advising clients on their occupational needs. He has previously worked with DEGW, CBRE, Stanhope Properties and ISG plc. In 2003, he established Ramidus Consulting Limited to undertake client consulting and research work.

Andrew Harrison
DEGW plc
www.degw.com

Director in charge of DEGW's worldwide research and methods activities. Previous projects have included intelligent buildings research projects in Europe, Southeast Asia and Latin America. Andrew was responsible for the major study funded by The European Commission on Sustainable Accomodation for the New Economy (SANE), carried out from 2001 to 2003 and published in 2004 as *The Distributed Workplace*.

Mychelle Hynd
Scottish Enterprise
www.scottish-enterprise.com

Senior Manager at Scottish Enterprise involved in creating and delivering organisational change. Michelle is active in providing advice to a broad spectrum of organisations on workplace change and relocation matters and focused her research on the environments of workplace and associated changes in achieving her PhD and MBA.

John Hinks
Royal Bank of Scotland Plc
www.rbs.co.uk

Dr John Hinks is the Innovation Manager, RBS Group Workplace Operations. He joined the Royal Bank of Scotland from Glasgow Caledonian University where he had been Professor of Facilities Management. Previously, Reader in Facilities Management at Heriot-Watt University, John has been closely involved with the consolidation of the FM profession in the UK, and with the development of the global FM research community.

Despina Katsikakis
DEGW plc
www.degw.com

Group Chairman of DEGW plc. Trained as an architect, Despina's primary speciality is working with occupiers and developers to deliver innovative real estate solutions that enhance business performance. Despina is chairman of the global DEGW group, providing strategic direction for its ongoing development.

Andrew Laing
DEGW plc
www.degw.com

Dr. Andrew Laing is the Managing Director of DEGW North America. With over fifteen years of experience at DEGW, he combines an interest in research into the design and use of the workplace with active involvement in client relationships.

DEGW is now recognised as North America's leading consulting group in workplace strategy. Since establishing the North American office, Andrew has worked with many significant corporations including, Accenture, Fidelity, Google, GlaxoSmithKline, Microsoft and the United Nations. He is a co-author of *New Environments for Working* and *The Responsible Workplace*.

Adrian Leaman
Building Studies Limited
www.usablebuildings.co.uk

Adrian Leaman specialises in understanding the behaviour, attitudes and problems affecting building users from the users' point of view.

He has carried out groundbreaking research on health in buildings and productivity in buildings, and has contributed to the renowned Probe series of post-occupancy studies. As well as running Building Use Studies (BUS) and a research and consultancy company, he is also secretary of the Usable Building Trust, a charity devoted to disseminating the results from post-occupancy studies to practice and education.

Juriaan van Meel
Delft University of Technology
www.tudelft.nl

Dr. Juriaan van Meel is an Assistant Professor at the Department of Real Estate & Housing of Delft University of Technology (www.re-h.nl). He specialises in briefing and office design. Juriaan is also partner at ICOP, a Dutch real estate consultancy firm (www.icop.nl). He has written a number of articles and books on office design, including *The Office, the Whole Office and Nothing but the Office* (1999) and *The European Office* (2000). His co-authors are Hans de Jonge, Professor of Real Estate Management and Development at Delft University of Technology, and Geert Dewulf, Professor of Planning and Development at Twente University in the Netherlands.

Lora Nicolaou
DEGW plc
www.degw.com

Lora Nicolaou trained originally as an architect, followed by post-graduate study in urban design. She currently holds the position of Director of Development Planning at DEGW. Her work has focused on Urban Strategies, Briefing and Design, both at city- and site-specific levels. Recent work includes city strategies for Rotterdam, Dublin, Cambridge, Utrecht, Hereford and London and a number of estate strategies for the private and public sectors including health and education. Lora is a CABE enabler and has taught at Oxford Brooks University Joint Centre for Urban Design.

Philip Ross
Cordless Group
www.cordless.co.uk

Philip Ross is the CEO of the Cordless Group and editor of UNWIRED™. He is a consultant, commentator and researcher on technology and workplace futures and has pioneered research on the impact of new technologies on work, the work process and workplace. In 1994, he wrote and published *The Cordless Office Report*, and ten years on published the *Wireless Workplace Report* that looks at the impact of new technology, primarily wireless, on people's behaviour within the built environment. He has written two books on the future of the workplace, *The Creative Office* and *The 21ˢᵗ Century Office*, both co-authored with Jeremy Myerson.

Tony Thomson
DEGW plc
www.degw.com

Director of Workplace Strategies in DEGW's London consulting operations. Tony has been with the company since 1987. Using the basic methodologies of DEGW, his work has involved developing new techniques for establishing users' needs in rapidly changing organisations. Prior to joining DEGW, he was for ten years UK Property and Facilities Manager with Hewlett-Packard Ltd. He has a degree in Applied Physics and a Masters Degree in Project Management, and is a Fellow of the Institute of Facilities Management.

Barry Varcoe
Royal Bank of Scotland Plc
www.rbs.co.uk

Barry Varcoe is the Head of Group Workplace Operations and is responsible for maximising the business return from approximately £2.5billion asset value for the Royal Bank of Scotland Worldwide.

Prior to joining The Royal Bank of Scotland Plc in October 2002, Barry was Director of Global Strategic Planning and Innovation within Johnson Controls, Inc. Integrated Facility Management. This global role involved the assessment of medium- to long-term industry trends and possible futures, and their impact on and translation into business strategy, value proposition, including the research and development function.

Barry is a Fellow of both the Royal Institution of Chartered Surveyors and the British Institute of Facilities Management, and an active member of CoreNet Global and was co-chair of its recent Global Business Development task force. His career has resulted in many years' experience in building economics, real estate and facilities management.

Geoff Woodling
BusinessFutures.com
www.BusinessFutures.com

Geoff Woodling studied geography at Cambridge and later organisational behaviour at the London Business School. He specialises in business futures. Most recently, he has spent three years putting the future into practice, as Director of Commercial Innovation for Hutchison 3G Telecom, leading the establishment of their new third generation mobile networks in Sweden and Austria. This provided valuable new insights for his ongoing Real Estate Business Strategy consulting practice, which he developed with colleagues in BusinessFutures.com, the firm he founded with his partners from Stanford Research Institute where he had been a European Director in the eighties. He has recently renewed his relationship with Jones Lang LaSalle, with whom he had previously established the corporate real estate services business, to co-develop their Property Foresight Programme in Europe.

John Worthington
DEGW plc
www.degw.com

John Worthington is a founder of DEGW, and holds the Graham Willis visiting professorship in architecture at the University of Sheffield. John's specialist interests are the design and briefing process, with a specific interest in urban design and estates strategies.

The majority of John's career has been concerned with supporting business organisations and cities in making the most effective use of resources, by matching available space and buildings to changing organisational demands. He trained at the Architectural Association, London, and subsequently spent two years as a Harkness Fellow at the Universities of Pennsylvania and at the Berkeley Campus of the University of California. From 1992 to 1997, he was Professor of Architecture and Director of the Institute of Advanced Architectural Studies at the University of York.

INTRODUCTION: THE CHANGING WORKPLACE

John Worthington
Co-Founder, DEGW
Graham Willis Professorship
School of Architecture, University of Sheffield

RESPONDING TO ECONOMIC CYCLES

In the early 1980s, I startled a gathering of sixth form business studies teachers by predicting that the jobs in banking and insurance for which they were grooming their students, like the jobs in shipbuilding which they had previously promoted, might well wither away under the impact of the new information technology. Having just come to terms with education for the service economy, they were highly sceptical. Fifteen years later when *Reinventing the Workplace* was first published, we had already seen exactly that change. The financial services industries, whilst increasing its revenues, had already shrunk dramatically in terms of staff required and premises occupied. The systematic application of information and communications technology had allowed for 24 hour on-line banking and new products. Like manufacturing in the 1970s, office work was going through a fundamental restructuring as we moved from a service to a knowledge-based economy.

By 1990, white collar work in advanced European countries accounted for approximately 60 per cent of the working population. Since 1975, the number employed in manufacturing had declined by 20 per cent whilst those in the service sector had increased by 22 per cent. However, manufacturing productivity had improved dramatically compared with the service sector where productivity was almost static. After the restructuring of the early 1990s many firms realised that to stay competitive they would have to rethink the way they worked and how they used technology. Simply to superimpose the new technology on old working patterns was not yielding results. *Reinventing the Workplace* set the agenda for change and provided some examples of how leading edge companies had responded. The new paradigm of work, given the transition from a service to a knowledge economy had resulted in a radical shift in expectations. Whilst the service economy had been concerned with organising data and its products (within a road, rail and telephone infrastructure, supported by bureaucratic organisations), the knowledge economy's main asset turned out to be information and ideas, enhanced by a world-wide information and communications network within an organisational structure of communities of interest. The global production line has become a reality where, through collaborative and concurrent working, design, manufacturing, and support have become a continuous sequence undertaken in a variety of centres. Organisations are now working across space and time through fluid networks rather than a strict hierarchy of centres.

Midway through the first decade of the twenty-first century, the knowledge economy is well established. Innovative ways of working and managing corporate real estate have become accepted; computing is ubiquitous, and the 'mobile' with all the convergence of computing and communications technology that such devices depend upon, has become a key component in the knowledge worker's arsenal.

CHANGING TECHNOLOGY

Much has been written about the seductive vision of teleworking at home, from which idyllic and rural bliss one only has to venture forth occasionally for critical client meetings. The National Economic Development Office's 1986 estimate that over one million Britons would be tele-commuting by 1995 was well short of the mark.[1] By 2001, 2.2 million people in the UK (7.4 per cent of the total labour force) worked from home[2] at least one-day-a-week and used both a telephone and a computer to do their work. Just less than 50 per cent of these people are selfemployed, many running independent businesses from their homes. Around three-quarters work in the private sector, most being in professional, managerial and technical occupations. About 25 per cent of the teleworkers work in real estate, renting and business activities. The number of those working from home, both in the UK and other countries, is increasing dramatically. In Finland, the home of Nokia, 17 per cent of the workforce is classified as teleworkers, and 11 per cent are home-based workers who spend at least one-day-a-week working at home, compared with 5 per cent in the UK. From the binary vision of twenty-years ago where the choice was either being an office or a homeworker, the reality is now much more diverse: mobile technology and the internet have opened up the choice of multiple working locations, with the home as just one of many desirable locations – including hotels, trains, airports, cafes, and clients' offices. Recent US statistics[3] reveal the degree to which ICT has become accepted within the home. In 2003, approximately 62 per cent of the US households had a computer, 55 per cent with internet connections and 20 per cent using Broadband. More dramatically, the number of households with Broadband connections more than doubled from 9 to 20 per cent in the period 2001–2003. Most knowledge workers today have some form of workplace at home. As the mobility of office technology has developed, distributed work has become a reality. Corporate assets have metamorphosised from buildings and infrastructures to people and networks.

NEW REAL ESTATE OFFERS

As added value migrated from hardware to the design and servicing of products, and as knowledge became the major asset, many corporations sought to reduce risk and improve the quality of their services by outsourcing their accommodation. IBM, the leader of the computing industry through much of the twentieth century, anticipated the restructuring to a knowledge economy in the early 1990s and recognised the need to reinvent itself as a knowledge-based service provider

1999	Capitalisation	Fixed Assets	Revenues	Net Income
IBM (Founded 1911)	$214 billion	$19.6 billion	$81 billion	$6.3 billion
Microsoft (Founded 1975)	$407 billion	$1.7 billion	$19.7 billion	$7.7 billion
Amazon (Founded 1995)	$11 billion	$29 million	$609 million	($124 million)

▲ 0.1   Organisations are changing in profile and divesting themselves of inflexible real estate assets

in order to continue to compete, but found itself captured by a rigid and hard-to-shift real estate portfolio. A comparison with Microsoft illustrates the dilemma (Figure 0.1). IBM, a global company with four times the revenues, and ten times the fixed assets of Microsoft, had half of Microsoft's capitalisation and was less profitable. IBM, which, like other companies from a previous era, had viewed property as a valuable asset on their accounts but was nearly throttled by premises that turned out to be surplus to requirements. Within ten years, under the leadership of Lou Gerstner, IBM has succeeded in transforming itself into a consultancy and service provider, completely rethinking its real estate strategy along the way.

Today's model for accommodating the flexible firm is a portfolio of properties with a mixture of tenure arrangements to provide the most appropriate space at the right time.[4] The new kind of property portfolio consists of three categories of space (Figure 0.2). Core space, say 30 per cent of the holding owned or on long leases, is symbolic of the values of the organisation, providing hearth and home; Flexi-space, on short leases, in adaptable generic space, with outsourced services, responding to 30–40 per cent of the space demand thus providing the ability to respond to rapidly changing market demands as new projects are initiated while others decline; finally, space on demand such as serviced offices like Regus where work stations and meeting spaces are available on short-term licences. Moreover, some companies are now recognising the value, as they consolidate their core functions, of sharing facilities on an as-needed basis with partners. Health, catering, library, computing, meeting facilities and support services can all be shared and provided separately for up to 30 per cent of a company's accommodation needs, with potentially major savings. The resultant property offer is not just real estate combining, space, flexibility of tenure and support

'Fixed'	'Flexi'	'On demand'
• Long lease • Corporate brand • High quality • Predominantly office • Representational space • Outsourced FM	• Short lease • Provider brand • Flexible • Office • Support • Outsourced FM	• Licensed • Service brand • Ready to use • Office • Support • Service company
30%	40%	30%

▲0.2   Changing patterns of tenure and function

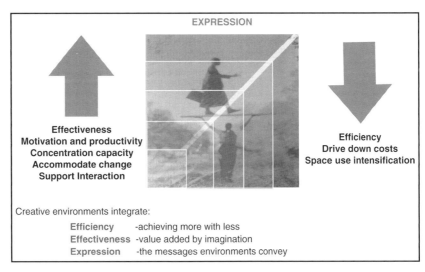

EXPRESSION

Effectiveness
Motivation and productivity
Concentration capacity
Accommodate change
Support Interaction

Efficiency
Drive down costs
Space use intensification

Creative environments integrate:

Efficiency	-achieving more with less
Effectiveness	-value added by imagination
Expression	-the messages environments convey

▲ **0.3**   Efficiency, effectiveness and expression

services, but increasingly the guarantee that the quality of amenity in the immediate neighbourhood will match the expectations of tenants (Figure 0.3). Consumers are looking for long-term partners whom they can trust, and who will provide whatever services are required to accommodate their businesses, to ensure financial, functional and physical flexibility and to increase their chances of commercial success.

Companies who recognise the value of those who work for and with them, whilst still being concerned to minimise costs through improved *efficiency,* are also seeking to improve *effectiveness* – through the quality of service and amenity provided, and through increased staff satisfaction and improved performance. Finally, through the *expression* of design, management and planning the working environment can be a potent tool for transmitting corporate messages externally and supporting creativity internally.

ACCOMMODATING THE VIRTUAL ORGANISATION

The virtual office is already a reality and is having a major impact on the type of buildings and the amount of space required. Organisations still require buildings but with a change in emphasis. External appearance as represented by great corporate iconic statements, such as ING Bank's headquarters in Amsterdam may have less relevance than providing a sense of place where corporate culture can be reinforced and staff can meet and exchange ideas. The new corporate centre is becoming a kind of corporate hearth where stories are exchanged and myths reinforced (see section 2.1). Ready Mixed Concrete's corporate headquarters in Staines, designed by Cullinan Associates, is just such an example. Developed on an historic site in the green belt, the complex provides for a small headquarters staff and is the focus where all employees can come for training, meeting and relaxation. The entrance establishes the function. On entering, staff or visitors are confronted by squash courts, a swimming pool, a magnificent view to the landscaped and flooded reclaimed gravel workings beyond and by discreet meeting places. New corporate centres are likely to be very different to the corporate palaces of previous decades.

CHALLENGES AHEAD

Designers, managers and users of the workplace are now faced with a complex and changing world in which binary choices between *options* are seldom appropriate. The issue is accommodating, often conflicting, but frequently supportive of interests. In an increasingly paradoxical world, organisations want to be both centralised and dispersed, private and collaborative, outward looking but inwardly secure, economical with resources whilst generous to employees. Standard solutions that fit all situations are rare. Greater mobility and flexibility of service allow appropriate solutions and locations to be chosen to match particular requirements. Diversity is recognised as an asset, to be achieved by a rich range of settings within flexible building shells. The societal pressures to become more environmentally, economically and socially sustainable, are being addressed through using space that already exists much more intensively. Lean thinking through shared use, extended periods of usage, yield management and parallel working are all embedded in new concepts of working. DEGW and our Dutch partners Twynstra were, for example, asked to provide a learning centre for senior managers of Shell from around the World.[5] The brief was that the facility should be within 45 minutes of drive to Schiphol airport, that it should be available from Monday evening to Thursday night, though never on Fridays nor weekends nor during the eight week summer holiday period. The centre was to have a life of only 5 years. The solution was a deal with Holiday Inn who were nearing completion of a new tourist hotel with a nine-hole golf course close to Schiphol. The hotel could use the facilities during weekends and during the 8 weeks in the summer, and would be returned the facility after 5 years. By projected logos, changing nameboards, and the construction of a small raked theatre for the formal training sessions (which became a cabaret theatre at weekends), both the parties could maximise the use of space in a simple solution that saves resources and pleases both the parties.

Changing workplaces mean continuous reappraisal of the way we work, the spaces we occupy, the technology we require and the ways in which services are delivered. For providers and their architects, the challenge is to avoid conventional solutions. Working simultaneously both physically and virtually is certain to result in workplaces that are very different from the norm.

SECTION 1
CHARTING A FUTURE

There can be few white collar workers today who have not in some way experienced the changes that are occurring in organisations and their workplaces. Since the mid-1990s 'outsourcing', 'downsizing', 'job sharing' and more recently 'nomads', 'independents' and 'team workers' have become part of the terminology of the workplace environment. Much has been written about change, but what really are the organisational outcomes and the physical characteristics of the new workplace?

Many of those concerned with charting the future argue that the only assured fact is that it is unpredictable and will inevitably change. However, pointers to the future exist today. In all sectors of business, leading edge companies are exploiting new markets, technology and know-how, and are thus a model of where others could be tomorrow. Hamal and Prahalad in Competing for the Future (Harvard Business School Press, 1994) suggest that the success of organisations, as we enter the twenty-first century, will be dependent on competing for the 'acquisition of industry foresight'.

This section sets out scenarios for the city, the real estate industry and the settings in which we work. In the future, the ability to organise the logistics of space and time will be as important as the design of buildings. The future role of real estate will be evaluated by its ability to add to business performance and support organisational change. A review of office organisations and workplace design since the turn of the century enables us to understand where we are, and to speculate on the options that lie ahead. Finally, we reflect on the more recent past to set out an agenda for the future workspace.

How fast, and in which direction, we move towards the future will depend on our ability to recognise and take creative advantage of paradigm shifts. Mankind spent generations trying to fly by strapping on complicated wings, and flapping like a bird, only to plummet to earth. It was not until we perceived that hawks actually soared on air currents that hang-gliding was invented. In our understanding of how to accommodate the changing world of work, we are poised to take advantage of many new possibilities. The first edition of this book has stood the test of time well. Ten years later what a few leading edge organisations were doing then has become mainstream.

The 'networked city' with many combining physical and virtual settings is a phenomenon which many planners have already accepted as central to the shaping of future urban environments. Established office developers are now squarely in the service business. Businesses seeking the competitive edge have embraced flexible working, as well as increased mobility and individual control. Flexible real estate strategies now really are focussed more on amenity and service than bricks and mortar.

This second edition of Reinventing the Workplace reinforces our original challenge. It is now up to office providers and office designers to respond imaginatively.

1

THE LOGISTICAL CITY

Adrian Leaman
Building Use Studies

SUMMARY

In this chapter, Adrian Leaman, a researcher and consultant who has observed the breakdown in performance of increasingly highly serviced and complex workplaces, reflects on the wider implications for the 'logistical city'. He argues that the freedoms afforded by developments in information and communications technology – to organise things to be in the right place at the right time – take over from spatial factors as the dominant constraints influencing settlement geography. The focus on 'just in time' rather than 'just in case' puts great emphasis on minimising the cost of wasted time. The result will be on greater demands for better building performance not less. Building criteria will focus on health, safety, comfort, energy efficiency, ease of management, cost of operation and above all, on flexible access by public transport.

Leaman sets an agenda for the workplace in the wider city and regional framework. He proposes that to address the workplace of the future means second-guessing change rather than merely responding to it. Current complex, high technology, energy-hungry solutions merely displace risk from the developer to society at large in the form of pollution, noise and waste. Risk/value trade-offs, through the application of continuous feedback, will become more important.

Leaman proposes that the logistical city will be characterised by time replacing space as the main factor affecting locational decisions; intensification of critical business functions in highly serviced, secure locations; waste avoidance; greater use of public transport, with less predictable journey to work patterns; more working from home; and a more dynamic and opportunistic approach to time management. This holistic view of the context for the future workplace is a major challenge for workplace planners and designers.

INTRODUCTION

This chapter deals with working environments, and how social, technical and organisational changes affecting workplaces are likely to affect buildings in the near future. It argues that we are moving into a fundamental new logistical age. It uses 'Logistical City' as shorthand for significant new trends underlying changing settlement geography. These also impact workplace and individual behaviours. It draws on a private study of foreseeable changes in the demand for energy in buildings[1] and the experience gained from post-occupancy surveys of buildings and their occupants.[2] The conclusions reflect UK conditions, but there are also wider implications.

APPROACH

In a nutshell, buildings create value (either realised or potential) for human activities which in theory should be greater than the sum of their parts. As complex systems, buildings are organised in functional layers, with large-scale, geographical characteristics like sub-region, urban infrastructure and location setting constraints which influence characteristics at smaller scales – site, shape, size, orientation, form, accessibility, height and so on. These in turn, set the context for building services, such as heating and lighting systems, which then affect conditions created for users and occupants, for example, working at desks or in workgroups. In this sense, buildings have one layer at the largest scale setting the constraints for the next level down, and then so on down the layers.[3] The layers also correspond roughly to the professions that deal with them in the planning and design process, with planning operating at the larger scales, architecture and building services in the middle and interior design at the smaller.

Too much separation between the layers usually means that a building may not work properly as a whole – the integration between different layers not being sufficiently effective. Too little separation creates conflicts between the intended functions of the spaces (affecting the activities carried out in them) and the intended functions of services (such as providing effective heating, cooling, ventilation and lighting in the right places at the right times). Where close integration fails, buildings can become unmanageable, creating vicious spirals of deterioration which are often extremely difficult to put right.

There are many examples of functional failures caused by too much or too little integration or by new constraints introduced unintentionally, including:

- 1950s and 1960s high-rise public housing in the UK, where over-reliance on single technologies such as lifts (which frequently broke down and stranded people) or even something as seemingly straightforward as electric-only heating (which many tenants could not afford) quickly became unmanageable and induced worse slums than with the high-rise dwellings replaced, because the high rises were less manageable by their occupants.
- UK office buildings of the 1960s, whose 'restricted floor-to-floor heights exaggerate the problem of inadequate building services...' thereby leading to premature obsolescence.[4]
- Historic buildings, whose 'accessibility and ownership may be much more important to their survival than the actual techniques or cost of restoration...'.[5] A perfectly serviceable building may deteriorate beyond repair solely because of factors like lack of rights of access.
- 'Sick' buildings, where chronic performance problems affecting the perceived health of building occupants are often the result of technical complexity in the building systems outrunning the capabilities of occupiers to afford to manage them effectively.
- Vandalism, which may start in a relatively trivial way but will soon escalate if not dealt with quickly. Often remedial systems are not in place to deal with it.

The layers are important from the perspective of how buildings are both designed initially and then subsequently managed. It seems to be vital to both:

- To separate out sub-systems with different functions (thus clearly concentrating on how they function individually), but also and just as importantly...
- To integrate them with the lowest achievable functional penalties and side effects, thus creating stable, adaptive systems which are as failure-tolerant and efficient as possible.

As a consequence of not carrying out both of these properly, buildings are beset by failures, usually of a chronic (low-impact but frequent) type, resulting in inefficiency and lower human tolerance. This happens because:

- Buildings do not seem to adapt properly to even marginal fluctuations in the underlying constraints, such as the management resources available to maintain them from being lower than expected.

Premature failure, vicious circles of deterioration, total obsolescence or complete bafflement about why things are not working as they should do, may result. For example, newer displacement ventilation systems can be more vulnerable to tenant changes.

- Complexity that has been added in response to calls for greater flexibility, for example, cannot be efficiently managed, unwittingly leading to downward spirals of performance and less flexibility if not more. For example, large office floorplates with floor areas which are free of columns may work well in theory on the space plan but may introduce difficult-to-resolve management problems.

The approach here is systemic, looking at the total context within which the buildings operate. This obviously includes both cities and settlements at the largest scales, and the individual user at the smallest. Understanding where constraints lie helps to make it easier to think strategically both about the future and, in the case of individual buildings, about how best to prepare briefs for their design. In the following section, we look at changing constraints at the larger scales and then move on to the smaller scale of the workplace.

THE LOGISTICAL CITY

Our main theme is that society is entering a new era, for which we offer the term 'Logistical City' to describe the aspects of it which affect buildings and settlements. In this perspective, time and logistics — organising things to be in the right place at the right time — take over from spatial factors as dominant causes influencing settlement geography.

The Logistical City is coming about because the constraints which govern city forms and building types are changing their relative positions.

This is shown in Figure 1.1, which has four constraint lines:

1 transportation (of physical goods);
2 communications (of information);
3 environment (availability of land and resources);
4 existing infrastructure (buildings, settlements and their services).

Each of the four constraint lines has different degrees of effect at various times, but they are all present at any given time. For example, until the advent of canals and then railways in the eighteenth and nineteenth centuries in the UK, transportation represented a major constraint on settlement development. The pattern of cities, towns and villages was relatively small-scale and closely packed. Economic geography was

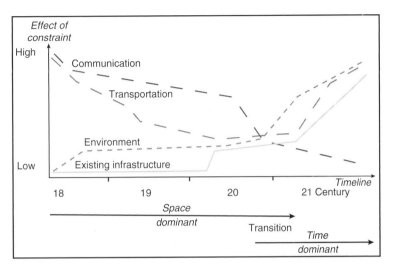

▲1.1   As we enter the twenty-first century, communication has become easy at the expense of the environment

dominated by the high cost and difficulty of transportation of physical goods. Similarly, communications were beset by slowness, inefficiency and relatively high cost. There were few environmental constraints: witness the easy availability of land and the relative indifference to pollution prior to public health regulations, for instance. Infrastructural constraints became significant later, in the 1920s and 1930s, when town planning Acts were introduced to cope with some of the undesirable effects of rapidly expanding cities like London.

Bearing in mind the time line across the bottom of Figure 1.1:

1 The order of relationships between the constraint lines for transport, communication and the environment has stayed roughly the same throughout the nineteenth and most part of the twentieth centuries, but . . .
2 The lines have been converging, and . . .
3 The infrastructure line does not impact as a factor at all until the mid-twentieth century, and . . .
4 The lines cross at the end of the twentieth century, which is the crucial difference.

These factors created the pre-conditions for, first, the industrial cities of the eighteenth and nineteenth centuries (as a result of better communications, better transport, cheaper energy, cheap land, no real environmental constraints); then, as convergence continued, the development of the twentieth century central business district/suburb city (given cheap energy, higher densities, contours of land values, intensification of uses, daily patterns of commuter movements from city centre to suburbs). Then, increasingly, the existing building stock and its infrastructure has itself become a constraint, especially in historic city centres and other concentrations of listed buildings.

Constraint lines are factors governing resource deployment. Technological improvements allow constraints to be manipulated in different ways. For example, technological innovation made movement of goods and people much cheaper and more efficient in the nineteenth century. More recently, in the late twentieth century, constraints on communication have been radically relaxed, prodigiously changing the capacities and speeds of information networks. Conversely, (because they are connected by a feedback loop) greater accessibility introduced by technical improvements and economic prosperity has introduced increased environmental constraints as a result of the waste, pollution and health risks associated with them. Geographical inertia – the effect of buildings and infrastructure already existing – has also been an increasingly important factor.

Convergence of the constraint lines in Figure 1.1 is driven primarily by technological development, economic change and environmental side-effects – it is often hard (and probably not relevant) to know which is chicken or egg. The upshot is that constraint lines are now crossing over, which partly explains why so many commentators on business affairs and the environment have dubbed the recent past the 'age of paradox'. More importantly, it is this crossover that is setting a new pattern of constraints which underlies the Logistical City.

The characteristic city form we now process – the central business district (CBD) and suburban pattern – evolved with these features:

- Initially slow, but gradually improving communications infrastructures (mail, then telegraph, telephone, radio and eventually television);
- Step-change improvements in the speed and capacity of transportation systems (from horse to canal, steam and electric railways, then road and air);
- Less environmental restraints (but these began to change with the first public health acts in the UK in the mid-nineteenth century);
- Few restrictions on land use.

The horizontal scale of Figure 1.1 describes a time line from the first development of the industrial city in the eighteenth century through to the late twentieth and twenty-first centuries. Early city growth was characterised by rapid improvements in transportation of goods and people, and extraordinarily rapid demographic change, combined with agglomeration in densely-packed cities and industrial towns clustered around cheap sources of energy (such as coal or water). There were also improvements in communications technologies. This growth tended to be unconstrained by environmental considerations. In fact, dirt and poverty were their hallmark.

These conditions were widely exploited, often ruthlessly. Damaging effects on human society were increasingly evident. These prompted in the mid-nineteeth century the first significant environmental legislation concerned with public health. At the same time, model settlements, amongst other philanthropic and utopian initiatives, were founded. By the first part of the twentieth century, evolution of transport technology, first in electric tramways and railways, then in road and air transportation, underwrote rapid expansion of cities into the space- and energy-hungry settlement model familiar not only in urban America (Chicago is the classic example, with Los Angeles the latter-day sub-type) but also around the world (Melbourne is an almost perfect case).

Two recent trends have far-reaching consequences:

1 Innovations in information and communications technology create new potential for the storage and movement of information, with digital data structures increasingly taking over from analogue for many types of media – alphanumeric, voice, video, graphical and so on.
2 As the long-term effects of unsustainable industry and agriculture become socially more destabilising, far more radical restrictions are being contemplated or imposed on polluting and damaging activities, amongst which transportation is the most destructive.[6,7]

This is leading to the situation as shown in Figure 1.1, where the communication, transportation and environmental constraint lines are exchanging places, with communication not only increasingly freed from the tyranny of distance, but also neutralised and countered by likely new, onerous restrictions on activities with high externality costs and risks, such as carbon dioxide and related emissions pollution from, for example, coal-fired power stations. Eventually, these trends form a new stable pattern (which will be much clearer from the year 2010 or thereabouts) – setting the pre-conditions for the Logistical City. However, at present they can seem contradictory, paradoxical and anomalous.

The Logistical City will have these drivers:

• Hugely improved communication infrastructures ultimately constrained by bandwidth spectrum limits and, conceivably, the electricity requirements of servers and their infrastructure;

- Transportation systems with limits and costs imposed by congestion as well as unwanted externality effects;
- Significant, sometimes onerous, environmental constraints designed to protect, for example, biodiversity;
- Major restrictions on land use.

The likelihood is that because road and air transport systems are the worst offenders, they will be more severely penalised. However, they present a much greater political problem, as greater costs of free movement are often equated with threats to democratic freedoms. Movement of people and goods will have to be carried out increasingly efficiently, especially when externality and opportunity costs are built into overall cost equations.[8,9] For example, the trend towards larger and slower aircraft will be accelerated. However, higher constraints on antisocial environmental damage will be mitigated by much greater freedom to move information around cheaply. As information becomes better packaged, more dynamic, more organised and more reliable to send and receive, the need to be profligate with energy and space-intensive travel (like commuting or international business travel) will be reduced. Although this trend has been obvious since the mid-1990s, it has been slower to take effect than many expected, partly because of the emergence of deregulated, cheap air travel and the continuing, and perhaps surprising, cheapness of oil. This will not last. Wireless broadband, either from fixed hotspots or third-generation mobile telephony, will deliver on-demand bandwidth which will also fuel these trends, perhaps acting as the main catalyst for them in the short-term. Yet the energy consequences of the 'weightless' economy are non-trivial; it can sit more heavily on the environment than it appears.

Given more physical restraint, people will be more likely to move shorter distances on a day-to-day basis, cutting out as much regular commuting as they can. However, though they are likely to still spend an average of 1.5 hours a day travelling – walking or cycling or local commuting on a metro or light rail system, perhaps, rather than driving or a longer commute, they will make more recreational, social and family-related trips, but rather less associated with their jobs and non-recreational shopping. In the short-to-medium term, projects such as TravelSmart, dedicated to less environmentally damaging journeys to school and work,[10] will reinforce the trend.

Instead of the main constraints manifesting themselves spatially (through friction of distance and agglomeration effects) they will appear much more time-related because logistics will have become crucial. For example, operations management techniques[11] like electronic point-of-sale

(EPOS) databases (which record sales and automatically generate orders for new stock in an integrated supply chain eventually reaching back to the factory) affect many more walks of life, especially where stockholding, warehousing and distribution are concerned. These technologies help to ensure that supply chains are run as efficiently as possible, even in situations where catastrophic failures may occur. As systems become more dependent on each other, disaster recovery and risk management strategies are needed to either get damaged systems up and running again as quickly as possible or to prevent disasters happening in the first place. The downside is that failures of tightly coupled systems can be more problematical to businesses in the short term. For example, the UK retailer MFI has experienced serious difficulties with a new system linking point of sales information to furniture production and ordering,[12] thereby endangering its core business.

However, improvements in supply-side economics through value engineering and operations management are not enough. Similar step-change efficiencies are sought on the demand-side, with greater efforts to fit demand patterns to supply, with as little waste as possible. Minimising waste is critical because waste is the common denominator between improved sustainability (involving the elimination of polluting or environmentally damaging outputs) and reduced costs (stripping out inefficiencies). In this light, building designers will be forced to juggle risk/value calculations. They will have to justify extra redundancy added in for health and safety reasons (like extra structural capacity or air conditioning to meet worst case load factors), while removing redundancy for value engineering reasons (that is, taking out features which are perceived as too expensive). At the same time, they will be exhorted to reduce environmental impact, which may involve reducing redundancy, possibly for the wrong reasons. The problem for them will be to avoid creating buildings which are too tightly coupled: that is, buildings whose operation is unstable rather than robust in the face of unpredictable inputs.

Thus, risk/value trade-offs become more important. This also means that feedback from buildings in use[13] must also improve, otherwise designers have no rational way of assessing risk beyond their own anecdotes. For example, do we reduce environmental risk by giving buildings the potential for natural ventilation but, by so doing, reduce the density of occupation, thereby supposedly decreasing the perceived short-term value to the client? We need to know precisely what risks and benefits are involved.

Buildings play a major role in delivering better value, because so many of them are now used inefficiently, with space left permanently under-unoccupied, or with gluts and famines of occupancy, yet still serviced with full capacity energy-hungry lighting and air-conditioning systems to meet low levels of demand. Often conventional strategies for building design (using energy-intensive materials and technologies) displace much of the risk to society at large in the form of pollution, noise and waste.

If a developer tries to adopt an environmentally responsible strategy – perhaps using significant recycling of waste – some of the risk will be transferred to the developer and the landlord and/or tenant. What happens when the waste water management system breaks down, for example? As yet, because of untried systems and lack of economic incentives, few are prepared to bear the costs of these perceived risks. Thus the risk-free option to the developer is usually the environmentally damaging one. Perhaps, entrepreneurial environmental risk capital – where developers take on some of the environmental risk themselves – is the way of the future.

The Logistical City will have:

- Time replacing space as the main factor affecting locational decision-making with time-intensive activities becoming the norm 24/7 with much more stress on, for example, time management and space utilisation;
- Intensification of critical business and organisational functions in highly serviced, secure locations, working in tandem with diversified functions elsewhere (these trends are obvious now with, for example, teleworking, outsourced information technology services and risk avoidance strategies especially to the fore);
- Less emphasis on CBD functions and single CBDs, with smaller, polycentric CBDs emerging in the main metropolitan areas, probably based on existing transport nodes like airports and railway/metro junctions;
- Waste avoidance across all aspects of society, especially affecting transportation as the single most damaging pollutant;
- More emphasis on integrated urban transport, possibly along the lines of the existing Dutch model, especially in areas of high population density;
- Less predictable journeys to work, thus avoiding rather than creating the time penalties of congestion;
- Greater use of the home, but also of safe, well-serviced and well-connected neighbourhoods (which may be in existing village, town and city centres, but may also emerge around clusters of hotels, for example, or convenient shopping centres with good public transport access);

- More emphasis on the extended family, but not necessarily based on spatial propinquity or on single-occasion family gatherings like Christmas;
- Greater emphasis on re-use and multiple use, especially in existing city centres (for example, converting offices to residential) and in areas with obsolete property (converting industrial to residential);
- A more dynamic and opportunistic approach to time management, with less emphasis on fixed appointments and more on exploiting opportunities created by such innovations as texting and satellite navigation, which offer greater flexibility in time management, but time also becoming an increasingly precious commodity.

SOME IMPLICATIONS

The Logistical City at larger scales places far greater demands on building performance at the smaller. Buildings already need to be more healthy, safe, comfortable, energy efficient, adaptable, cheap to run, easier to manage, accessible by people without cars and proven to be such. These factors will eventually become even more important, so that, for example, rental cost or first cost, the staples of the past, will cease to be the major factors which they are now.

THE WORKPLACE

The accelerating trend towards diversification of workplaces is also connected to increased intensification.[14] In the mid-1990s, British Telecom (who have a vested interest in self-fulfilling prophecies!) forecast that there would be 3.3 million teleworkers in the UK in the year 2000, with one worker in six using the home as an office.[15] The actual figure turned out to be rather lower,[16] but the trend is still clear and growing. In 2004, there are probably about 2.5 million teleworkers (perhaps 8–10 per cent of the UK workforce). This has been growing at over 10 per cent per year since 1997, within an overall average growth rate for all employees of 1.6 per cent.

Teleworkers utilise their homes more effectively, perhaps stimulating local demand for services close to them. When they travel, they do so less predictably with a more varied pattern, perhaps geared to avoiding peak-hour congestion. However, the environmental impact of their travel is not necessarily less than the average commuter because they may choose to live in less accessible places and use cars more.

Their headquarters workplaces will often be smaller and more intensively utilised and managed, often by staff who will be younger than is usual at present. Staff who attend their office workplace every day will be those who need supervising, training and overseeing – those who do not share the same assumptions as their colleagues. For example, project teams work together for a period, ensuring that they share a common purpose, then split up and work alone or in smaller groups. Those who know each other well may never need to meet face-to-face at all. This fuels demand for facilities which are increasingly seen in hotels – conference and exhibition suites, with office facilities supplied in support. It is also claimed that teleworkers in the main are happier and more productive, but they work longer hours (usually because they commute less) and can feel isolated from the social aspects of work.[17]

Minimising the costs of wasted time will also be more important, especially with workforces with highly skilled, mobile knowledge workers crucial to the core business. This is a key feature of the Logistical City, considerably enhancing trends that are already clear in the growth of time management, for example. More attention will be given to structuring information and knowledge in ways which use expensive staff time effectively – rather like the use of consultant surgeons in hospitals. This means greater filtering of information, more reliance on information science, probably more use of knowledge-based systems and more attention given to the value and potential of information.

How does this affect the design of the workplace? Some of the trends are already clear. Figure 1.2a and 1.2b are developments of the den/club/hive/cell model.[18] This gives four workplace settings characterised by the relative positions with respect to the axes.

Logistics and information is low interaction/intermittent occupancy. People come in for short periods to check their mail, synchronise diaries, log in and download/upload information, make calls and so on.

Meetings are high interaction/intermittent occupancy, with intensive peer group or one-to-many training activities, often time-constrained and goal oriented.

Tasks are low interaction/continuous occupancy, again goal-oriented, but more individual in character such as report-writing.

Projects are high interaction/continuous occupancy, but of variable duration and intensities.

Most modern office buildings have spaces which accommodate all four of these setting types, so all four types may be found in many office buildings. However, many buildings also use a restricted palette, so to speak.

A designer's office may be mainly a project setting, with most people working in teams, but a few, like the company secretary, having to put up with less than ideal conditions in order to accommodate the majority. Many offices are now like this, with one setting type having to serve for everyone, even if it does not fit individuals' tasks very well.

The same dimensions can also be used not just to describe the work settings, but also individual tasks that are carried out in those settings. In Figure 1.2b, the diagram has been nested to show how individual work tasks fit within work settings. For example, a logistics setting (like an area of touchdown workstations in a headquarters office) is not the best place for task-oriented, continuous occupancy work (AI), sales-force staff may successfully use a meeting setting occasionally at headquarters (BI) for logistics-type activities, some tasks may be well-suited to a task setting designed for them (CI), but project work in a task setting may not work so well (C2) as may be the case for task work in a project setting (DI). Many more work tasks and sub-types can be added.

The design of an appropriate workplace setting Figure 1.2a depends on understanding work tasks and how they cluster on the diagram (Figure 1.2b). Many modern organisations do not include all the func-tions within one building. Low interaction/continuous occupancy tasks, in particular, have higher potential for remote working. A basic analysis of work tasks (from Figure 1.2a and 1.2b) will show which work settings are appropriate for a particular organisation. Most organisations will have different requirements, depending on their size, structure and work/ task mix. The challenge for designers is to create work settings which are sufficiently adaptable to meet changes in work tasks (for example, secretaries are fast disappearing) without imposing unmanageable overheads.

Other building types such as laboratories and factories are becoming more like offices. The proportion of space devoted to offices is increasing. For example, over 25 per cent of usable floorspace at the University of York (a small campus university in a low density parkland setting) is given over to office space.[19] Office-like spaces have people plus technology of varying complexity, value and sophistication. Just as the computer has escaped the purpose-built, air-conditioned machine room and invaded the office floor, so also has equipment in laboratories, factories, hospitals and universities. The design and management problem is knowing which of this is specialised, thereby needing more intensive management, and which can safely be treated as generic and placed in relatively simple spaces with domestic levels of servicing and support. Special needs have tended to invade everywhere and make buildings much costlier to run

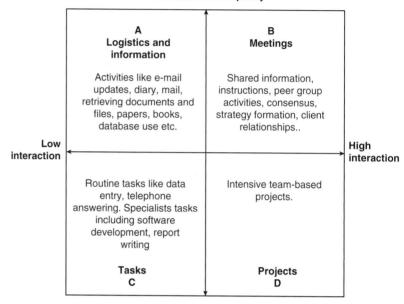

▲ 1.2a

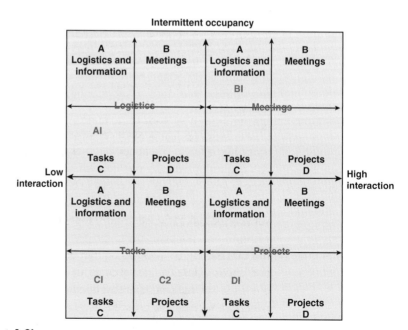

▲ 1.2b

and manage effectively, especially when the expectations of the occupants are higher.

ENVIRONMENTAL SERVICES

As workplaces have become more office-like, they have also diversified. The 16 setting/task variants shown in Figure 1.2b create an extensive vocabulary for office design, not simply within a single building or cluster, but across the organisation as a whole, perhaps involving many sites, permanent or temporary. As space sub-types are diversifying so too are environmental services, with many more types of heating, lighting and air-conditioning systems becoming available. For instance, mixed-mode systems – hybrids which combine natural ventilation and mechanical ventilation and cooling – are now more common, offering the potential for 'tunable' buildings with longer life, greater adaptability, less waste, lower cost and less management overhead.[20] These are evolving in response to more stringent requirements from clients, especially with respect to meeting improved comfort, health and energy efficiency standards as well as increasingly dynamic requirements of diversified space types (especially for occupancy changes, zoning, controllability and rapid response).

In theory, environmental support systems are becoming more demand-responsive, switchable, less of a management overhead and more capable of re-configuring at low cost. In reality, they are still surprisingly poor at matching demand to supply. As environmental risks continue to threaten, there may also be the need for buildings to offer the potential for far greater energy savings, even if they are not running efficiently at present (say a 50 per cent reduction by the year 2025 in electricity use). There is more scope for technological improvements to bring about efficiencies (through the use of solid-state, low-voltage technology in computer systems, for instance).

ORGANISATIONAL CHANGE

Organisational change, especially from organisations providing all their own support services (vertically integrated) to those contracting out support services (horizontally integrated), should result in smaller buildings with higher levels of physical and informational interaction between them (perhaps using just-in-time logistics to organise the interactions more efficiently). As yet, there is little available evidence to show that this is, in fact, occurring, although there is plenty of talk to suggest that it might.

Organisations in the UK with large portfolios of sometimes complex buildings, especially universities and hospitals, have been most active recently in re-evaluating their property strategies.[21] But whether this is leading to fewer buildings or buildings divided more clearly into generic and specialist types is not yet clear. Campus-style developments (for retail, universities, business parks, science parks and hospitals) are no less common as we enter the twenty-first century than they were in the 1960s, 1970s and 1980s, so the attractions of economies of scale and spatial propinquity may still be strong.

The difficulty in predicting how organisational change will affect buildings is the effect of transport. If, as widely expected, constraints on transportation (either *via* the marketplace price of fuel, government legislation, congestion or combinations of these) significantly restrict movement of goods and people, then logistics will rapidly come to the fore. Companies such as British Airways (BA), which already invest heavily in yield management (i.e. optimising revenue from passenger journeys) may ultimately make more profit from expertise in logistics than from flying and maintaining planes, where profit margins may quickly disappear altogether as the environmental costs of flight become even more onerous. Whatever their fate, companies with global informational infrastructures like BA will be tempted to seek the advantages of low cost, high-skill labour markets like India.[22]

CONCLUSIONS

In the first instance, trends in building use and design are more likely to be set by cost reduction drives. These cost-reduction strategies almost inevitably seize on people or buildings, or both. A part-time work-force operating from home, or overseas, carrying their own overhead costs, can take an attractive slice off bottom-line costs. However, a cost-based approach will usually miss out the finer nuances of strategic advantage for organisations and businesses. The trends clearly point to buildings which are more intensively used, but also linked to a diversity of other buildings with much greater responsiveness to change, less risk carried by the building owners and less environmentally damaging.

Where will all that risk go? Increasingly, it seems that a self-employed, perhaps part-time, workforce will carry more of it (in the form of lower incomes, unemployment, stress, illness and unsocial hours).

Environmental costs are also offloaded on others – increased movement and interaction creates greater congestion costs which in turn places greater burdens on infrastructure services such as road building. Many view these processes as having finite limits, expressed not only through congestion costs, but also pollution, waste, lost time and opportunity costs, and for the individual, depression, anxiety and anomie.

In this light, the importance of logistics will become pervasive. Windows in diaries are no longer yuppie jokes but a major factor in organising business and family life. Many of these trends are already visible. For example, it is relatively commonplace to find people spending the working week living from a pied-à-terre apartment and then commuting home at weekends. Sometimes home may be in another country! Such arrangements place severe stresses on people and their families, making it extraordinarily difficult to organise seemingly trivial but life-forming events, like attending a child's nativity play. These events, and the consequences of not being there (absence costs) then take on increasing potency. People benefit in one way from cheap and reliable transportation – giving easier physical access to their jobs, but suffer in other ways – in their family and other relationships, for instance. Trade-offs between career, family, relationships and where they live are increasingly forced on people. Such decisions are increasingly burdensome and, for many, difficult. Only the privileged minority are able to optimise all of them, usually because they have the money, and some good fortune, to do so. Increasingly, people give priority to different facets at different life cycle stages – relationships and careers in their twenties, family and career in their thirties, and perhaps a nice place to live in later life.

Regular routines and patterns of life are disappearing quickly. Additional complexity – more types of job contract, more technology, more consumer choice, less perceived security at work and at home, greater perception of risks (even if risks are misjudged) and more perceived or actual stress are quickly redrawing the boundaries of work and family life to create scenarios which were unimaginable even one generation ago (especially relating to travel and global communication).

Re-inventing the workplace means second-guessing and grasping the consequences of these changes rather than merely responding to them. Organisations are becoming more distributed over wider geographical areas, using smaller buildings. Complexity is managed more successfully, so that generic and specialist building types are increasingly separated by function, with more zoning of the result. Services need zoning more effectively, not just to deal with demand patterns which are less predictable and more onerous, but also to deal with greater occupancy over 24-hour periods, such as day/night control centres or night-time-secure car parks. All buildings have to operate much more efficiently in the consumption of energy: energy budgets 50 per cent lower by the year 2025 seem achievable. Better energy efficiency will be fruitless without much greater transportation efficiency, with the ability to convert at least task – and occupancy – intensive work to remote locations thereby offering the possibility of reduced commuting burdens.

END NOTE

This chapter is a revised and updated version of a paper first published in 1994, although much of what was written then still holds. The major difference has been to change the tense of the chapter from the future to the present, as we appear to be moving ever more firmly into the logistical age.

2

NEW PATTERNS OF WORK: THE DESIGN OF THE OFFICE

Andrew Laing
DEGW North America

SUMMARY
Knowing where we have come from is essential to understand where we are today, and what our options are for moving forward. This chapter identifies the major changes that have occurred in the last fifty years in the way office work is done pointing out the paradox of how little, physical work settings have changed in the same period. Concepts of office organisations from the early 1950s to date are analysed and the spatial and workplace layouts that have been proposed to meet different organisational forms are compared.
Information technology since IBM's legitimisation of the personal computer in 1981 has opened up many new options for work organisations, shifting the office from a data processing factory to a centre for the creative application of ideas and information. Different attitudes to office design and tenure are highlighted contrasting Northern Europe, where buildings are planned and built around specific users and organisational concepts, with the UK and North America, which prioritise flexible office space with a focus on exchange value.

THE SEPARATION OF OFFICE DESIGN FROM USERS

The design of office buildings has often not been closely related to the needs of the organisations who use them. First, the speculative nature of most office development has encouraged design focused on maximising economy and flexibility of space; second, even when a particular client has been directly involved, the design has all too often focused on corporate image expressed in reception spaces and facade design; third, the very shape and design of the office building has been heavily restricted by planning legislation.

The 'International Style' of the Modern Movement, for example, rarely confronted in detail the relationship between the building and the activities of its occupants. This lack of concern was exacerbated by the separation of the interior design of the office from its structural design, the architect merely providing flexible space for subsequent interior design. The break between the building as a container and the activity within it was complete. This tendency reached its climax in the 1980s with the North American post-modern skyscrapers: 'the retreat of the architect into the skin trade, the abdication of responsibility for deciding what the building is for, how it is going to be used and how it will be serviced'.[1] The exceptions to this rule are few and far between and have often thereby become landmarks in thinking about the office, such as Frank Lloyd Wright's Larkin Building of 1907, or Herman Hertzberger's Centraal Beheer Building, 1972.

It is all too easy to be hoodwinked into believing that the fundamentals of office design have changed over the course of this century. A contemporary image of the Larkin Building compared with a modern office interior (Figure 2.1) would certainly lead us to believe that everything has been re-thought: the modern workstations are different, new technologies have proliferated throughout the space, the lighting and furniture are entirely updated. Yet when one compares in detail the pattern of the space use and the core assumptions of the occupancy of the space over time, very little has changed. The changes are cosmetic and superficial.

As Duffy has argued, the process by which office buildings and their interiors are procured has hardly changed since the early manuals of office administration and layout were written at the beginning of the twentieth century. The design of the office has been governed by outmoded stereotypes, partly a result of the lack, until recently, of really

Atrium of the Larkin
Administration Building, 1906;
Buffalo, New York;
Architect: Frank Lloyd Wright;
Courtesy Buffalo and Erie
County Historical Society

▲ 2.1   Image of the Larkin interior, c1907 (top) contrasted with a
modern office interior

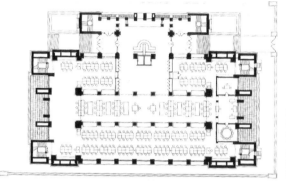

Ground floor plan of the
Larkin Building; Redrawn by
Joseph Bruno, Charles Rhyu,
Toby O'Rorke, Dragan Mrdja,
and Brian Messina; Courtesy
the Museum of Modern Art,
New York

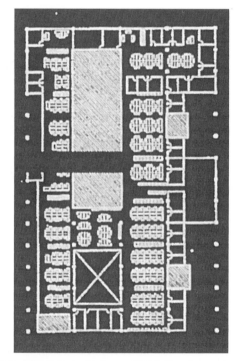

▲2.2   Plan of the Larkin building, 1904 (top) contrasted with a 'Broadgate' type contemporary office layout, 1990

new ideas in the field of organisational theory itself. Furthermore, even as new ideas of organisation emerge, the furniture and construction industries remain supply-side dominated and fail to respond to changing demands. 'Taylor's ideas of the mechanical, top-down, inhuman, status-rich, invention-poor, alienated workplace live on, manifested in every workstation, ceiling tile and light fitting.[2]

Conventional offices are still briefed, designed, built, serviced and occupied without regard to the emerging characteristics of new ways of working, which include:

- Highly mobile and nomadic work patterns;
- The use of multiple shared group work settings;
- Diverse task-based spaces;
- Extended and erratic periods of working;
- Varied patterns of sometimes high-density space use;
- More shared and temporary ownership of settings within the office combined with teleworking and homeworking.

This disassociation of the building from the interior life of the office only began to break down and therefore to demand a greater reconciliation between the building shell, its environmental services, and the settings appropriate to the life of the organisation, with the revolutionary impact of information technology (IT) in the 1980s. The pressure of change of organisations and the continuing development of IT through the 1990s has meant that these complex demands by users continue to require radical and holistic approaches by architects and designers to the office environment.

We have consistently found in our research with organisations, that they are thinking very hard about rethinking their ways of working and have sought to translate their innovations into office design. They are very often ahead of their architects, designers and suppliers in their thinking. While the suppliers and designers of buildings, interiors, and office furniture have rigidly and unanimously looked to the past, advanced organisations have grabbed hold of the opportunities of new technologies and have re-designed their work processes as well as work spaces. Often the most innovative solutions have been achieved with little professional design support and with limited input from conventional office suppliers. Examples include the pathbreaking offices of Digital in Finland and Sweden in the late 1980s, and the more recent offices of SOL in Helsinki.

These leading-edge offices have often had to achieve innovation in spite of, rather than with, the help of design professionals and suppliers. This explains why so many of the most avant garde offices incorporating new ways of working with new technologies look much more like domestic environments or other kinds of places. Their inspirations have been the relaxed intimate spaces and furniture of the home; the flexible and efficient space occupancy of the hotel; the sense of opulence, sociability and prestige of the gentlemen's club, the restaurant, and the airport business lounge; the ultraergonomic, fast-paced, high-density design features of the executive airplane seat or the check-in desk; and the manoeuvrability, re-configurability, and transience associated with the stage set, the film set or the art gallery installation.

The design of the office must therefore be re-thought in the same way that the structure and shape of organisations are being transformed. Fundamental to this rethinking is to break away from the idea of the work space as an individual desk occupied full time from nine-to-five every day. As soon as this basic stereotype of office design is questioned, then a new world of work patterns and office design becomes a real possibility. Design must correspond to the highest levels of strategic management: it must be used to achieve managerial objectives and to lever organisational change.[3]

What has been the historical logic of this highly damaging separation between office design and the work processes of the organisation?

HISTORICAL BACKGROUND: 1950s–1960s: FROM POST-WAR PAPER FACTORY TO BÜROLANDSCHAFT AND THE ACTION OFFICE

The offices of the early 1950s were places for the collection and routine processing of paper-based information. They have been called 'paper factories' because in their approach to organisation and even in the layout of their plans they shared many characteristics with the design of factories. Two major types of 'clerical factory office' existed in Europe: the narrow-depth cellular office and the Bürolandschaft open office which emerged in Germany. In the USA, the office building type evolved gradually from the narrow slab tower towards deep planned space, predominantly open plan for clerical use with executives in enclosed perimeter offices.

USA: post-war office boom and deep plan office space

A major post-war boom in office development occurred in the USA. The landmark Lever House building in New York, designed by Skidmore, Owings and Merrill in 1952, represented the new building type: a thin slab office tower on a podium base.[4] As Duffy remarked on the Seagram Building of 1954 in New York: Mies van der Rohe was 'more interested in the formal possibilities of reflective glass than any real organisational requirements or actual developmental possibilities'[5] (Figure 2.3).

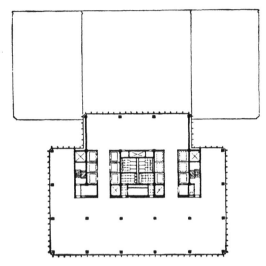

▲ **2.3** The Seagram Building, Tower Plan. Mies van der Rohe and Philip Johnson, 1954

By the 1960s, deeper plan buildings were made possible by air conditioning and fluorescent lighting and were further encouraged by the development of the open planned office. The architect of the office now worked alongside a space planner and an interior designer.

Europe: the traditional cellular office

Europe was generally reluctant to adopt the 'American' open plan office in deep plan spaces[6] although many of the innovative Bürolandschaft offices were designed as large deep open spaces. This was partly a result of higher energy costs for air conditioning and lighting but more importantly was the result of cultural differences and expectations about the workplace. The typical European building remained narrow in depth and cellular in plan, with small offices served off a central corridor (Figure 2.4).

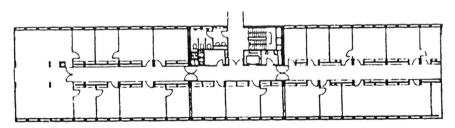

▲ **2.4** Typical 1950s European cellular office

The Bürolandschaft landscaped office

The Quickborner team in West Germany in 1959 analysed work patterns of the office organisation and pointed to the need for better communication supported by the design of the office. The flow of paper-based and visual communication between individuals and groups was used to determine the layout of the office. The concept resulted in very open layouts, all interior walls being removed. The large deep space was used to accommodate concentric rings of lines of communication between groups. The first installation of this type of office was for the Bertelsmann Publishing Company at Guttersloh, West Germany, in 1960 (Figure 2.5).

In 1967, the concept was introduced to the USA as 'office landscaping'[7] where it evolved in new directions: casual meeting places and coffee bars on the office floors were dropped, clerical workers remained in the large open spaces while managers retreated once more to their private enclosed offices. Space standards became centralised and uniform across the open planned areas. Variants of this landscape office concept became established throughout Europe and North America. Duffy popularised the idea of Bürolandschaft in the UK in a small book published in 1966.[8] Real estate managers of North American multinationals moving into

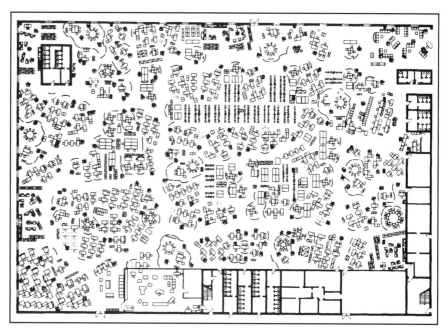

▲2.5   The Bürolandschaft office: 1960s, GEG Versand Kamen building

Europe sought to apply their familiar office concepts across the European continent. The 'Bürolandschaft', originally invented in Germany, returned to Europe as 'landscape or open plan'. Duffy made a critique of the landscaped office concept in 1975.[9]

The essential promise of Bürolandschaft was that 'it seemed the closest approximation to a service which it was felt architects and interior designers were failing to supply – the detailed planning of interior space by people who understood something of design and organisational structure'.[10]

Herman Miller Action Office

Following the development of the Bürolandschaft office concept, Robert Probst (working for Herman Miller in the USA) re-defined the direction of office furniture design. His 'Action Office' system (Figure 2.6) was introduced in 1964 and his book *The Office: a Facility Based on Change* appeared in 1968. The idea was that office furniture should be a kit of parts responding to the varied tasks of office work and recognising the conflicts between privacy and communication inherent in office organisations. The approach focused on sets of components designed to permit individual discretion in office design, assuming high levels of autonomy. The concept of the furniture system was less concerned with any one over-arching concept of the organisation and its work processes.

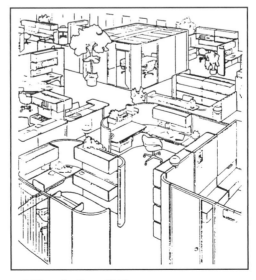

▲ **2.6**   Herman Miller Action Office

The problem of change was solved by giving management responsibility to the user. The furniture itself began to take on some of the subdivisional functions of the building shell and allowed designers to break away from the right angle in their layouts. The hardware was modular so that the worker could select and adapt different components according to changing needs.

1970s: A DEVELOPING CULTURAL DIVERSITY

Reaction against the office landscape

After the American-dominated approach to office design of the 1960s, in the 1970s European designers began to develop a distinctively independent approach. The multinational companies realised that Europe could no longer be considered 'one country'. For example, in 1978, DEGW undertook a study for IBM comparing differences in national concerns about the work environment. The study identified the tension between corporate allegiances and individual aspirations. It showed that the new open-planned offices did not generally provide well for individual concerns for privacy, environmental control, and personal identity and it questioned the overly deterministic assumptions of Bürolandschaft. Not all office organisations are the same, and 'not all office layouts should be equally landscaped'.[11] Indeed, not all organisations are necessarily communication intensive, and 'office landscaping appeared to offer unlimited freedom but in fact created a whole series of problems in planning and in maintaining surprisingly fragile layouts and in defining spaces for groups of office workers within endless office floors'.[12] The complex requirements of users for a variety of space types began to be recognised, and a reaction against large, undivided spaces began to set in.

The Centraal Beheer archetype

An archetypal office that sought to balance the tension between these corporate and individual aspirations was that designed by Herman Hertzberger: the Centraal Beheer at Apeldoorn in the Netherlands (Figure 2.7). The office provided open spaces for ease of communication, yet also defined space in such a way that small groups and individuals had identifiable personal zones. Duffy argues[13] that Centraal Beheer was brilliant in its use of the building shell to define but not enclose units of space, but noted that it did not make the most economic use of space. Surely an equivalent degree of space definition and structure could have

▲**2.7**   The Centraal Beheer building, Herman Hertzberger

been provided without 'quite such vigorously articulated and presumably expensive architecture'.[14]

Innovations

Germany, The Netherlands and the UK developed innovative office concepts in the 1970s through custom-designed buildings and interiors. The idea of the office building was evolving away from that of a static building shell towards the concept of a self-regulating structural grid within which working groups grow and change. Furniture began to be used to define spaces within deep open plan areas and to respond to the needs of small autonomous working groups. In Northern Europe a reaction against very large open planned spaces began to reverse the Bürolandschaft layout concept.

At the same time, rigorous space planning and management methods began to be imported from the USA into Europe, and office furniture design stimulated by North American suppliers was raising environmental standards at the workplace. Computers, however, were still centralised in computer rooms. A hint of the future was the commissioning of DEGW in 1979 by a Swedish furniture company, NKR, to brief the development of prototype furniture specifically for the use of information technology (IT).

1980s: THE PC REVOLUTION

1980 was the year in which IBM introduced the Personal Computer (PC) and the world of office work and office design was changed forever. The computer began its escape from the confines of the computer room and its proliferation on office desks. The consequences continue to drive innovation in office use and design.

ORBIT studies

Information Technology clearly demanded a radical re-thinking of the use, servicing and base building design for the office, and in 1983, DEGW and others began the ORBIT (Figure 2.8) studies (ORganisations, Buildings and Information Technology) to consider the issues. Multi-client studies in the UK and North America established new parameters for office buildings able to cope with IT and the changing nature of the corporate organisation on both sides of the Atlantic.

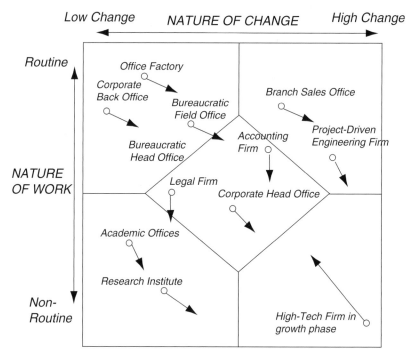

▲ 2.8   Organisational classification model from ORBIT (ORganisations, Buildings and Information Technology) 1985

The office is where you are

As the office workforce began to demand higher standards, greater personal identity, and more privacy, and as 'knowledge work' and other more creative forms of office work began to take precedence, some began to question the traditional design concepts of the office. The outstanding contribution here was that of Stone and Luchetti with *The Office is Where You Are* (1985)[15] (Figure 2.9). They posed the fundamental

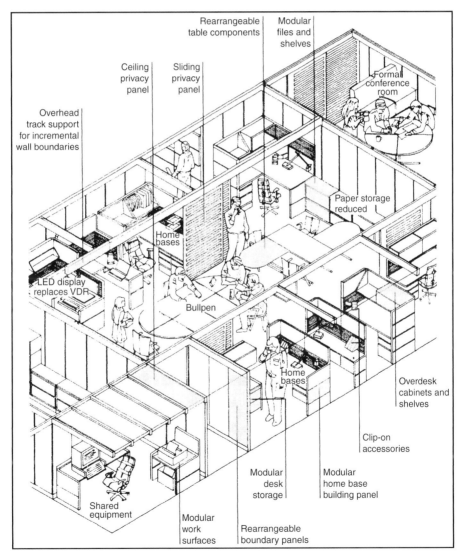

▲2.9   Your office is where you are

question that would drive innovative thinking about the office for the next ten years: with increasingly ubiquitous information technology the space and time of the office could be used in new ways. A variety of work settings could be provided to handle the needs of isolated work or interaction, with the individual moving between them. The idea of one individual work place within the office, or of one seat per person, was challenged.

Two traditions in building supply

Two major variants in office procurement design and use were confirmed in the 1980s: those of Northern Europe *versus* the UK and North America.

NORTHERN EUROPE VARIATIONS

In Northern Europe, the Combi office concept emerged to provide high levels of personal enclosure at the building perimeter as well as shared spaces for interaction and group work in the internal space. This kind of office responded to the high-quality environmental standards demanded, and legislated for, in several North European countries, such as those of Scandinavia and the Netherlands, and in Germany. In their high degrees of enclosure, these Northern European offices reversed completely the open landscaped office concept. Very narrow highly cellular buildings re-emerged in Northern Europe, more sophisticated versions of much older office building types. Other variants include the Group Room layouts for 10–15 people (e.g. the GEW Building, Cologne or the NMB PostBank in Amsterdam). A further innovation was the introduction of the internal street and atrium to serve as a social centre and circulation space for the building (such as the SAS Building in Stockholm).

Three types of space layout can be identified (Figure 2.10):

- Highly cellular;
- Combi office;
- Gruppenräume or group rooms.

Design driven by owner occupancy

The design of Northern European offices was driven by the system of procurement that favoured owner-occupied development and highly customised building designs tailored to the particular needs of the end user. The dominant building form was therefore highly influenced by

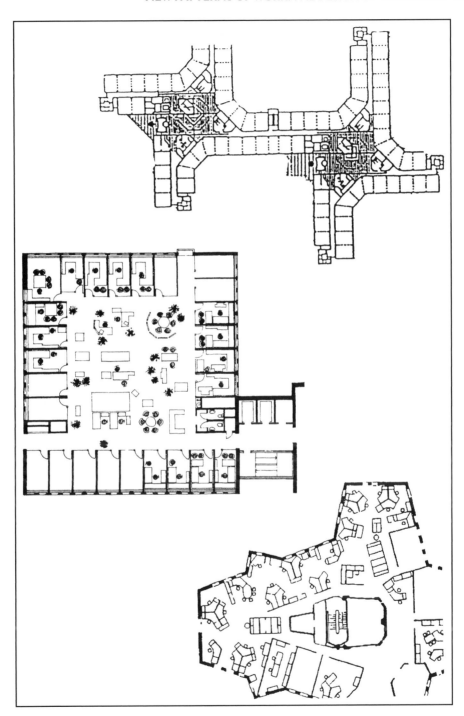

▲2.10   The new cellular office (top), Combi office (centre) and
group room (bottom)

users' demands: resulting in narrow rather than deep plan forms, very high degrees of cellularisation (as in the Combi office described above) and in extremely high standards of amenity, comfort and space per person.[16]

The particular significance of the Northern European office model is that the high degree of shaping by direct user influence (a result of highly professional briefing, the design competition system, and the powerful influence of the Workers' Councils), results in them being very much focused on the achievement of organisational goals. Their very expensive design solutions are an attempt to create offices that very closely match the needs of the total organisation, as contrasted with the USA/UK speculative model which can at best offer only an approximation of the needs of unknown end users. The Northern European buildings, at whatever cost and usually with high levels of spatial inefficiency, are intended to add value to the organisations that use them. It was this distinction between buildings that added value to organisational performance *versus* those that provided spatial efficiency that Duffy argued was the central problem to be solved in future workplaces.

NORTH AMERICA AND THE UK

The North American office building type, developed in miniaturised and less-efficient versions in the UK throughout the 1960s and 1970s, evolved towards ever more cost-effective standards throughout the 1980s. The supply-side dominated development industry enabled large office buildings to be produced as simply and cheaply as possible. The typical North American office building was the deep floor plan central core skyscraper. These buildings were designed to be highly standardised and were suitable for the simple and highly routinised demands of office work.

From the middle of the 1980s in the UK, however, the stereotyped North American central core office tower was replaced by the innovation of a new building type, best represented by the 'ground scraper' atrium buildings developed at Broadgate in the City of London (Figure 2.11) as well as by the low-rise 'high-tech' buildings developed for suburban business parks, such as the pioneering Stockley Park (Figure 2.12) outside Heathrow Airport (the concepts for both developments having been researched by DEGW for the developer Stuart Lipton of Stanhope).

These similar building types, invented in the UK, one suitable for downtown locations, the other for business parks, were both nevertheless also speculative developer products which in their procurement methods

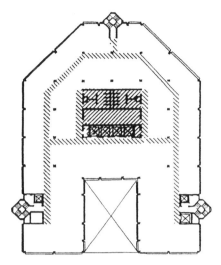

▲2.11 'Broadgate' type building

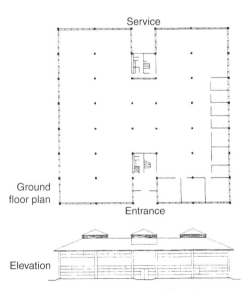

▲2.12 Typical low-rise 'high-tech' building type such as
Stockley Park

and high spatial efficiency standards share the dominant characteristics
of the USA model described above. In this sense, both the central core
skyscrapers at Canary Wharf, London or the World Trade Center in
New York, as well as the Broadgate buildings in the City of London,
are all more similar to each other than to the SAS Building, Stockholm;

the Colonia Building, Cologne; or the NMB PostBank, Amsterdam, in Northern Europe.

1990s: ENDING THE TYRANNY OF SUPPLY

The recession of the late 1980s and early 1990s, the associated collapse of the office real estate boom in Europe and North America, and the need for corporate organisations to reinvent what they were doing in order to survive, threw the world of office work, office design and office development into a tailspin. All the old certainties disappeared.

The North American and Anglo-Saxon standardised models (Figure 2.13) of the speculative office building, designed for unknown tenants, whether of the central core skyscraper or the groundscraper plus atrium variety, were no longer valid. Neither, however, could the high cost of the tailor-made, owner-occupied, Northern European office building be sustained. Only the very richest organisations could afford to cater to the unique preferences of their particular culture in the design of their own buildings.

The Northern European organisations are now being forced to rethink their needs for expensive custom-designed buildings for their exclusive use; the North American and UK developers have been forced to link up more closely with end users through joint ventures or pre-lets. A double shift has therefore occurred in the expectations of what buildings should offer end users: on the one hand, the developers are forced to pay more respect to the complex, varied and changing needs of end users; on the other hand, the end users are demanding buildings and office environments that can both add value to the ways they want to work but in ways that minimise their costs.

New ways of working and the future office

In other words, the tyranny of supply-driven development that dominated the UK and USA throughout the 1980s has been broken. In its place a new world of office organisations, with ways of working both in and out of offices, has placed entirely new demands on the ingenuity of designers at all levels for the provision of the workplace environment. The emphasis is now on adding value by improved productivity through the effective application of information technology, and greater flexibility of use: organisations can choose to manage work across time zones, on multiple sites, in a variety of settings.

	Bürolandschaft offices	Traditional British speculative offices	New 'Broadgate' type of British speculative office	Traditional North American speculative office	The new North European office
No. of storeys	5	10	10	80	5
Typical floor size	2,000sqm	1,000sqm	3,000sqm	3,000sqm	Multiples of 2,000sqm
Typical office depth	40m	13.5m	18m and 12m	18m	10m
Furthest distance from perimeter aspect	20m	7m	9–12m	18m	5m
Efficiency: net to gross		80%	85%	90%	70% (lots of public circulation)
Maximum cellularization (% of usable)	20%	70%	40%	20%	80%
Type of core	Semi-dispersed	Semi-dispersed	Concentrated: extremely compact	Concentrated: extremely compact	Dispersed: stairs more prominent than lifts
Type of HVAC services	Centralized	Minimal	Floor by floor	Centralized	Decentralized: minimal use of HVAC

▲2.13   North American, UK, North European building types

CONCLUSIONS

How are we to understand which kinds of organisations can move in these new directions? In the *New Environments for Working* study completed with the BRE in 1996, DEGW explored alternative models of work patterns (Figure 2.14) for different types of organisations in order to understand their different impacts on space use, environmental services demands and the suitability of alternative building types. Four organisational types were identified corresponding to distinctive patterns of space occupancy (Figure 2.15).

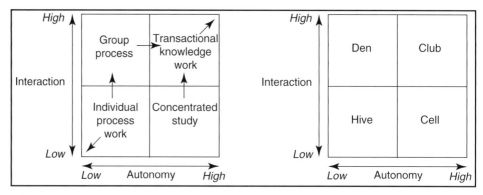

▲2.14   Patterns of work: four major types

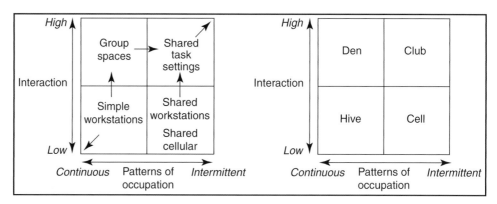

▲2.15   Patterns of space occupancy

The direction of change is away from non-interactive routine work towards both more collaborative and more highly autonomous styles of working. Much routine work is becoming automated or exported to lower cost economies. Creative knowledge work demands a combination of highly concentrated individual work alongside interactive team work. The environment in which this complex combination of activities can best be supported has been called 'the Club'. The Club concept refers back to the traditional Gentleman's Club in which a variety of rich and highly specific settings provided for many different social and individual activities. The key characteristic in making the modern Club both effective and efficient is that the richness of its setting is shared by hundreds of people over time. In this sense the Club approach overcomes the dichotomy between the expensive user-friendly North European office and the cost-efficient North American speculative office. It is this innovation of rethinking the time utilisation of space that is the major means by which architectural design can provide buildings and workplaces that better support users' emerging organisational needs.

ACKNOWLEDGEMENT

The author would like to acknowledge the specific source of many of the arguments in this chapter from the general research tradition developed at DEGW and in particular from the many papers of Francis Duffy.

3 REAL ESTATE AND THE FUTURE

Rob Harris
Principal, Ramidus Consulting Limited

SUMMARY

Rob Harris argues that the real estate agenda of the future will address relationships. Following concentration on building design during the 1980s, and the emphasis on building performance during the 1990s, in the next phase we may expect much more attention to relationships between employers and their employees, workers and their places of work and occupiers and suppliers will shape the future workplace. Drawing on his experience of working as the operations director for a major interior contractor and service provider, and earlier as research director for a leading developer, the author outlines the drivers of change, and postulates how these will effect the ways in which real estate is designed, delivered, occupied and managed.

A framework comprising drivers and outcomes at the level of the workplace, operations support, and the asset is described. Each level has its own distinct drivers and outcomes which require holistic thinking and planning. As organisational planning demands more and more flexible approaches to the development of resources, a need grows for a more coordinated approach to resource planning. As corporate planners consider best practice, knowledge systems, change management, and cost control measures, they will expect integrated approaches and strategies of delivery from their providers.

Many talk about the demise of the office – Harris argues that there has never been a greater need for new settings to support knowledge workers' creative well-being. More flexible ways of delivering the appropriate accommodation are also essential. If future real estate strategies are only driven by the need to cut costs and defend existing paradigms, the office certainly will be doomed. The business of real estate must shift from trading assets into creating valuable ways of enhancing business performance.

AN EMERGING REAL ESTATE AGENDA

Demand for real estate is the byproduct of the production of goods and services. As goods and services change, so the environments in which they are produced and supported need to change. As organisations are constantly adapting to changing markets, demands on accommodation are in a permanent state of change. In this sense, the perfect workplace is a chimera, and just as micro-level changes constantly alter the nature of demand within organisations, so macro-level changes bring about whole-sale change to workplace needs. For example, in the economic expansion of the 1980s, a changed political agenda and technological developments led to a steep change in demand. Similarly the 1990s saw recessionary pressures force occupiers to minimise their cost bases and reduce their exposure to costly real estate. Figure 3.1 places change in demand for offices into a long-term perspective.

It is possible to describe the past two decades as having had two distinct real estate agendas. The 1980s focused attention on the product. Rapid technological advancement, globalisation and corporate change demanded new kinds of buildings. The supply industry responded with

	Pre-War	1950s	1980s	2000s
Workplace	Production line Labour intensive Task oriented Hierarchical	Data processing Departmental Corporate	High specification Extended hours Large, open floors Cellular space	Mobility Core/periphery Hotelling Flexitime/place
Systems	Simple lighting Simple heating Natural ventilation	Mainframe Data processing Typewriters	The workstation BMS PCs and networks Fax/teleconference	Individual control Integrated BMS Natural ventilation IT convergence
Culture	Small scale Uniformity Task oriented	Multi-layered Corporate identity Large scale	Delayering Outsourcing Individualistic Meeting space	Flexitime/place Group areas Employee welfare Networking
Finance	Owner occupiers Long leaseholds Large estates	25 year, FRI lease Mortgage finance Debentures	Non-recourse Off balance sheet Debt finance	REITS Management Flexibility

▲3.1   Long-term change in offices

buildings very different from those of an earlier vintage. Then the economic pressures of the 1990s focused attention on performance. Most organisations and corporate real estate managers had the overriding priority of getting more out of their buildings: lower costs, flexible occupation and efficiency became the new watchwords.

As we look to the decade ahead, it is clear that the real estate agenda is shifting once more. There is some evidence to suggest that the office economy is maturing, and that the phenomenal growth in office jobs seen over the past three decades is likely to slow down in the years ahead. Groshen and Potter[1] have presented compelling evidence of a jobless recovery in the USA, while Parker[2] has suggested that the trend towards off-shoring jobs to low-cost locations is likely to increase. Consolidation and reorganisation are likely to be more pervasive trends than unfettered growth. This of course has major implications for occupiers themselves as they seek to balance their occupancy with changing organisational needs, and also for the property supply industry which has enjoyed a long (albeit interrupted) period of growth in demand for its product.

If the office economy is reaching a mature phase, then the new agenda is likely to focus on relationships — those between employers and their employees, those between workers and their places of work, and those between occupiers and suppliers. Coyle and Quah's analysis of the new economy[3] provides a useful framework within which to consider the dynamics of these relationships and their implications for demand for office space. One approach to considering the drivers and outcomes of change is shown in Figure 3.2. The approach distinguishes workplaces, operations and assets, and identifies some of the key drivers of change and their outcomes for the ways in which real estate is designed, delivered, occupied and managed.

WORKPLACES

The relationship between employers and employees focuses on the workplace itself. Of course, the principal role of the workplace is to provide a physical environment in which organisations configure themselves efficiently and effectively to support operational imperatives. But the key drivers of change reflect the much broader agendas and pressures on the organisations themselves. Growing skill shortages, labour costs, competitive pressures, rapid change and uncertainty are all leading to new approaches to management. Re-engineering and widespread delayering

	Drivers	Outcomes
Workplaces	Labour/skill shortages Consolidation Flexibility Uncertainty	Distributed workplaces Hotelling and flexible work Spaceless growth Networked organisations
Operations	Technological change Mobile workforce Distributed workforce HR issues	Simpler buildings Technological obsolescence Economic obsolescence Outsourcing
Assets	Underperformance Consumer pressure Government pressure Supply chain	Greater acceptance of flexibility New ways of getting value Innovation in product Integration of delivery and management

▲ **3.2** Drivers and outcomes of change

are resulting in flatter and more flexible organisations, with horizontal networks replacing vertical hierarchies. Highly trained, group-based knowledge workers are replacing clerical, departmentalised information processors. The workforce itself has changed, with more women and more part-timers: a trend which is forecast to continue. The full-time eight-hour day, five-day week form of employment is being challenged with the spread of flexible working, and the notion of a 'core and periphery' workforce has become established as cost pressures have encouraged outsourcing.

These drivers of change are having a profound impact on the workplace. New methods of space management are very different even from those of the recent past. For example, the practice of a permanent place of work with a fixed, dedicated workstation for each individual is no longer a given for everyone. Hot-desking has become established as an efficient and effective means of occupying space to address highly cost-competitive and fast-changing business environments. Whereas previously a person's office space reflected their status, today space allocation is more closely aligned with tasks and how they are best accomplished, with the appropriate space distributed accordingly. Similarly, cellular offices which are seen to reinforce hierarchies and individualism are increasingly yielding to group areas that encourage interaction, co-operation and innovation.

As more flexible work environments spread, so desktop PCs are starting to disappear. They are being replaced by portable laptops, touchdown stations and wireless environments. This will have an impact on workstation requirements and configurations. Unified messaging technology has arrived, with combined e-mail, fax and voice messaging accessible from an Outlook-type interface on laptops and PDAs. Voice messages will be accessed either as attached recordings or will be transcribed into text by voice recognition software. Voiceover internet protocol (VoIP) will spell the death of the telephone. This technology transmits the voice over the internet, allowing companies in multiple locations to keep in contact for much reduced costs.

Such technology has also reached the domestic market. Telcos and ISPs are joining forces to launch mass market for voice over the internet products that allow consumers to manage all their home communication – phone calls, webcam, e-mails, texts and instant messaging – together in one place on their PC. Multi-way video is expected to be added soon. Such genuinely converged multi-media communications packages will have ramifications far beyond the household. Developments such as these have already made communication between office and home very simple, and new products will push flexibility further.

All these trends enable greater flexibility in the use of space by taking out the 'fixes' that make change in the workplace more difficult and expensive to achieve. They also allow an organisation to change and evolve without having to make fresh commitments to new real estate. By getting more people working from less space, a growing number of companies have begun to talk about 'spaceless growth', the idea that headcounts can grow while the amount of space consumed remains the same. This phenomenon breaks, for the first time, the historic correlation between increased output and increased demand for space. Figure 3.3 shows the historic relationship between output and

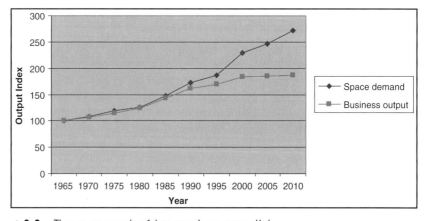

▲ 3.3   The concept of 'spaceless growth'

space demand, and the potential for space demand to slow down relative to business output.

Personal interaction or cultural interchange have always formed an integral part of the office experience, and current trends suggest that this aspect will increase in importance over the coming years as the ways in which people interact change. As mobility has become more pervasive and as more people spend at least part of their working week away from the office, it is increasingly important to consider the design and management of the workplace in terms of 'hotel' facilities. Hotelling involves individuals in booking space, technology and support services through a 'concierge' service. It can be little more than hot-desking for visiting employees or it can be a full service adopted throughout a company where no employee has their own space. Property developers are also looking at building offices on the 'hotel' model for multiple occupiers, where services can be provided under hourly, daily and monthly licences.

Despite the rapid spread of technology and more flexible ways of working, the role of the office is evolving rather than disappearing, and the relationship between employer and employee is changing as a result. The notion of a single place of work, is yielding to one in which work is distributed through time and space. Real estate will need to respond with products and services that reflect the new relationship.

OPERATIONS

The relationship between workers and their places of work focuses on the operational infrastructure necessary to support new forms of work and distributed or mobile workers. It seems inevitable that more people will be spending less time at a designated desk. More and more people will be pulled (by quality of life factors) and pushed (by employers eager to save overhead costs) to work at least part-time from home. There is also anecdotal evidence that the number of selfemployed and small limited companies is increasing in key sectors, reflecting the ease with which individuals can now operate commercially outside the bounds of larger companies. While estimates of the number of people actually teleworking vary widely – anything up to 10 per cent of the workforce – the fact is that more and more people are mobile, either within the office and involved in collaborative work, or away from the office undertaking, for example, client work. In either case, traditional approaches to the provision of facilities services will need to evolve into demand-driven regimes.

Financial resource trail	**Business**
Human resource trail	**People**
Physical resource trail	**Property**
Information resource trail	**Knowledge**

▲ **3.4**   Four generic trails to the future[4]

Facilities services are part of the *experience* of an organisation, whether for employee, customer or visitor, and so they must reflect the values, processes and brand of the organisation.

As the practice of the distributed workforce in distributed workplaces gains ground, there will need to be more sophisticated and responsive approaches to supplying the services and support infrastructure. This will in turn require greater co-ordination with other operational areas such as human resources and technology. Facilities managers can no longer work in isolation, simply providing the traditional menu of hard and soft services. They must be working in an enabling role, providing support to complex business processes through space and time, and working in an integrated manner with other corporate resource areas (Figure 3.4).

Wireless fidelity (WiFi) will be a key enabler in this area, and is set for explosive growth, further loosening the bonds to a fixed physical environment. WiFi enables companies to extend their networks to impractical or costly locations (homes, hotels, transport interchanges, etc), allowing easy internet and network access to remote or mobile workers.

With the increase in contract work where individuals and teams from one or more companies come together for the duration of a project, the organisation may more easily be seen on the computer screen than in the physical world. When it has no physical existence, an organisation is said to be 'virtual'. But the virtual company still has to operate and needs technology, support, and usually a meeting place. The trends would seem to indicate that when a virtual company is established, its 'parent' companies do not disappear; they simply spawn another organisation for the project which in turn needs space. If virtual companies do occur on a large scale, there should be significant cost savings but new management skills and working practices will be needed to manage an organisation which is 'not there'.

A further impact of flexible work patterns combined with developments in technology is the prospect that for many organisations, the demands that they place on their buildings in terms of energy use and environmental controls will lessen. The property boom of the 1980s and early 1990s was caused partly because of the obsolescence of much of the office stock built during the 1960s and 1970s. Suddenly, the complexity of buildings and building services grew in order to accommodate the ever more intense deployment of technological infrastructure used by occupiers. However, recent trends suggest that the intensity of technology in many buildings will reduce.

Buildings will continue to have wired networks but they will increasingly use fibre optics rather than copper cable, and WiFi will have a growing significance within buildings. The former will be used where a totally reliable connection is needed and to carry bandwidth-hungry information such as video conferencing. The greater adoption of mobile working and plug-and-play devices linked *via* the internet will mean that the huge communications rooms in basements will become much smaller. Thus it is likely that, for most businesses, the demands that they place on their physical surroundings will diminish rather than intensify. Connectivity is now the single most important criterion, and WiFi and Bluetooth technology, together with laptops, PDAs and computer tablets will distribute demand, and reduce the need, for example, for raised floors and expensive-to-maintain air handling systems.

The impact of wireless technology is not limited to the work process, but is also impacting building services. For example, Motorola's ZigBee technology enables the automation, control, monitoring and maintenance in buildings to take place in a wireless environment, thereby lessening the demand for huge risers packed with cabling. The most likely impacts of such trends are that occupiers' needs will become more diverse, with implications for services infrastructure, while smaller units will become more important and space will become more commoditised.

As well as technological obsolescence, there is also the question of economic obsolescence on operational efficiency. Corporate occupiers have become much more adept in recent years at specifying their requirements and they have also begun to question the whole life costs of buildings. It has become commonplace in 'Private Finance Initiative' (PFI) deals, for example, to specify the running costs of buildings. The outcome of these trends is a demand for certainty over cost, and for the 'de-specifying' of expensive features that increase running costs. Everything from air handling systems to glazing systems to marble receptions are now reviewed for their cost implications.

ASSETS

In addition to performing as workplaces, offices are also owned and traded for the purpose of earning a return through capital growth and rental income. The relationship between occupiers and suppliers focuses on the office as an asset, or as an investment. The problem is that for many years, offices have underperformed. For example, in real terms, office rents are no higher now than they were in the 1970s. Consequently, institutional investors have reduced their holdings in property from around 20 per cent to around 7 per cent today, and most property companies operate at a significant discount to net asset value. This will become a more pronounced driver of change as owners and investors seek better returns. They will, for example, find new ways of securing value. Signs of this are evident in traditional property companies, who now provide services alongside their development and leasing activity.

In 2004, two key UK property markets – the City of London and the Thames Valley – suffered vacancy rates up to 15 per cent. This followed three years of strong economic performance and full employment. Such dynamics suggest that something structural rather than cyclical is happening within the office market, and the property supply industry will have to respond with greater flexibility and more innovative products and services. Within the context of these market dynamics, consumer pressure will be a key driver of change in the years ahead. The business of real estate management has professionalised over the past 20 years, to become an effective lobby for change. The fact that Government is intervening in the area of leases is symptomatic of consumer pressure. Greater flexibility in contracts is likely to emerge as suppliers recognise and respond to the changing dynamics of the market. Occupiers have also become more effective in defining, measuring and monitoring their occupancy needs. Such approaches use sophisticated MIS systems that link space to financial performance measures, allowing constant review of the disposition and cost of space. The impact is to act as a brake on the acquisition of new space.

Government influences on property, both at the national and European level, are likely to become more evident in the years ahead. Policy frameworks aimed at sustainable development, for example, are likely to influence everything from construction materials, to energy use, to travel to work. There is likely to be a greater emphasis on town-centred development that maximises the advantages of public transport, and on developments that contain a richer mix of uses.

The Enron and WorldCom debacles have led the US Congress to enact far-reaching measures to introduce transparency and accountability into public companies. The 2002 Sarbanes-Oxley Act (SOX) applies to all quoted US companies and puts in place CEO/CFO certification of accounts; improved financial disclosures, and newly defined roles for directors, accountants and attorneys. Given that real estate has a material impact on many companies' financial statements, new priorities will emerge. For example, corporate real estate executives (CREs) will need to provide better, up-to-date information on their portfolios; they will need rigorous processes tracking acquisitions and disposals; they will need to normalise definitions, assumptions and metrics in transactions; they will need to document comprehensive real estate expenditure, and ensure accounting standards are applied to all excess space in the portfolio. All this will lead to a much tighter control of real estate assets, and probably to less willingness to lease real estate without a very clear business case being prepared and approved.

One further area of change likely to impact real estate as an asset is the re-organisation of the supply chain. This began in the mid-1990s but still has some way to go. The key driver is that owners have begun to recognise that delivery of the asset is no longer sufficient to secure a worthwhile return. We have already seen the emergence of PFI and its various private sector look-alikes, but we are likely to see more examples of the integration of the delivery and management of space.

RESPONDING TO CHANGE WITH RESPONSIVE WORKPLACES

It has been argued here that the real estate agendas of the past two decades, which have focused on the design of the product and then on its performance, are giving way to a new agenda based on relationships. The relationships between employers and their employees, between workers and their places of work, and between occupiers and suppliers will become increasingly important in determining the form and function of the emerging office environment. Perhaps one of the most direct impacts of this relationship-based approach is the need for a more integrated approach to the management of an organisation's three strategic resources: people, technology and space.

Traditionally, these aspects of organisational planning have existed as separate managerial silos, but as organisational planning demands more flexible approaches to the deployment of resources, there will be a need for a more co-ordinated approach to resource planning. As corporate planners consider areas such as best practice, knowledge management, change management programmes and cost control measures, they will require integrated approaches and strategies for dealing with them. One of the implications of integrated infrastructure management is that management tools will become more generic so that they can be used together.

The new, relationship-based agenda will call for new skills among real estate managers, who will need to be able to translate the needs of stakeholders into the language of the business, thereby allowing them to communicate effectively with managers of the business. And as the management of office space becomes more sophisticated, and as demands become more diverse, the office supply industry will need to respond in kind. In other words, as the office economy matures, there will emerge a growing imperative to leverage more value out of what exists rather than to rely on growth or an inflationary backdrop to justify creating anew. This will ultimately lead to the demise of the traditional, 'let and forget' approach to real estate provision and lead instead to a model in which investment in property is accompanied by intensive, occupier-focused management, and the growth of a service-led philosophy.

4

THE FUTURE WORKPLACE, OPPORTUNITIES, REALITIES AND MYTHS: A PRACTICAL APPROACH TO CREATING MEANINGFUL ENVIRONMENTS

Nicola M. Gillen
DEGW plc

SUMMARY

Nicola Gillen, an architect and workplace strategist with considerable experience in working for major global corporations in Europe and North America, reflects on the need for space to both communicate the values of organisations and to meet functional demands. She uses the example of the global pharmaceutical company GlaxoSmithKline, to describe how the language of urban design is being transferred to the workplace in the search for new ways of accommodating collaboration, exchange and communication. The allocation of space to individuals by function and status is subsumed by analysing patterns of work, and creating menus of settings from which staff can choose for themselves the most appropriate ambience to achieve their specific business goals. 'The street' provides for casual encounters, visibility and the chance to linger, whilst the 'kitchen table' is a focus for informal small group discussions. Information technology is freeing up the place of work. Settings are no longer tied to one building or a single geographical location but can be spread across localities, under different ownerships, within a virtual office environment. Office building typologies, Gillen argues, in addition to reflecting the function, sophistication of servicing and infrastructure required, must also be defined by management and tenure structures. An organisation's accommodation needs may be met by a combination of four types of space. 'Iconic', reflecting the long-term values of the company; 'Event', high-quality space for hire; 'Home base', flexible, pragmatic space for back office functions and the 'Serviced office' on short lease to match sudden changes in demand. Currently, most firms are still predominantly housed in front or back offices with fixed tenure. Consequently, we should anticipate a greater flexibility of tenure and even greater differentiation of settings.

INTRODUCTION

The need to accommodate office workers from 9.00 to 5.00 is being replaced by the need to accommodate dispersed communities of more or less independent collaborators across virtual and physical space. Distinct work patterns and characteristics of space occupancy are emerging. Unfortunately our existing office building stock has been largely designed and managed to support a much more static workforce which may be rapidly disappearing.

Work environments are in a state of transition from something familiar and predictable to something not yet defined, multi-locational, virtual and physical. This state of transition has led to many predictions about the future of work and office buildings. Ten years on from the first edition of *Reinventing the Workplace*, this chapter aims to develop some of these predictions and to challenge the reality of others.

As virtuality and dispersal increase, organisations will become more demanding and discerning about where and how they choose to locate buildings. The old model of an office building as a command and control structure is being replaced by offices as a way of bringing people together. Organisations are trying to do more with increasingly scarce resources, less time, less money in the context of more competition. Paradoxically, as activities become more dispersed, physical space and meeting face to face are becoming not less valued but more.

It has been proposed that dispersed and flexible working may reduce the need for space. Is this true? We have seen the nature of space change inside office buildings in terms of flexible space planning and hotelling systems of sharing space. We have seen the management of office buildings change in terms of ownership and lease length, as with PFIs (Private Finance Initiatives) for public services, highly serviced offices such as Regus and, moving forward, the integration of facilities management other operational services such as IT.[1] We have seen space shift elsewhere, with outsourcing, people working from home, and more recently, moving work offshore. There may not be signs that the need for space is reducing. They could simply indicate that the management, configuration and experience of office space are changing. There has been a trend to discuss dispersed working in a bi-polar fashion. However, the question may not be either/or but rather what is appropriate at which moment in time.

Are distributed working and flexibility realistic? Naivety is common in the literature on flexibility and distributed working. Rather than these new ideas being a panacea for everyone, such opportunities and choices are not available to all workers in all sectors. Well-educated knowledge workers living in the most developed parts of the world, with access to the technology and resources that give them choices, are the lucky ones who can take advantage of distributed working and flexible work policies.

This is not new; multi-nationals have needed to work across boundaries of time and place for some time. Geographically dispersed teams are already a reality for many global organisations. Yet real estate strategies are still largely based on the assumption that workers can only be accommodated in one place at a time. People have been working in dispersed ways for some time, but have they always had the tools and systems in place to support them? Do organisations really understand and respond to the realities of working with virtual communities? Without the proper support systems, organisations tend to operate in two worlds: physical hubs and virtual networks,[2] maximising the efficiency and effectiveness of neither. A handful of businesses have seriously begun to address this over the past 10 years, such as Accenture, British Petroleum (BP) and GlaxoSmithKline (GSK).

How and where organisations locate is of increasing importance to con-sumers and shareholders. How an organisation treats its employees, suppliers and partners will become more closely connected to how it does business. Corporate Social Responsibility (CSR) is visibly higher on organisations' agendas.

There is no doubt that this new emphasis on place and community will make the contribution of design more important. With mergers and a blurring of boundaries between sectors, organisations need to work harder at distinguishing themselves from others. The need to provide spaces for geographically dispersed communities to come together puts new pressures on real estate teams and office buildings. The traditional specifications of office buildings need to be questioned. Research shows that allocating 30 per cent of a building to support spaces such as confer-ence rooms and canteen, is typical today. What is the appropriate ratio likely to be in the future – perhaps as much as 40 or 50 per cent? Do new work patterns call for new office typologies? Using the city as a metaphor of the workplace is one way of planning work environments in a more meaningful way. Corridors are being replaced by 'Streets', formal meeting suites by 'Piazzas' and seas of open plan desks by 'neigh-bourhoods' of mixed use spaces. Placemaking really is becoming more important as the knowledge economy grows.

COMMUNICATING VALUES AND BRAND THROUGH SPACE

Organisations express their values through the work environment, both by branding with artefacts, or by branding through protocols for the use of space.

Branding through artefacts means using elements such as products, logos, advertising campaigns or art collections to communicate collective values. An organisation's artefacts can be physical or virtual and should communicate what the business stands for. Buildings can be powerful symbols of business values.

As organisations become larger, more complex, and become more distant from manufacturing processes and closer to services and sales, it is understandable that they feel the need to remind their own staff as well as everyone who visits their buildings of the products they create and sell. Physical products, displayed in work environments is the most common method of branding through artefacts. However, products being placed in display cabinets can be problematic as this means removing products from their normal context.

Another common approach is to create an exhibition of the history of the organisation, its brands, good works and its impact on society. One of the best examples of this is the award-winning Guinness Storehouse in Dublin. The Storehouse is a visitors' centre as well as a three-dimensional brand experience. Described by Diageo as a 'Media Beacon', it is an unusually elaborate example of a corporate-branded environment. Other examples are Autostadt and the Cadbury Village, places more closely aligned with Disney or Gracelands than conventional corporate environments.

Using three-dimensional work environments as a canvas to express brand values can be one of the most successful ways of using artefacts as communicators. Perhaps this is because the use of the work place as a communication device can go beyond the simple display of the brand to the direct engagement of the people behind it. Wally Olins[3] sets down a series of guidelines for successful branding, arguing that organisations should brand through four vectors, 'product, environment, communication and behaviour'. These vectors are the four 'senses' of brand.

Branding through behaviours means that an organisation is committed to demonstrating its values through the way it does business, how it treats its staff, its promotion of environmental policies including where it chooses to locate. Organisations are increasingly concerned with the way they do business, making Corporate Social Responsibility part of their core business strategy in order to be perceived favourably by investors and consumers. Sustainability registers track energy consumption; international agreements like the Kyoto Protocol set the scene for change, highlighting protagonists and dissenters.

Demonstrating brand values through behaviours and ways of operating can have a much more profound impact than the single emphasis for the brand in its own terms. A message delivered through people has much more integrity.

Changes in technology such as wireless LANs and attitudes to employment such as portfolio working [4] are resulting in fundamental changes in work patterns. Sustainability, flexibility, travel, personal wellbeing and greater longevity are creating a demand to which organisations need to respond. Many consumers want the procurement process to become more transparent, to know the origin of raw materials, how they are transported and how local producers are treated.

Such demands infiltrate the workplace. If an organisation claims to be open and accessible as an example, then everyone will expect employees to behave in a consistent way. Prospective employees may raise their eyebrows if 'open and accessible leadership' is hidden behind layers of secretaries and closed doors. How the workplace is designed and how people behave within it can be extremely powerful ways of demonstrating brand values.

Choosing between communicating brand through artefacts or through behaviours is not the issue. Combinations matched to the profile of different businesses are much more likely. Olins[5] describes branding as having two roles, 'persuading outsiders to buy and persuading insiders to believe'.

URBAN TYPOLOGIES IN INTERNAL ENVIRONMENTS

Irregular working hours, inner city rental costs pushing organisations out to the edges of cities, transport challenges, the need to retain talent by creating a sense of place have all contributed to reinventing settings within the building. BA's well-publicised Waterside head office near Heathrow is one of the first UK office buildings to have created an internal 'Street', a central spine of activity connecting people and providing downtown services such as restaurants, or grocery store and dry cleaners. The convenience and informality of 'Street Cafés', the focal point of a 'Town Square', the scale and mix of uses in 'Neighbourhoods' are all typologies that respond to new organisational needs. Some of these 'urban' environments offer variety and interest but not all. There are probably more examples of unimaginative borrowing from urban typologies than genuine successes. A wide corridor stretching the length of a building punctuated with a few coffee points and meeting rooms is not a sustainable 'street'.

However, the pharmaceutical company GlaxoSmithKline (GSK) has successfully made use of an urban typology in its new global headquarters in Brentford. The GSK Street is a focal point for the organisation globally, a place where the wider community works, socialises, exhibits and where frequently individuals bump into people they have not seen in a while. The street is curved, it rises and falls and is supported by a grocery store, bank, hairdressers, art gallery and a series of restaurants. The street café (called 'Kix') is more informal and fast Figure 4.1. Indeed, this 'street' is so attractive that it has been criticised for drawing too much activity from the work floors.

Also some departments now want to recreate their own community space (one called a Piazza) in their own team areas Figure 4.2.

A 'Piazza' is intended to provide a space for exhibition, gatherings and, chance encounters in a more meaningful way than is possible in a conventional corridor. Such neighbourhoods respond to variety, scale, individuals and teams. They are the antithesis of seas of open plan desks. The Neighbourhood as a typology is becoming so widely used that it has also become a design process now known as 'Neighbourhood Planning'. 'Neighbourhood Planning' is a process by which a business creates a mix of open and closed, individual and group spaces based upon the needs and work patterns of particular teams.

The *principles of neighbourhood planning* are:

1 **Understand work patterns**, and what people actually do. Work patterns must be understood at an organisational level taking each department separately. Early strategic research with GSK revealed the work patterns (Figure 4.3).
2 **Match work patterns to settings**. A setting can be a space such as a small meeting room, an office or a coffee point. A setting can be virtual as well as physical, a chat room for example. This matching exercise is often done in an inclusive way, i.e. through focus groups with the users.
3 **Develop a menu of spaces**. From the huge variety of settings that may or may not be appropriate for a particular organisation,

▲4.1 'The Street Café Kix' GSK House Global Headquarters

a short list should be created. This short list is then presented in the form of a menu of spaces. The menu illustrates the range of spaces necessary to create a flexible, reconfigurable set of neighbourhoods specific to individual teams. This menu can be assembled in a variety of ways depending on the group. The example (Figure 4.4), was developed for GSK, clusters settings along two axes, from types of work on the vertical axis (individual and collaborative activities) to types of spaces on the horizontal axis (individually owned and shared spaces).

▲**4.2**   'The Piazza' team area GSK House Global Headquarters

Work Pattern	Characteristics
Global senior manager (cross-functional)	Communicator. Manages teams and functions across multiple sites globally.
Project manager (cross-functional)	Team leader, communicator. Manages project teams across sites and based within a key team or function
Virtual (Within a function)	Connects virtually to GSK. Spends time working remotely e.g. entire team is based elsewhere, Sales function or Clinical Trials
Team resident (Within a function)	Balance of individual and team work. Based within a team on a GSK site
Research resident (Within a function)	Dominant individual work. Based on a single site but works predominantly alone

▲**4.3**   Hypothetical work styles based on early research for GSK's Global Workplace Guidelines 'Space Programme'

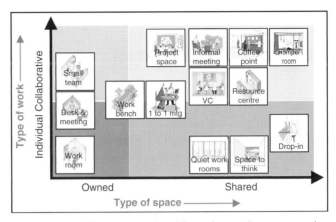

▲**4.4** A GSK-specific menu of settings based upon work patterns

4 **Develop neighbourhoods of spaces**. Configure the menu into a series of neighbourhood layouts depending upon the whole range of work patterns within a department. Some departments may, for example, have much more enclosure than others. The benefits of Neighbourhood Planning are that it allows variety according to work pattern while maintaining choice. The menu can be created as a generic model or with a specific building in mind. When working with a specific building, settings must be designed in a modular way in line with the existing building grid to allow flexibility as settings offer change. The example neighbourhood (Figure 4.5) is generic, that is with no particular building in mind. It shows spaces clustered in another way into 'Hot', noisy interactive spaces and 'Cool', quiet, controlled spaces.

Up to this point in the process, Neighbourhood Planning is functional, allocating space on the basis of what people do. Now design, form and style become important. The functional elements must now be given a set of design characteristics including, for example, consideration of whether elements should be solid or transparent, traditional or modern.

5 **From Neighbourhoods to 'Workscapes'.** Looking to the future, the natural extension of the Neighbourhood Planning approach is to take into account spaces outside the office as well as inside. For some people, time will be split across a variety of locations, while others will be largely based in one place. In order to address this, the idea of neighbourhoods can be taken further to what has been described as a 'Workscape'.[6] Workscapes are effectively a summation of all the spaces any individual worker might operate within. The Workscape environment is for a 'Global Senior Manager' (Figure 4.6) and reflects the fact that such individuals spend most of their time either communicating

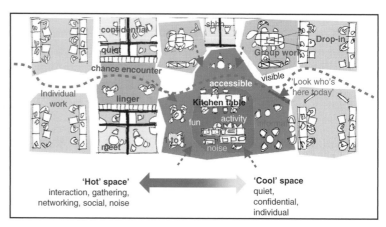

▲4.5   A team- or department-specific neighbourhood based upon the menu of settings

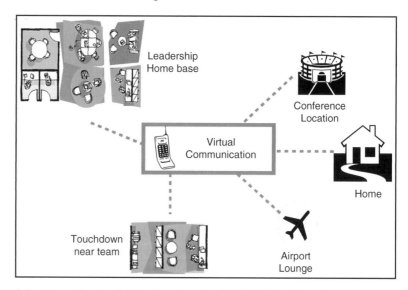

▲4.6   Hypothetical Workscape for 'GSK Global senior manager'

with others or travelling. The range of spaces they use can include the office, airport, hotels, conference centres and home. The web that holds all these spaces together is virtual communication.

The second example is for a 'GSK Team Resident' (Figure 4.7). This profile involves individuals spending most of their time at their designated 'home base' accessing other facilities as needed.

Dealing with this range of spaces quickly highlights the importance of servicing and management in work environments. High-quality design needs to be matched with an equally high level of servicing.

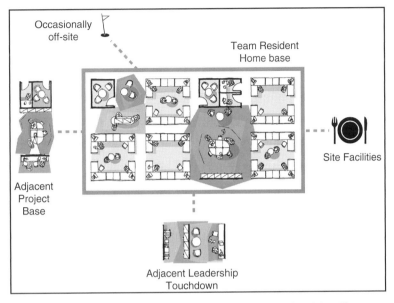

▲4.7   Hypothetical Workscape for 'GSK Team Resident'

The members of the Facilities Management (FM) team who run GSK House take the levels of services in their building seriously. They are accessible and proactive, their office being located directly on the street. The Site Director has a background in the hotel industry. They practice what they preach, leading the way in terms of sharing desks and challenging hierarchy.

6 **From Workscapes to a distributed Real Estate Strategy**. Beyond Neighbourhood Planning and the creation of Workscapes leads us ultimately to a consideration of Real Estate Strategy. In order to realise the efficiency and effectiveness of this demand-led approach to design, it is necessary to consider the implications for each business building's policy. The benefits of this approach can only be realised if work environments respond to how organisations manage and procure buildings. Business drivers such as multiple locations, virtual teaming, rental prices and transport links have an impact on the location, quality and quantity of an organisation's real estate. These emerging patterns demand not just new building typologies, but also new systems of management including lease lengths.

Figure 4.8 sets out a hypothetical Real Estate Strategy designed to respond to two very different work profiles. The vertical axis maps Core Space, (managed by an organisation) against the horizontal Non-Core Space, (managed by others). The boxes traversing on the diagonal, represent a range of work patterns from Physical Team working to

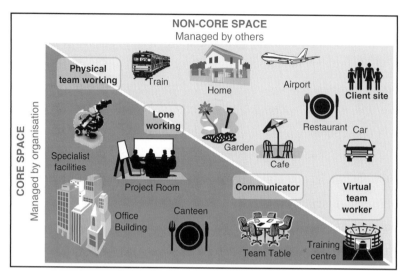

▲4.8   Allocating real estate on the basis of work patterns

Virtual Team working. Physical Team workers would probably spend the majority of their time in the office building where they are based. A Virtual Team worker by contrast may spend a lot of time travelling.

A CONCEPTUAL MODEL OF BUILDING TYPOLOGIES

Diversification of office space and the infrastructure challenges of accommodating work in the city is discussed by Adrian Leaman in Chapter I. The ideas of building typologies are developed with 'generic, sheds and specialist buildings' emerging. The drivers for these typologies largely reflect upon function, sophistication of servicing and infrastructure required.

To build upon this argument an additional driver is proposed, that of image value or expression. Expression is concerned with the iconography and symbolism of a building or location. This factor will effect location, occupancy, duration of occupancy and design. Expression is increasingly important for businesses as links with colleagues become more virtual and less intermittent. Swiss Re's Headquarters in the City of London, commonly known as the Gherkin, communicates powerful messages about the position of Swiss Re within the City of London and the financial industry. Increasingly, organisations are concerned about what their workplaces and locations say about their values. Often, greater the image value of

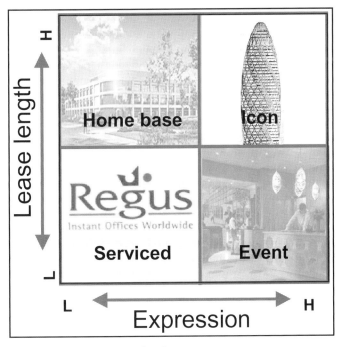

▲4.9   'Occupancy expression'

buildings, greater is the cost of occupancy. The model (Figure 4.9) explores the relationship between expression and lengths of leases and of occupancy within a fourfold building typology: Icon, Event, Serviced Office and Home Base.

'Icon', in the upper right-hand box, indicates strong expression and a long lease in an iconic building. Icon buildings are often designed by signature architects. The investment that goes into an icon building tends to result in either ownership or lengthy occupation. An example of this typology is Lloyd's of London.

An 'Event' is a high-quality landmark building available for hire. Classic examples of this type are private clubs and historic buildings. Flexibility is not so important because occupancy is only for short periods. The main objective in going to these places is to create a memorable experience.

'Serviced Offices' are now common. They offer businesses instant accommodation on terms matched with the needs of the business. One of the best-known examples is Regus.

'Home Bases' accommodate back offices or out-of-town functions. This type is often found in business parks and on the edges of cities. This is where the longest leases occur. Home Bases need to be very flexible in

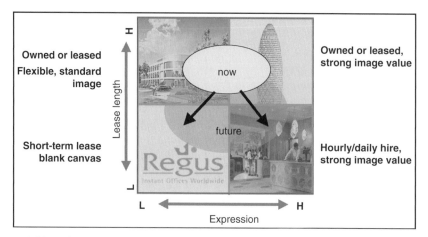

▲4.10 'Occupancy expression'

their building grids and IT infrastructure. Classic examples are Stockley Park and Chiswick Park, both in West London.

Mobile work patterns, dispersal and increased collaboration between businesses result in people working across all these types. The Icon building can be the front door of an organisation, the place to host visitors and to woo new recruits; the Home Base is for back of the house activities; Event spaces are for special occasions; Serviced Offices are for one-off projects or for setting up an office in a new location. While many businesses already occupy all four quadrants, few have consciously devised their Real Estate Strategies accordingly (Figure 4.10).

SOME REALITIES OF THE DISTRIBUTED WORK PLACE

Flexible and dispersed ways of working are still the preserve of a minority of well-educated, wealthy individuals who live in the most developed parts of the world. Much of the literature concerning the future of work mistakenly treats choice and flexibility as given. The reality is that few people have access to the resources that allow them to make such choices. Richard Sennett[7] discussed the negative impact of constant change and flexibility on our value systems.

While the advent of the wireless LAN in 1997 [8] made it possible for those with access to mobile technology to live in a nomadic way, it is simplistic to think that such technologies and lifestyles, free individuals from the need for community. People are attached to peoples and places, partners, children, towns and countries. While the freedoms that these technologies and lifestyles allow are convenient, they do not provide a permanent or desirable way of life for everyone.

In fact, virtual spaces have opened up new possibilities for connecting and collaborating. Some of these opportunities allow work to happen in a more efficient and sustainable manner, with less travelling and more time. But much of the debate about virtual and physical space has been bi-polar in nature, and this does not represent a true picture of the issues. It is not a question of choosing between virtual or physical space but rather deciding which is best suited to particular activities.[9]

Given the volume of literature available on the future of work, it is curious that few offer insights into how virtual communities can be sustained. Fewer still address the new management styles that are necessary to work effectively in dispersed ways. While technology and choice offer more freedom in terms of where and when we work, they also challenge us in terms of our effectiveness.

Does collaboration need to become more scheduled and less *ad hoc*? Good virtual collaboration tools are widely available, such as Instant Messenger. These tools can work as effectively as face-to-face collaboration, and perhaps even more so for certain populations.[10] However, much social networking is done at coffee points or over lunch. Serendipitous interactions can be lost when technology mediates the connection. Collaboration needs to become more scheduled when people are not physically present. Scheduled events tend to follow an agenda and have stricter timescales. A scientist who spends most of her day in front of her PC in NetMeetings, video conferences and teleconferences remarked that 'the worst thing about virtual meetings is that no one brings tea and biscuits'. While she spends most of her day collaborating with others online, physically she sits alone in an office rarely seeing anyone.

What is the impact on head offices? Looking forward, the reality is that many organisations will have a mixed population partly of full time, physically present people and partly of people working flexibly or remotely. For people to work effectively from afar, their time needs to be well planned. Their colleagues need to know, how and when to contact them. The same principles apply to those 'based at head office' but, since it is easier to find and connect with people who are physically present, scheduling can be looser. Most organisations balance predictable and unpredictable work loads. In organisations with a large proportion of flexible or remote workers, the pattern can emerge from those who are physically present having to deal with the unpredictable as well as their own predictable workload. People who are physically present can find themselves under greater pressure than those who work remotely.

Dispersed working raises the question of whether virtual space will result in organisations providing less physical space. Since people will always need to be located somewhere, the answer is not less space but rather different types of space at different times in different places.

CONCLUSIONS

Our proposition is that organisations will become more concerned with the nature and quality of the spaces they occupy. The challenge is to provide effective and meaningful work environments for an increasingly diverse work force. To maximise effectiveness, organisations will need to be more integrated in how they manage their tools and resources. For example, travel budgets should be connected to technology budgets, reinvesting savings from one to the other. Desk observational studies over a ten-year-period show that office buildings are not intensively used, 35–45 per cent is a typical maximum occupancy level of a desk and a 65–70 per cent occupancy level for an entire building. Such spaces could be consolidated, the excess disposed off and released funds invested in better and more appropriate spaces. Moreover to make the most of resources, businesses need to stop duplication, by, for example, managing IT and space separately with separate budgets and priorities. It may be more important to equip mobile workers with the latest and best technology than with office space. Until organisations start to leverage their assets more holistically, the true potential of virtual and physical spaces will not be realised.

Organisations will increasingly seize the opportunity that their buildings and locations offer in terms of communicating their values. Office buildings will have to accommodate communities with all the spatial variety implied rather than providing anonymous environments for anonymous individuals. The development of Urban Typologies and Neighbourhood Planning in office environments is a reaction to the pent-up demand for more meaningful work places. Commercial organisations are clearly concerned with maximising shareholder value. It has been said that the desire to create a self-contained 'city' in the office is more about keeping people at work rather than giving them choices. However, office buildings that create more memorable workplaces can only support and enrich the lives of the people who work there.

The argument that organisations will need dramatically less space in the future to accommodate networks of autonomous workers oversimplifies the issues. Organisations will need a more diverse portfolio of real estate that will have to be managed in an integrated way. HR and IT will become more closely involved in real estate issues and real estate will contribute more to the behaviours, values and tools of businesses. Building briefs of the future will not only deal with quantitative and qualitative matters but also with people and the management of space. The way ahead is cross-disciplinary, dynamic and more conscientious. These changes are an opportunity to bring design thinking back to the centre not just of real estate projects but of business strategy.

SECTION II
REAL ESTATE DILEMMAS

Today, everyone involved with the production, management and marketing of property is faced with multiple and seemingly conflicting interests. Charles Handy, in The Empty Raincoat[*] discusses the shift from a value in material to intellectual property, and identifies these shifting values as a key feature of the 'age of paradox'. The decisions we make today are no longer that of 'either . . . or' but rather 'both . . . and'. Since the first edition of Reinventing the Workplace, designing for a world of paradox has become even more important. Companies are striving to speed up innovation and to harness intellectual capital; to be both individual and collaborative, to provide for both privacy and interaction, and to have centralised meetings whilst enabling people to work in a distributed network of settings. Leaman, in Building in the Age of Paradox[†] predicted that the balancing of conflicting interests will be at the heart of solving the challenges of the twenty-first century. He foresaw that the biggest paradox will be 'between continued economic development and the new agenda of sustainability'. He suggests that ' . . . as we progress towards 2010, the agendas of business efficiency and environmental responsibility can become complementary: they are both ultimately about waste avoidance . . .. Information technology can provide the means to meet the goals of improved economic performance and sustainability simultaneously . . . Systems which were previously incompatible or in conflict suddenly become connected and start working towards the same ends'.

In the changing world of office design, the challenge is to find physical and organisational forms that balance conflicting but complementary interests. In this section, we explore the impact that national cultures have on perceptions of the workplace. Conflicting interests can be seen as opportunities to provide a diversity of settings that address both status and function. We address the paradox for corporate real estate of retaining property value whilst adding to the success of the business.

New perceptions of work open up fresh opportunities for innovative real estate solutions. Potential conflicts, when viewed not as binary choices between this

---

*Handy C (1994) The Empty Raincoat. Random Century London.
[†] Leaman A (1995) Building in the Age of Paradox, IOAAS.

or that, but as opportunities for conflicting demands to co-exist, suggest very different accommodation approaches, such as distributed work, shared space and new partnering arrangements. Dilemmas are also challenges. The property industry, in the midst of the dilemma faced by corporations to improve business performance not despite declining property values will see the role of real estate providers as not merely brokers of property but as global facilities managers. Corporations may outsource property provision, management and services to global facility operations. The key to property investment must therefore lie in adding value to property through better management services.

Since the first edition of this book, outsourcing of not merely building facility management, but complete real estate portfolios has become the central focus to the property market. The trend has also been hastened by central government's embracing of Public Finance Initiatives (PFI), transforming contractors into service providers and property developers into partners with the potential of sharing in their tenants' long-term business success.

5

OFFICE CULTURES: INTERNATIONAL DIFFERENCES IN WORKPLACE DESIGN

Jurian van Meel and Hans de Jonge, Delft University of Technology
Geert Dewulf, Twente University

SUMMARY

The world of office design is more international than ever. Corporations are expanding into new markets and transferring both production and office work to the other – cheaper – end of the world. They need sales offices, research facilities, call centres and local headquarters, and such requirements seem to be similar wherever they are located. The business imperative is that all these premises must be functional, flexible and cost-efficient. Meanwhile, the instant transfer of knowledge means that around the world, real estate managers are now familiar with the latest and most visionary examples of desk sharing, teleworking, club offices and hotelling. How global are these concepts? Can these theories be implemented anywhere, in any culture? It is questionable, whether these terms have the same meaning all over the world. Does the word 'efficiency' have the same meaning in Hong Kong as in Amsterdam? Do American facility managers refer to the same layout solutions as their German counterparts when they talk about 'flexibility'?

Juriaan van Meel from the Department of Project Management and Real Estate at Delft draws on considerable research experience with corporate real estate managers in both Europe and North America to show that office architecture and workplace design are shaped as much by local conditions as by international corporate practice. European, office cultures differ strongly from the US. This chapter identifies how 'tribal' needs for status, territoriality and interaction can contradict global standardised workplace concepts. The authors highlight the cultural, legislative and economic differences that real estate professionals encounter when working across borders. In this context, the importance of 'soft' factors of culture and psychology is tempered by 'hard' technology-driven demands of corporate real estate directors. This chapter ends by debating how far these differences might persist in a globalised world, particularly given the growing influence of new office cultures emerging in India and China.

GLOBALISATION

We seem to be living in what Marshall McLuhan called the 'global village' where national cultures are disappearing. The worldwide popularity of branded consumer goods such as Prada shoes, Heineken beer and Starbucks coffee underlines this trend. Tastes, markets and hence culture, seem to have become similar everywhere.

Globalisation is reflected in the built environment. Many writers have commented on the fact that cities are becoming more and more alike, with chains of standardised hotels, franchise restaurants, brand stores, fitness centres and multi-screen cinemas.[1] Strolling through the interior malls at Canary Wharf in London's docklands, at Potsdamerplatz in Berlin and the underground Manege Square in Moscow is fundamentally the same experience.

The same comment can be made about the office environment. Looking at the slick-skinned, air-conditioned office towers that dominate the skyline of virtually every major city, one can argue that globalisation translates in the cityscape as 'the replication of an architectural language symbolic of international corporate triumph'.[2] Anyplace where the flow of international investment touches the ground, clean and shiny business district arise. When Norman Foster built the Century Tower in Tokyo, architectural critic Diane Ghirardo wrote: 'Whatever its merits, this (. . .) building could have been built anywhere, even though the design was conditioned by local site constraints'.[3]

Yet, when we look at these same buildings from the inside out, we are exposed to an underlying reality of diversity, which results from the various cultural and economic contexts in which the buildings are produced. The design, layout and use of the actual work environment may be very diverse, even within the same company.[4] Floor plans can vary from high-density, cubicle-filled open plans in Bangalore and Silicon Valley, to spacious cellular offices in Frankfurt and Brussels (Table 5.1). In China, the form and layout of workplaces may depend on the decision of a feng shui master, seeking harmony and equilibrium, while in Amsterdam offices may be refurbished by a 'hip' consultant according to the latest management trend.

DEALING WITH DIVERSITY

Globalisation has a strong impact on the real estate profession. On the supply side, we find architects involved in international competitions,

Table 5.1   Space utilisation per worker: the net usable area divided by the planned headcount for which space is intended

Country	Space utilisation standard per worker (square metre)
Germany	22.5
Netherlands	21.0
Belgium	19.0
Paris	17.0
UK	10.5–11.5
US	20.7–22.1
Japan (Tokyo)	11.6
China (Hong Kong)	13.0
China (mainland)	10.0–12.0
India (Mumbai/Delhi)	12.0

Source: DTZ Research, 2002.

investors looking for new markets, and real estate consultants following their clients abroad. On the demand side, real estate managers are leasing and building new offices to facilitate the internationalisation of their organisation.

Internationalisation generally leads to pressures for standardisation and homogenisation. In particular, American corporations have a tendency for developing uniform workplace standards. Yet, real estate strategies that are successful in your home country may be difficult to translate into effective practice in other regions of the world. Real estate managers are likely to be confronted with different 'office cultures': local standards, expectations, regulations and power-relations concerning office design.

Some of the international differences in office culture may seem trivial, close to clichés. For example, in a Dutch office building, you will always find spacious parking space for bicycles, matching the popular image of the Dutch as being always on bikes. Other local characteristics, however, may be more fundamental and more difficult to deal with. Telework, for example, is not as easily implemented in Southern Europe as in Northern Europe or the US (Table 5.2). This 'digital divide' is caused by various factors, ranging from the limited available space in private housing to the quality of the technical infrastructure. But it also has to do with cultural differences in managerial style and social interaction. In France, for example, 'teletravail' is more likely to be hampered by managerial paternalism than in, say, the UK or Finland.

Table 5.2   Teleworkers (working at least one day from home) as a percentage of the total working population

Country	Teleworkers (%)
Netherlands	21
Denmark	18
United States	17
Finland	16
Sweden	15
United Kingdom	11
Germany	8
France	4
Italy	3
Spain	2
European Union (average)	7

Source: SIBIS, 2002.

Real estate managers have to deal with such differences. They have to find a balance between uniform corporate policies and local particularities. Acting as 'office anthropologists', they should observe local differences, and assess to what extent, and in what way, they should be taken into account. Below we will discuss four factors that are worth noticing since they are likely to leave a strong imprint on local office design:

- workplace culture
- market conditions
- labour relations
- legislation.

Workplace culture

The term 'workplace culture' refers to employees' norms and values concerning the work environment. These norms and values guide organisational behaviour, but also affect office and workplace design.[5] Deal and Kennedy wrote: 'a company's investment in bricks and mortar inevitably says something about its culture'.[6] One of the most crucial cultural factors is status. It is well-known that workplace design can be used as a status symbol. Everybody is familiar with the stereotypical image of self-important managers who occupy large corner offices at the top floor of their office building. This type of over-stated status symbol may be denounced in all international management books, but they have not faded away. The importance of status depends very much on culture.

In hierarchical cultures, managers and their subordinates see each other as unequal. Geert Hofstede, a Dutch expert on organisational culture, noticed that visible status symbols are expected and even encouraged in such cultures.[7] Managers are not likely to give up their spacious offices for a shared desk or a universal footprint. Italy, France and Germany are European examples of particularly hierarchical cultures.

The impact of status on office design can be observed in the headquarters of German car manufacturer Opel, outside Frankfurt. The brief for the building stated that it had to be a non-hierarchical workplace. The British *Architects' Journal*, however, commented wryly that 'the resulting building achieves this within the limitations of common German practice. The fact that the office suites of top management are only slightly larger than those of middle management is seen as pretty revolutionary'.[8]

Working in an hierarchic culture does not necessarily mean that open and universal workplace concepts are doomed to fail. But, it will require more energy and effort. Commitment often wanes when dues have to be paid. Senior executives can change their tune when told to move out of large, private rooms. Middle managers may not be thrilled with the idea of sitting amidst their subordinates.

In egalitarian cultures, new workplace concepts may be easier to implement along all management layers. Such cultures can mostly be found in Scandinavia, where extreme competition for hierarchical advancement and status seem less dominant. Workplace layouts tend to emphasise equality and uniformity rather than hierarchy and power. A good example is the new headquarters for NCC (Figures 5.1 and 5.2), one of Scandinavia's leading construction companies. In their new building in Copenhagen, junior employees and senior executives occupy the same open office space, and all workplaces have natural daylight, natural ventilation, and access to meeting rooms and break-out spaces.

Another crucial cultural factor is the desire for privacy. The development of a person's attitude toward privacy is part of a socialisation process; it is a cultural value. This can be illustrated by two opposite cultures: the German and the Japanese. According to American sociologists, E.T. Hall and M.R. Hall, Germans have a strong sense of privacy. They tend to prefer cellular offices, having their own, rather spacious, territory and they tend to leave their doors closed.[9] Real estate managers are likely to meet resistance when implementing new, more open concepts. Employees are probably too aware of what is 'personal space' and what is 'communal' to give up their attained privacy easily. For this reason, most innovative offices in Northern Europe consist of a mix of spaces

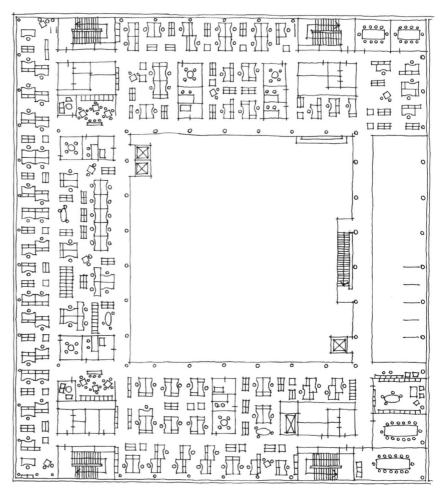

▲5.1 NCC headquarters in Copenhagen (design: Schmidt, Hammer and Lassen). All employees, including top management, work in an open plan, sharing break-out rooms, meeting rooms and pantries

(Figure 5.3): open, enclosed and semi-enclosed, providing possibilities for different types of work. Large open plans remain rare.

In Japan, however, the open plan is an intrinsic part of workplace culture (Figure 5.4). Large spaces with lots of desks are common. While every employee has his or her own work to do, each is very aware of everything else that is happening in the office. The Japanese do not think of this as an invasion of privacy or as eavesdropping on someone else's business. Anything happening in the office is *everybody's* business.

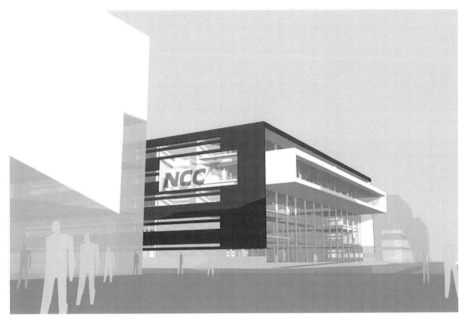

▲**5.2** Exterior NCC headquarters

Market conditions

It is not only 'soft' cultural factors that affect office design. 'Hard' financial conditions also affect the layout of the office. Rent levels are a crucial factor. The cost of office space differs strongly from city to city. In global cities like London, New York or Hong Kong, costs can be twice as high as in Amsterdam, Stockholm or Milan (Table 5.3). These differences are likely to put pressure on accommodation budgets, and therefore on space standards and design efficiency. Differences in rent levels probably explain why the use of space per employee in London is half of that in Amsterdam where rents are half as high. A Dutch employee working in London comments: 'At my previous Dutch employer I had a spacious room. In the heart of London you can forget about that. Most employees are accommodated in a cubicle . . . Fans of Dilbert know what I mean. Such a roofless office pen is small and noisy, and it does not have much of a view'.[10] A survey of Cushman Wakefield Healey & Baker (2002) showed that London employees tend to rate the quality of their office lower than their counterparts in Amsterdam or Frankfurt (Table 5.4).

The impact of high rents can also be felt in major Asian cities like Hong Kong or Tokyo, where space remains a luxury item for most business.

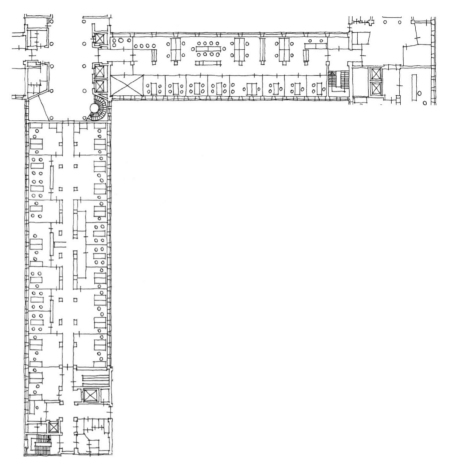

▲**5.3** Fragment of new workplace layout at the Dutch Ministry of Agriculture (design: van den Broek & Bakema). Employees work in a mix of open spaces, enclosed offices, informal areas and meeting rooms

Another crucial market factor lies in the ownership of buildings. In the US, and to a lesser extent, the UK, the office market is dominated by developers and investors. As they aim for low risk, they flood the market with rather conventional, risk-free formulaic buildings. 'Spec' buildings are quick and cheap to build with generic floor plans open to any kind of users. Floor plans tend to be deep and large to 'squeeze' as much rentable space out of an office building as possible.

It is this type of development that has spread throughout most parts of the world. China, for example, has been quick in copying the

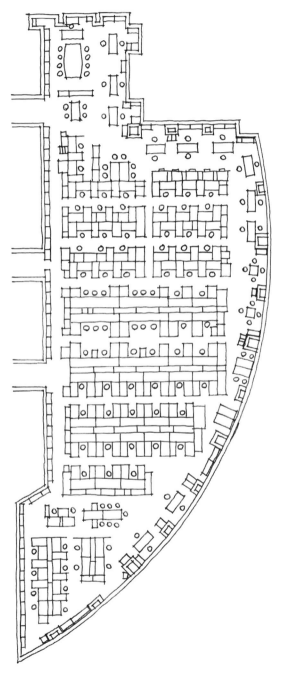

▲ 5.4   Typical high-density open plan in a Japanese office

Table 5.3   Rent levels for several major office locations in the world, indicating huge differences from place to place

City	Class A net rent 2003 (Euro/square metre/year)
Amsterdam	160
Brussels	190
Frankfurt	198
Copenhagen	201
Beijing	324
Stockholm	356
Mumbai, India	386
New York (Mid Town)	440
Hong Kong	485
London (West End)	725
Tokyo	941

Source: Colliers International, 2003.

Table 5.4   Office scores: employees in various European cities were asked to rate the quality of their office buildings

City	Average score
Frankfurt	7.7
Brussels	7.5
Barcelona	7.0
Paris	6.9
Amsterdam	6.6
Milan	6.4
Madrid	6.3
London	6.0

Source: Cushman Wakefield Healey & Baker, 2002.

developer-led office development. The market is less mature and experienced, but it builds cheap copies of the classic shiny American skyscraper in amazing quantities at an amazing speed. Again, however, the focus is on quick return on investment rather than user satisfaction.

The 'old world' is an exception. In continental Europe, developers have never had such a dominating position. Although it is changing, corporations in continental Europe have a tradition of funding their own purpose built office buildings. The developer culture, seeing buildings as tradable commodities rather than objects of use, is only slowly picking up.

This has resulted in office culture that is less standardised and more user oriented. In combination with relatively high economic prosperity and low rent levels, it has resulted in buildings that are more spacious and diverse, and less efficient, than elsewhere.

It has also resulted in a culture where architects have developed different strengths. Dealing with owner-occupiers instead of developers, they have had more freedom to experiment with office typologies. Countries like the Netherlands, Sweden and Finland have been laboratories for workplace innovation. Think of the icons of innovative office design like the (former) NMB headquarters (The Netherlands), Centraal Beheer (The Netherlands) and SAS (Sweden). This situation contrasts strongly with the United States. Frank Duffy states: 'They (American architects) are no longer paid to think. They cannot afford to invent. There is no time to listen to users. What a supply side dominated system forces them to do is to deliver the same formulaic buildings and interiors, over and over again, only ever more quickly and cheaply'.[11]

Labour relations

The power structure in the office market is closely related to the labour relations within companies. Again, there is major difference between the US and Europe.

Countries like Sweden, Germany and The Netherlands traditionally have a strong social democratic culture in which employees and unions are just as dominant as shareholders. According to local labour regulations, corporations are obliged to consult unions or workers' councils before implementing decisions that involve a major change for employees. In particular, during the 1970s, this had a strong impact on workplace design, resulting in high quality standards for space, privacy and indoor air-quality.

These days, the powers of trade unions and workers' councils are considered to be diminishing all over Europe. But, as an architect or consultant, you still have to deal with a social democratic decision-making culture. Top-down implementation of a new workplace concept will not easily be accepted. Radical changes will require many, sometimes painstaking, discussions with employee representatives about the use of space per employee, the type of desks, or smoking policies within the building. Changes are likely to cost more time and energy than elsewhere. A good example is the briefing and design process of a new building for an American insurance company in the Netherlands. Local top managers liked the cubicle-filled open plan that they had seen in their new London office. User representatives and middle management, however, objected strongly to what they called these 'bull pens'. Since they were part of the project group they could dismiss the idea. To come up with more acceptable open workplace layouts, the hired workplace consultants had to go through with over 32 workshops, 24 presentations, and many meetings with the project group, middle managers and employees.

Such an elaborate implementation and consultation process is not likely to take place in the US. American corporations are traditionally more focused on the capital market than their employees, having one overriding goal: to maximise returns to shareholders. Cost control and improving the balance sheet are the key energisers of real estate decisions. Not that the opinions and interests of users are neglected, but they do have to fit within the overall corporate framework.

Legislation

Every country has its own codes and regulations that affect office design by establishing requirements for fire escape, health and safety and construction. But some countries have more regulations than others.

In particular in Northern Europe, foreign architects and real estate managers are likely to get lost in a bewildering web of requirements from co-existing standard bodies. An architect from the British architectural firm, Nicholas Grimshaw & Partners, working in Germany, commented: 'we are working in much more highly regulated climate than we are used to. I sometimes think that Germany is the fountain of all regulation, and that has been a bit of shock to us'.[12] Some of these regulations have a direct impact on workplace and office design, setting strict standards for floor-to-ceiling heights, corridor widths, dimensions of desks, provision of fresh air and so on.

One of the most influential requirements concerns access to daylight. In the Netherlands, daylight is mandatory, while in Germany visual contact with the outside world is also required ('eine Sichtverbindung nach außen'). This requirement results in much more narrow floor plans than most American developers are used to. In the US, employees may sit within 14–16 metres (or even more) from a window, while British employees are used to sitting within 8–10 metres (See e.g. Figure 5.5), and most continental European employees within 4–6 metres.

Another requirement with which workplace designers are likely to be confronted concerns the size of workplaces. The Netherlands, for

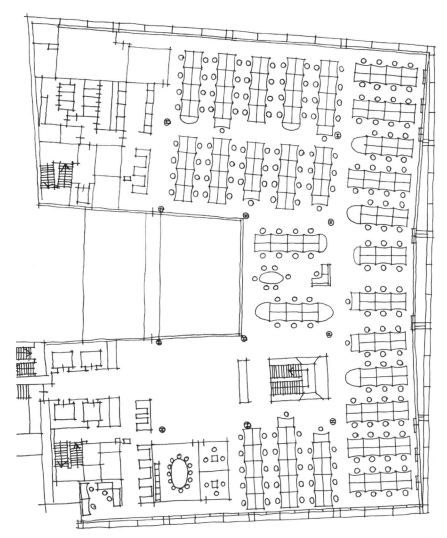

▲**5.5** Bloomberg headquarters in London (design: Axis design and
Powell-Tuck Associates). Bloomberg is an international distributor of
business and financial information and services. Employees work in
a high-density open plan, that has a pantry as its central hub to
encourage people to congregate. The exterior is 'Jazzed-up' with
glass floors, videowalls, colours and art installations

example, probably has the most complex regulations concerning use
of space. The minimum size depends on different variables: type of
work, type of computer screen and the number of filing cabinets
(see Table 5.5). In contrast, British legislation says little more than that

Table 5.5   Dutch workplace regulations concerning size

4 square metre	Workspace (including chair and circulation space)
+ 1 square metre	Flatscreen
+ 2 square metre	Crt-display
+ 1 square metre	Space for reading and writing
+ 2 square metre	Space for laying out drawings
+ 1 square metre	For every filing cabinet or file pedestal
+ 2 square metre	For every meeting place

every workplace 'shall have sufficient floor area, height and unoccupied space for purposes of health, safety and welfare', without giving any exact sizes.

Other laws that vary from country to country concern energy-usage and green design. Again, continental Europe is most stringent. High energy prices have forced European countries to become much more energy conscious than most other countries. The best example may be Norman Foster's Commerzbank Tower that has been heralded as a model for sustainable high-rise design. The building features operable facades, extensive natural lighting, wintergardens and meets the strictest environmental laws.

US legislation is much less strict and puts hardly any pressure on developers to create buildings that are 'greener' than the current fully air-conditioned, tightly sealed office blocks. As a result, the energy performance of buildings differs significantly from that in Europe (Table 5.6).[13]

THE NEW GLOBAL OFFICE?

The international differences discussed in this chapter show that globalisation does not necessarily homogenise the work environment nor erase the salience of cultural labels. It shows that offices are not just a physical by-product of functional requirements, but also symbols of the context in which they have been produced. Just like the architectural remains of past civilisations or exotic tribes, these modern buildings tell us something about the contemporary local norms and values, the economic system and power-relations. In Northern Europe, they tell a story about powerful unions, economic prosperity, and stringent regulations. In the US, they symbolise shareholder capitalism, developer-dominancy and economic flexibility.

Table 5.6 Energy performance of commercial buildings in the US and Europe

Building type (commercial)	Energy performance ($kWh_e/m^2/year$)
Average US building	675
New US buildings	200–500
Best-in-Class US standards	175
New EU buildings	150
Emerging low-energy codes	45–60

Source: Garforth, 2004.

International real estate professionals have to deal with these local circumstances. To create productive offices, they have to promote corporate policies on efficiency and flexibility within the context of potentially divergent office cultures. The more they understand the local context, the more likely they are to respond intelligently by providing local businesses with satisfactory buildings.

Yet, you can question to what extent the international differences we have discussed will persist. Most of the differences concern countries like the US, Germany and Japan – prosperous, developed countries with a strong service economy. In emerging service economies like China and India, local culture does not seem very relevant in office design. In these countries, developers and corporations have been quick to copy American or 'international' office standards. India, for example, may be a country of great poverty and chaotic run-down cities, but you can also find well-designed business parks with immaculate green lawns and modern amenities such as coffee bars and gyms. Inside, office buildings may differ little from those in Houston or Silicon Valley. Just like in their American counterparts, you will find centrally air-conditioned open plans filled with cubicles and state-of-the-art technology. Hafeez Contractor, one of India's main architects, says: 'Vernacular architecture... is dead. Globalisation effectively means that you are making the entire world into one small city. It means that Bangalore and New York are just different districts. A man travelling between these cities experiences the same comfort level as far as appearance, systems, practices and technologies are concerned'.[14]

The international character is further emphasised by the clear borders within the local context. Just like 'gated communities', modern offices tend to have sophisticated security systems, fences and guards to separate the clean corporate workplace from its local environment. New York seems closer than the shanty town next door.

The question is whether these countries are copying the right office model. Are vast office complexes with shiny facades and central air-conditioning the proper office concept for the future? How happy should we be that systems furniture, cubicles and suspended ceilings with artificial lighting are considered as international standards?

The concept may work well for accommodating call centres or programming shops and help desks. But sooner or later, these countries will also do high-end jobs like financial analysis, research, product development, marketing, design and graphics. The emphasis will shift from routine jobs to intellectual, creative tasks. White-collar sweatshops are likely be replaced by buildings resembling universities, ateliers and laboratories. Office cultures will move away from standardisation and uniformity towards diversity and creativity. Office buildings will tell a new story, and managers, designers and consultants should listen carefully.

6 NEW REAL ESTATE MODELS TO SUPPORT DISTRIBUTED WORKING

Despina Katsikakis
DEGW plc

SUMMARY

Most major organisations have now recognised that their real estate can be either a hindrance, if not properly considered, or a support, when integrated with wider business objectives.

Despina Katsikakis, drawing on her experience, globally, of advising corporate clients on appropriate workplace strategies, describes how companies are increasingly viewing their space as one component of a wider accommodation strategy which encompasses 'new ways of working', personnel issues, and the integrated use of space and time, through the support of mobile and personalised information and communications technology.

Companies today are faced with reconciling apparently opposing business drivers such as the desire to expand versus the need to minimise risk, the advantages of integrating individual self-motivation with team collaboration and the balance of short-term competitive success and longer term sustainability. A real estate strategy that focuses on recognising how work is being undertaken is changing and then provides relevant settings in appropriate and cost-effective locations, is the right way to reconcile these opposing drivers. An effective distributed workplace strategy reduces corporate property holdings and focuses attention on spaces that support business culture, enhance team spirit, express identity and transfer knowledge.

Despina Katsikakis argues that, unlike conventional real estate strategies which locate all functions in similar buildings in centralised locations, the new model aims to differentiate between fixed long-term core space and short-term flexible project space to offer a variety of different depth of spaces and to provide support services and high levels of amenity in the immediate neighbourhood. A strategy which recognises that all functions need not be co-located allows a wider choice of settings, in appropriate locations, and reduces overheads through the sharing of facilities.

Two case studies are presented to illustrate the opportunities for more innovative accommodation Accenture grew 20–25 per cent annually during the 1990s and despite the collapse of the dot com boom has continued to grow both headcount and profits, whilst reducing real estate costs. Its strategy has been to acquire a diversified real estate portfolio, that provides a wide range of property and tenure types to meet differing locational and functional characteristics in response to the company's varied business models. This wider range of settings in different locations, is achieved through sharing space and using time flexibly. Lateral thinking has broadened Accenture's portfolio of settings to include coffee houses, clients' offices, work on the move and at home. From a supplier's perspective, a correspondingly innovative approach has been taken by Stanhope at Chiswick Park. The premise of the development is to match the demand of companies to attract and retain the best staff, through creating an enjoyable place to work. The 'enjoy-work' brand at Chiswick Park plays down the architecture of individual buildings to concentrate on the high quality of services provided in the public and semi-public spaces which support the shared identity and culture of all tenants on the site.

INTRODUCTION

International competition has forced businesses to rethink their organisational structures and developments in technology are making it possible to use time and space in new and creative ways. Office work has become more varied and creative as straightforward procedures are being automated or exported to developing economies. The defining characteristic of the knowledge economy is the recognition that intangible assets are the key to competitive advantage for business in the future; intellectual resources for many organisations represent their most significant intangible asset. While debate continues about what percentage of the workforce are knowledge workers, from a corporate perspective, knowledge workers are held to account for 97 per cent of the corporate profits.

The growth of the knowledge economy will place increasing emphasis on the importance of communication and collaboration. The automation of processes through the introduction of technology further changes the nature of the work that we are doing and has significant consequences on the design of physical space (Figure 6.1).

Technology is not the only enabler of change. Organisational/management theory over the past ten years has also generated several direct consequences for the redesign of the physical environment of work in order to best support physical and virtual collaboration.

The inevitable conclusion is that offices will become more saturated by information technology and will focus on supporting meetings and interaction. They will be more diverse in style and structure and able to be changed more rapidly. They will tend to be in less centralised, less predictable and more dispersed locations; physical place will be used to communicate explicitly and implicitly corporate values, and they will come increasingly under the control of, and be more responsive to, ever changing teams of intelligent and demanding end users.

Dr. Francis Duffy in his book *The New Office*[1] predicted a shift towards new ways of working that would result in organisations adopting a distributed workplace strategy. The contrast in the assumptions that have

What people should be doing	What machines should be doing
creating, communicating	documenting, recording, retrieving
deciding, judging, crafting	monitoring, controlling, locating
caring	configuring, following rules

▲6.1   Table

underpinned the conventional office and the expectations that are creating new office environments is very marked (Figure 6.2).

The new ways of working predicted in the late 1990s were confirmed in the recently completed research by DEGW for the European Union, 'Sustainable Accommodation for the New Economy' (SANE).[2]

The SANE research demonstrates that a distributed working strategy can help an organisation reconcile apparently opposing business drivers:

- The desire to expand *versus* the need to minimise risk;

	Conventional office assumptions	New ways of working
Patterns of work	Routine processes Individual tasks Isolated work	Creative knowledge work groups, teams, projects Interactive work
Patterns of occupancy of space over time	Central office locations in which staff are assumed to occupy individually 'owned' workstations on a full-time basis, typically over the course of the 9–5 day. The office assumes one desk per person; provides a hierarchy (planned or enclosed); and is occupied typically at levels at least 30% below full capacity.	Distributed set of work locations (which may be nomadic, mobile, in the office or at home) linked by networks of communication in which autonomous individuals work in project teams. Daily timetable is extended and irregular. Multifunctional work settings are occupied on an as-needed basis. Daily occupancy of space near to capacity.
Type of space layout, furniture systems and use of space and buildings	Hierarchy of space and furniture related to status. Individual allocation of space predominates over interactive meeting spaces.	Multiple shared group work and individual task-based settings. Setting, layout and furniture of the office geared to work process and its tasks.
Use of information technology	Technology used for routine data processing, terminals in fixed positions served by mainframes.	Focus on mobility of IT equipment used in a wide variety of settings. Technology used to support creative knowledge work, both individual and group. File servers serve a variety of IT tools, including PCs and laptops and shared specialised equipment.

▲6.2   The contrast between the assumptions that underpinned the conventional office and the expectations that are creating new office

- The need to decentralise geographically *versus* the need to work collaboratively;
- The need to maximise productivity *versus* the need to take the best possible care of people as the organisation's key resource;
- The need to compete *versus* the need to be sustainable.

A distributed working strategy can also help ensure that the potential benefits of IT investment are best achieved. It can help organisations respond to a growing market without the danger that a downturn will leave them seriously overcommitted. It can avoid the stop-go expansion-retrenchment merry-go-around by reducing the long-term investment in property traditionally needed to support growth. It can give more autonomy to staff whilst making the whole business operation of knowledge production much more efficient.

A distributed workplace strategy achieves all these because it reduces and focuses real estate holdings in those kinds of spaces that an organisation needs in order to maintain its culture, team spirit, identity and knowledge transfer. It allows the organisation to be 'light footed' in terms of its use of other kinds of workspace, allowing greater choice and autonomy to its staff and offering incidental benefits of cross-fertilisation in the wider business community.

THE DRIVERS CHANGING THE PATTERN OF DEMAND

- Technology developments, including broadband and 3G wireless communications, enabling office workers to be *increasingly mobile not only outside the office but also within;*
- The *space planning freedom* and the consequent reallocation of space over time made possible by these developments;
- The potential of distributed working in enabling office workers to shape their work schedules and thus their *life/work balance;*
- Increasing attention being given to *knowledge management* as a critically important component of office design, shifting from individual paper storage to proactively ensuring that all information, paper as well as electronic, is managed as a collective resource;
- The *growth of shared, collective, interactive spaces* as a proportion of the space budget and the corresponding decline in the area allocated to individual workstations;

- The *increasing importance of security*, leading to much greater control over access perhaps even to the extent of creating zones of high surveillance (as in the City of London);
- *Location Positioning Systems* as a means of tracking where and when distributed office work is carried out;
- Change management not only as a means of facilitating physical change but also of *using the design process as a means of accelerating organisational change;*
- The growing *focus on social and environmental sustainability;*
- The *use of the physical working environment as a means of expressing brand and culture* to office workers and to visitors.

THE SCOPE FOR INNOVATION – SUPPLY

Evidence clearly supports a radical paradigm shift in the supply of office environments. The majority of office real estate development still continues to look to the past, reflecting work patterns and organisational models that are no longer valid.

While the growth of 'office work' may continue – an increasing proportion of the workforce will be in 'office jobs' and a decreasing proportion of this activity will be accommodated in conventional workstations during the conventional working week. Both distributed working and workplace sharing will increase, permitting more intensive use of office space. Quite possibly the total demand for office space may diminish – a trend which may be aggravated by the displacement of certain kinds of jobs to economies where labour costs are lower.

New workplace strategies currently being adopted by organisations suggest that in the future, organisations will be less likely to permanently locate large numbers of staff in high-cost locations. This implies a much sharper differentiation between more boutique-like specialised offices in city centres and much lower cost, simpler office structures in suburban or campus locations. Demand for large office spaces in city centres will persist but these spaces will be used very differently. The overall character of development will change, polarising around high-value/high-cost locations and low-value/low-cost locations.

Occupiers offered more choices for operating reasons and to reduce fixed costs, will continue to press for much greater flexibility in terms of both type of space and length of leases. Businesses will differentiate between those parts of their organisations requiring stable long-term accommodation and those that can be housed in through more dynamic provision. This may not mean abandoning the lease structure but substantially modifying it.

Increased demand for space to support collaborative activities that can typically be accommodated in deep plan space will be balanced against increasing demand for spaces that stimulate – and have access to views and natural light and provide aesthetic and sensory variability. Greater mobility within and between offices, workplace sharing, space use intensification, and the growth in collective rather than individual workplaces will make it much easier to plan office floors in creative and stimulating ways. Increasing mobility requirements will force hardware developers to address power supply problems both through improving and/or replacing battery technology and through reducing device power consumption. These developments could have considerable impact on the demand for and distribution of small power supplies in buildings.

Development of the Ambient Intelligence concept is receiving considerable investment across Europe. The outcome of this research will be the creation of new infrastructures, devices, applications and services integrating the user experience of the physical building with their use of technology. Delivery of this vision will be dependent on closer linkages between physical building components and IT components.

Pressure for improved environmental performance is likely to increasingly come from government, public and business. Pre-fabrication and sustainable construction will be more commonplace and the design of buildings could well be turning inwards. Less glass on the facades for energy conservation could encourage the introduction of internal streets and atria.

Fresh solutions to vertical circulation, for example, in using small atria to create visual links between floors, may be used to support communication and knowledge flow in tall buildings with the introduction of concepts such as the vertical street.

More of the construction budget is likely to be allocated to interior fit out rather than the building shell. The trend towards adoption of new models of procurement will continue, creating new intermediaries in the supply chain. Businesses will increasingly seek to outsource management of their workplaces allowing them to focus on core business rather than property or workplace management.

The desire of tenants to reduce the cost of property, constrains the returns that investors in property receive from their assets. Shifting from a business model based on charging for occupation of space to one based on delivery of services opens the potential for greater returns. This will create the opportunity for landlords to provide additional services, such as design, facilities management and change management. Services that support the users of the building, rather than the building itself, will be more valued by occupiers. Modelling delivery of these services on the hotel, rather than conventional Facilities Management practices is likely to increase occupier satisfaction.

While traditionally many personal services and amenities have been clustered around the home, modern working patterns favour location around the workplace, creating opportunities for using the resources of cities to support working environments. Mixed use − such as housing, hotels, retail and entertainment − will need to be both themed and managed to support the attainment of commercial objectives like the attraction and retention of staff or the economies to be derived from shared facilities. The emphasis will shift from isolated development to greater integration with the city infrastructure, making more of the spaces between buildings and focusing on the creation of vibrant places.

The importance of location will shift from the building image, to the importance of place; building + services + amenities.

'In a world where technology enables you to work from anywhere − you will still have to work from somewhere'. Choice will be determined by: convenience, access to people and amenities and the desire for stimulating experiences in meaningful places.

CHANGING MODEL OF DEMAND: ACCENTURE

Aggressively shifting to a distributed workplace strategy and a diversified real estate portfolio

Accenture is dramatically reshaping its real estate portfolio and reducing its long-term property commitments for office space, moving towards a distributed workplace strategy relying heavily on virtual working for significant portions of their workforce and utilisation of spaces not paid for by Accenture.

The business climate of the 1990s enabled Accenture to grow at rates of 20–25 per cent annually. Despite the collapse of the dot coms and a very cost-conscious business environment Accenture has continued to increase headcount and revenue whilst reducing real estate.

Accenture recognises that:

- Emerging technologies will continue to influence real estate requirements;
- They must aggressively market legacy real estate assets to transform their portfolio's cost structure and align it with their new business strategies.

Accenture's new 'Flexible Workplace Blueprint' calls for reduced operating costs, increased efficiency and increased flexibility.

These ambitions are to be delivered through a *diversified* real estate portfolio, which enables them to cut costs whilst still fostering a culture of community. The concept of a diversified real estate portfolio is the key. At its simplest, this concept merely implies that Accenture will require different properties to perform different functions, in fact it represents a significant shift in thinking.

Prior to 2002, Accenture's staff were accommodated *either* at client sites or what they describe as 'large metro centres'. These centres housed a complete cross-section of the business's staff, functions and services delivered within a geographical area and were located in a relatively prestigious part of whatever city they were operating out of. The new Accenture strategy envisages a far wider range of property types, differing locational *and functional* characteristics, lease arrangements and standards of fit-out *which respond specifically to their varied business models* (Figure 6.3):

Accenture is also giving a higher level of importance to virtual/remote working as a means of reducing their property costs: mobility of their workforce enables greater leverage of their portfolio and also responds to employee needs for flexibility which contributes to improved work/ life balance. Their expectations are that a significant proportion of

	Location	Lease	Fit-out
Client Image Space	Central/Prestigious – major city	Long-term	Moderate- to High-level
Hub	Central/Transport – large city	Medium- to long-term – tiered options	Moderate
Satellite	Suburban/Residential	Short-term	Basic
Service Centre	Low cost	Long-term	Basic (some specialised)
Delivery Centres	Near shore/offshore	Medium- to long-term	Basic (some specialised)

▲6.3 Different models of real estate to support diverse business requirements

work currently being performed in Accenture's leased spaces will in the near future take place in spaces that have no direct cost to Accenture: homes, client sites, cafes, etc. Adoption of this strategy has already enabled the consultancy to reduce occupation costs by more than 50 per cent in some locations through 'right sizing' the amount of space they rent in expensive downtown locations. The new strategy also aims to shift a growing proportion of their real estate costs from fixed costs to variable costs. It is planned that future expansion of elements of their business will be accommodated through increasing the flexible accommodation costs, but not increasing the fixed cost base (Figure 6.4). Additionally, Accenture monitors occupancy of its facilities, often finding that increased worker mobility allows a larger population to be supported out of the same office space. Headcount growth does not necessarily mean real estate portfolio growth.

The emerging portfolio is shaped with varied facilities that are directly aligned with specific business functions. Increasingly, Accenture's offices are designed to support group work and collaboration. Technology allows individual and virtual collaboration to occur almost anywhere, often outside Accenture's facilities.

Whilst Accenture is perhaps the most aggressive adopter of a new distributed workplace strategy, other organisations are likely to follow. The key concern for investors in commercial real estate should be to ensure that their assets can provide the differentiated work spaces that large occupiers are likely to demand.

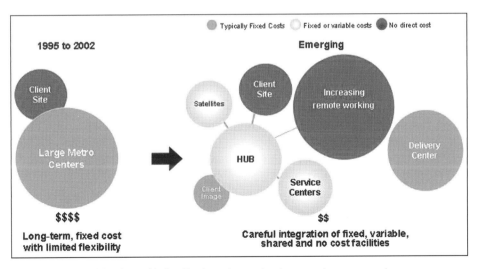

▲ **6.4** A diversified portfolio that acknowledges unique needs

CHANGING MODELS OF SUPPLY

Chiswick Park

Chiswick Park provides a highly branded environment with a large proportion of public and semi-public spaces used to support a shared identity and culture through events organised by the estate management group.

Located in Chiswick, west London, this 1.5 million square feet development, designed by Richard Rogers Partnership and based on Stanhope's experience at Stockley and Broadgate, was designed to provide occupiers with the best working environment both internally and externally. The first phase of three buildings, providing 375 000 square feet commercial space, was started in January 2000, and was completed on schedule in December 2000. This included the 86 000 square feet Regus centre, and a 40 000 square feet health centre and bar/brasserie for Esporta. Phase II started on site in early December 2000. The first two buildings, approximately 225 000 square feet in total, were completed in October 2001, with the third being completed in March 2002. Key features of the buildings have large floorplates, 3 metre floor to ceiling height, fully glazed facade, an environmentally friendly displaced air system and external environment control.

The scheme was designed to address the desire of companies to attract and retain employees. This is best expressed in the Park's slogan – 'enjoy-work' (Figure 6.5). The premise is that if people enjoy work, they do better work; if they do better work, you have a better business.

CHISWICK PARK **ENJOY-WORK.COM**

▲ **6.5**   Chiswick Park, a highly branded environment

The slogan is underpinned by an active on-site support team, collaborative planning and event management (CPEM). This team, drawn entirely from the service sector, provides a far wider range of support activities than those fulfilled by traditional FM functions. The CPEM team are responsible for reception in the shared occupancy buildings, security, maintenance and so on. However in addition they provide a programme of summer events, a sport programme and a lifestyle support programme.

Each of the buildings is linked by fibre optic systems and has access to the Chiswick Park intranet run by the on-site management team. The intranet provides access to preferred suppliers delivering such items as groceries, flowers, dry cleaning, etc – all designed to make working life easier.

Surveys of occupants indicate very high levels of satisfaction with the CPEM team. Occupants' responses suggest that the non-traditional one-team approach to service delivery is highly valued and seen as making a significant contribution to the experience of working at Chiswick Park.

7 COMPETING FOR THE FUTURE OF CORPORATE REAL ESTATE

Geoff Woodling
Businessfutures.com

SUMMARY

Other contributions in this publication have identified the paradigm shift that is occurring in office work. How will the world of corporate real estate respond? Geoff Woodling has advised major multinationals such as Electrolux, Apple Corporation, APV and ABB on organisational change and the impact on their property portfolios. He argues that property can just as easily become the rocks on which businesses flounder as the foundation for successful business growth. In times of rapid change the corporate real estate (CRE) function may be required to establish goals for the future, and identify flexible paths to success.

Woodling argues that the new corporate real estate function will need to respond to a world of dissolving bureaucracies. Corporations are changing into networked organisations, composed of creative knowledge workers with minimum hierarchy and flat organisational structures. The bureaucratic high profile corporate headquarters are being superseded by small dispersed groups of managers in high input corporate centres.

The corporate real estate challenge is to reinvent the management role to one of achieving performance improvement from operating a portfolio of sites and controlling the way space is employed. From the corporate perspective, it may be more constructive to consolidate the least attractive sites, as perceived by the property market, and to sell the 'jewels' of the portfolio. The emerging CRE function will be required to cover four facets: facilities operations, real estate strategy, development, and portfolio management. In the reinvented world of work, will corporations still need real estate? Can the function be outsourced to global facility operations where the property investment is in the total service of accommodation provision and management, not just in the land, bricks and mortar?

COMPETING FOR THE FUTURE

In Gary Hamel and C. K. Prahalad's celebrated book, *Competing for the Future*[1] the opening question is 'Does senior management have a clear and broadly shared understanding of how their industry may be different in ten years time?' Many in corporate real estate (CRE) would probably be unable to answer this question and, regrettably, property managers in corporations in general contribute even less to an understanding of the issues. Considering that property commitments can have such important long-term consequences for business, it would seem prudent for corporate real estate executives to consider whether possible futures for the industries they serve might make different demands upon property.

Regrettably, property has more often been the rock on which businesses have floundered than the foundation of future growth. The uncertain future most businesses face has highlighted the constraints which property imposes on rapidly changing patterns of operations. The challenge of managing corporate real estate (Figure 7.1) is first to remove those constraints, and second to anticipate when and where the resources will be required to accommodate future operations. This process is intuitive in small businesses. However, in larger organisations, where management no longer sees property as a necessary or profitable use of resources, the

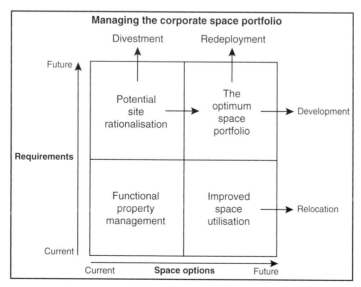

▲7.1 Changing characteristics of corporate space management

question is whether CRE will face competition from others to serve the need for space and, if so, how it will respond.

To help CRE meet this challenge, the future issues facing the organisations that CRE serves must be considered. If the trends among organisations can be identified, it is often easier to understand what is happening in one's own business and to anticipate the resulting needs for space.

DISSOLUTION OF THE BUREAUCRACIES

It must be recognised that organisations will adapt to the way individuals work together. Organisations exist to enable people to do things together which would be harder or more costly to do apart. Will this change? The cost of working apart is reducing. Therefore, it can be expected that the need to work together with the same people in the same place will decline. 'Dissolution of the bureaucracies' (see Figure 7.2) is just one of the challenges to the organisation. For example, there is no longer a need for large numbers of information 'servants' but, as government departments have found, reducing numbers can be a difficult exercise. Despite the risk of accommodating large concentrations of staff in one site, the practice is still surprisingly common among large firms. Evidence suggests that the need for space, changes faster in many cases than the time required to effect consolidation. Needs change has been confirmed several times over among City financial services, yet big projects embarked upon still find favour with management. The suspicion lingers that such schemes are more for image than reality.

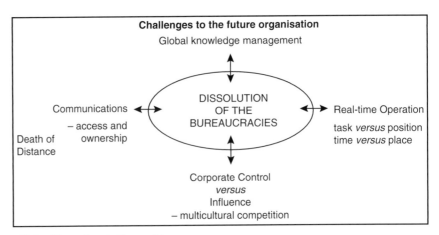

▲ 7.2   The dissolution of bureaucracy

One conclusion might be that large organisations will consist of many smaller groups which might not necessarily share the same space. This may lead to a shift of permanent staff from the headquarters to a new concept of the corporate centre (Figure 7.3).

The distribution of power and knowledge poses a serious challenge for CRE management attempting to accommodate diverse work patterns. It is more demanding to plan for a greater diversity of locations and space under different corporate centre scenarios, as Figure 7.4 begins to illustrate. However, the most difficult challenge may still be to come. The relatively uniform assumption that individual employees work exclusively for one employer and acquire residency rights with their job, may not prevail for much longer. There is growing evidence that activity

---

Transition from the Headquarters Model

"At the top of the organisation hierarchy, where the focus of corporate power and information is dedicated to the control of subsidiary operations"

Towards

"A centre of influence and knowledge exchange to co-ordinate and promote the development of group businesses and protect stakeholder value"

▲ 7.3   Transition from headquarters office to corporate centre

Centre concepts	Location Single	Location Multiple
Permanent	Concentration	Decentralisation 'separate development'
Transient	Distributed network	Competitive corporate centres

▲ 7.4   Alternative corporate centre scenarios

is shifting to smaller firms and even to the self-employed. These groups have far less dependence upon the traditional property industry, not least because it has always ignored their needs. Once larger firms recognise that workstyle has become a key factor in attracting talent, it may not be long before they also discover that an office, and the trappings of corporate life it signifies, are no longer so appealing. The need to accommodate the individual, not the organisation, may become the driving force for change in the provision of space.

FROM PROPERTY TO PRESENCE

Changes that can be expected in the nature of a business organisation's conduct will have an impact on the space and services it needs, not only for offices, but also for warehouses and factories. The result has been the 'dematerialisation of the industrial economy'. Fewer material resources are required to service needs, and in some cases, energy requirements are reduced. The result of this has been a rapid shift towards knowledge-based employment and activity. The office has become the factory of the present. Whether it will go the way of past factories is one of the critical uncertainties facing the property sector.

One of the main processes underlying the transition to a knowledge economy is the value of trade in knowledge exceeding its physical counterpart. In the engineering industry, the highest value added is often in small, complex products which can be made at one global source and assembled or fabricated in systems close to the market. This has profound effects on the need for production space. Most large industries now exist as a network of closely integrated suppliers. The best example of such complex logistics is in the electronics industry where each stage in manufacture can take place in different parts of the globe with many attendant needs for shipment.

The lack of spatial constraints, low cost of construction, and competitive subsidy to attract firms to new locations are all undermining existing asset values. This is a symptom of the relatively slow rate of adjustment of changing economic demands of the kind shown in Figure 7.5. Today, more than in even the recent past, it is a symptom of changing demand for office space. The sight of the former head office of a global agro chemicals company being razed to become a garden centre is symbolic of these changes. The concentration of 'production' among fewer large global firms and their network of local suppliers means that large amounts of surplus space will not be redeployed.

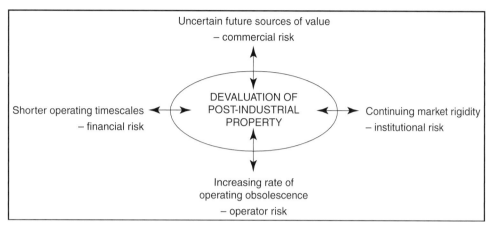

▲7.5   The uncertain context of post-industrial property

The declining need for 'production' space of all kinds has been further weakened by the rapid growth of off-shoring to take advantage of low-cost labour and telecommunications. Once many large organisations were left with a surplus of industrial property, much of it in older areas too unattractive or too isolated to develop for other uses. The more recent impact of such trends has been to release office properties even in supposedly high growth areas such as the Thames Valley.

The once much vaunted business park model is itself becoming outmoded. It is an extreme example of the vulnerability of the kind of property monoculture built to accommodate large concentrations of office work-ers in out-of-town locations with little other life. At a time when it is easier for distant groups to work together electronically, the need to meet at convenient locations is growing, not declining. The more people communicate, the more they want to meet. That demand is placing a premium on presence in the market. Places to meet are still found close to physical communications hubs, not in distant parks accessible only by car, and must offer a diversity of attractions to support nomadic lifestyles.

SITE OPERATING PERFORMANCE

To achieve improved performance through cutting facility operating costs, CRE must satisfy both those who occupy space and the corporate management responsible for ensuring that such resources are effectively employed. This is both to ensure that assets and liabilities are efficiently managed and to secure the best performance from the use of corporate property resources. However, it is notoriously difficult to identify how value is created in buildings. In most businesses, costs are incurred and value added where people work. Management accounts only rarely reveal where such costs and revenues are secured because businesses and sites are not the same unit. Increasingly, corporate management needs to know where performance improvements can be secured which means knowing how sites are employed. This role obliges CRE to concentrate on the way space is used, fundamentally determining the potential rental value of each site. CRE must develop the means to identify how value is added. Property records alone do not show this because they specify generally only the physical, legal and contractual characteristics of the space supplied. This does nothing to help corporate management understand how well each site is employed. To do so, CRE must identify how space is used, what drives the demand for space (the external trade links) and why operating margins vary. This approach begins to address the need to deliver better levels of competitive site operating performance. Timing is the critical issue: 'just in time' space means not just when space can be acquired, or even for how long, but how to optimise the use of space available at all times.

Based on a better understanding of the way space is employed, CRE will need to achieve the performance criteria to meet new corporate priorities. CRE also needs to influence total operating performance and not simply act as an internal agent of the property sector.

THE CRE MANAGEMENT CHALLENGE

One of the axioms of management is to think 'global' and act 'local'. Too often, CRE practice has evolved the other way round. CRE will be distinguished by its success in achieving performance improvement from the portfolio of operating sites rather than the provision of the space itself. Frequently, large multinational organisations have separate national real estate functions which vary greatly in size and have no corporate policy direction. Others have found it possible to manage a corporate global space portfolio with fewer than ten staff judged on measures of site operating performance. This is not so different from an institutional asset portfolio where the management of the individual properties is outsourced. Often, these two roles are confused.

In most cases, the confusion of purpose arises because the CRE role is based on a property management function whose structure (reflecting the property business with which it is closely identified as illustrated in Figure 7.7) conflicts with its purpose of achieving the performance criteria identified in Figure 7.6 for which the alternative process focus is required.

Although many now contract out facilities management, fewer have contracted out the management of their entire portfolio of properties.

- Enhance corporate capacity to invest in business, not property

- Ensure competitive operating performance from business use of space

- Enhance global management responsibility of corporate space portfolio

- Endow operational and financial flexibility

- Enable management to anticipate organisations' changing needs.

▲7.6 Goals of real estate performance

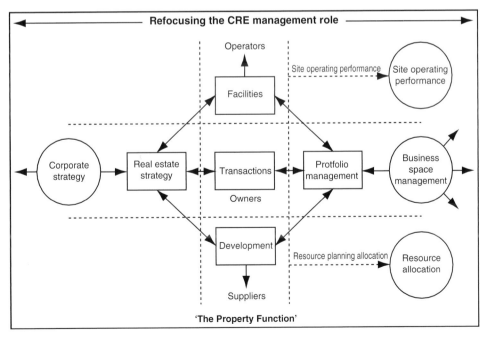

▲7.7 The changing role of corporate real estate management

CRE needs to manage a strategic resource portfolio to ensure that it meets specific performance criteria. This means that CRE must ensure that sites are well managed, if not in-house, then through contractors. However, facilities management, like real estate, emerged from the bottom-up and struggles to be thought of in the same way as IT management companies, which have developed from consultancies and from utilities in particular. Such companies often manage a complete infrastructure and, crucially, may own most of the hardware. They are accountable for value added. They control cost and deliver IT services *when* and *where* needed. A great deal of effort goes into managing change and in removing the barriers revealed by obsolete software and systems.

This begins to point towards a possible change in the way CRE's role is performed, i.e. along the lines shown in Figure 7.8. This model goes well beyond what is seen as traditionally the prime role of CRE – matching leasing locations and layout with function, time and space. It is increasingly uncertain that it will be possible to meet operational needs within the existing constraints of the property market. The separation of owner, occupier and operator at every location,

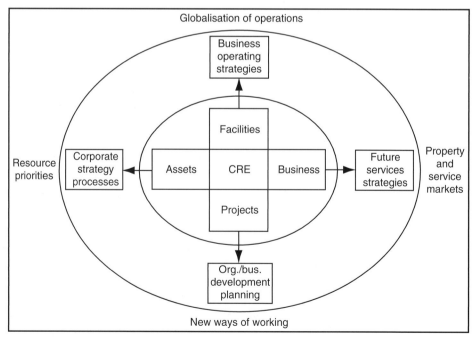

▲7.8   Strategic focus of corporate real estate management

where each has different and conflicting time scales and interests, is a complex solution.

Property suppliers, by their nature, are forced to charge more for the cost of capital than large occupiers, and are unable to offer products in more than a few locations because there is no such thing as a brand of space, apart from that offered on a temporary basis by firms such as Regus. Property companies are still a long way from recognising the need to operate their fixed assets, the buildings, to maximise productive use and profit as other industries do. It is not even clear whether the innovation of completely outsourcing the entire physical infrastructure and facilities function has done much more than transfer, at a price, the risk of a mismatch between the supply of space and the demand for it. It has not fundamentally changed the way that space can be employed and charged for in most cases.

COMPETITION FOR THE CORPORATE SPACE BUSINESS

In the final analysis, do corporations need real estate at all? In a more competitive and uncertain market with volatile profit streams, the covenant of large corporations to lease space for specific purposes is one of the most valuable assets such organisations have. Although many large multinationals operate what comes close to a global brand of space, few have made any money from owning it. Corporate (and institutional) owners have failed to recognise that the declining value of their property is partly a function of its shorter operating life and the relatively unproductive way in which most space is employed. Study after study has shown how less than one-third of 'occupied' office space in is normally in use. The value of these properties needs to reflect the way they are employed, like retail centres or hotels, which are valued more in line with the way they are operated. Perhaps, institutional investors will be obliged to become, or to invest in, active property businesses whose equities rather than properties are traded. Maybe they will finance the corporate infrastructure to be managed by global facility operators who will serve the occupier. Occupiers already award contracts for the use of the space and infrastructure it provides. It is unlikely that the CRE's role will be to maximise contract value for a guaranteed supply of space over time – like low-cost airlines. The more property becomes like any other business, the more that corporate occupiers can rely on the market to supply their needs.

▲7.9   Competing for the future corporate space business

In the 'space business' concept, illustrated in Figure 7.9. CRE could be either the catalyst or the victim of this change. Few, if any, property companies, developers, investors or facilities managers have shown the capacity to create a global brand of space. Global corporations with strong balance sheets and secure revenue streams can still create space more cheaply than anyone else. It is clear that they need to operate it in the same way as the rest of their business, leaving others to take the risk that the space will continue to meet both their own and others' operating needs. In place of real estate, corporations could find it more attractive to contract for a quality of space from communication providers who would maintain the network infrastructure thus generating greater revenue than the costs of the space people occupy. The 'space business' could even become the new communications marketplace, once network access is wireless and ubiquitous, and available to all at work, whatever be their affiliation.

SECTION III

THE OPPORTUNITIES OF INFORMATION TECHNOLOGY

Today we are all part of the knowledge society. The 1970s were typified by central mainframe computing, the 1980s were dominated by the personal desktop computer, the 1990s by the lap top and palm top, reflecting a move towards greater availability, mobility, and freedom of action and connection. Poised at the beginning of the twenty-first century, personal access to knowledge and global accessibility is cheaply available through the world wide web. Information technology has pervaded all aspects of life, resulting in a blurring of boundaries, and a widening of business opportunities. Computing is ubiquitous and user-friendly. We have moved from computing being an optional extra to a phase where it is integral to business, a tool to be harnessed to improve efficiency, increase effectiveness and enhance the quality of working life. Clerical functions, the bulk of office functions twenty-years ago, have been computerised to leave the creative functions of applying know how to add value through research, design, innovation and services. Productivity gains can be clearly recognised in those organisations which have been prepared to rethink their business model through applying technology and simultaneously reviewing their work practices and their space utilisation.

Ten years from the first edition of this book, perhaps the most significant development has been the impact of mobile telephony and its rapidly expanding range of functions. The freedom of location afforded by mobile computing and communication has allowed for work to be undertaken where and when it is most appropriate. The mobile phone with high-bandwidth wireless connections and with the power of the internet have empowered people and also have expanded corporate access to knowledge, ideas and creativity. However, unless companies are prepared not just to rethink the mechanics of how they work but also the culture they work within, the full potential of technological change may not be realised. For example, some commentators have agreed that increased access to information and empowerment through participation may be a mirage leading to a 'corrosion of character' (Richard Sennett).

The first contribution in this section, sets out the background to the development of the intelligent building as this concept developed from a random collection of high-tech functions to the conveyance of all such functions in the Computer Integrated Building. The final part of the story explores the impact that miniaturised, and mobile technology, combined with the web, has had on the distributed workplace, and upon real estate strategies for meeting these new demands. The final chapter, having given us a rapid tour of the emerging technologies that may impact on the workplace of tomorrow, leaves us with the thought that 'places for people and not paper will be the challenge for tomorrow'.

8

FROM THE INTELLIGENT BUILDING TO THE DISTRIBUTED WORKPLACE

Andrew Harrison
DEGW plc

SUMMARY

To maximise the opportunities afforded by the immediacy created by the convergence of information and communications technology, businesses have not only embraced the new technologies but also rethought the way they work. Andrew Harrison, who has led three major DEGW multi-client studies assessing the characteristics and trends of intelligent buildings in Europe, South East Asia and South America, and more recently has led the SANE study (Sustainable Accommodation for the New Economy), a major European Commission initiative, draws conclusions on developments in information technology and their impact on organisational form.

The intelligent building studies described the rapid convergence of building and business technologies within the 'Computer Integrated Building' where building, space and business management systems are intimately entwined. Harrison concludes his review of the Intelligent Building Studies undertaken between 1989 and 1996 by exploring the logical outcome of the process: the virtual corporation which is networked across cities and regions through wide area networks, remote monitoring and personalised video conferencing. He describes the barriers which still prevent the development of intelligent organisational networks and virtual corporations.

The major part of the chapter describes the distributed workplace model developed for the SANE study. Whereas the earlier intelligent building studies had focussed on the new technologies, SANE recognised that technology was now available and ubiquitous. The new challenge is to manage the relationships between the virtual and the physical, between private and public management and ownership and between functions that can be dispersed and those that must be centralised. If knowledge and its application to speed up innovation are the keys to success, then the challenge will be to fast track the exchange and assimilation of all available knowledge. The paradox is that technology allows us the freedom to work remotely but knowledge is best disseminated and created by social interaction within real places. The new working environment will offer distributed, often transient, settings supported by central spaces for the interchange of ideas and creative collaboration.

CONVERGING TECHNOLOGIES

Organisations use buildings not only to house their businesses but also to communicate messages about themselves to their clients, customers and peers. In the 1990s, there was a great deal of interest in sophisticated, high-technology, 'intelligent' buildings which utilised the latest in communications, building and office automation technologies. With time, it is thought that all these technologies will become integrated, producing a 'Computer Integrated Building' (CIB) able to support increasingly demanding organisations with a wide range of work patterns and technology requirements.

However, these technological advances may have long-term impacts which will challenge the notion of the intelligent building and will instead move the organisation past the physical envelope of the building into a wide range of locations and work settings. The intelligent building will become merely a node on intelligent organisational networks which may span cities, regions and countries. This will only occur if a number of major technological problems are overcome and if organisations adapt their work processes to take account of the multiple work locations that will result.

EVOLVING ORGANISATIONS AND SPACE REQUIREMENTS

Historically, organisations have generally had a very well-defined physical form. As companies grew, they invested in larger, usually grander, buildings which reflected their new prosperity. Such buildings had an important symbolic role as well as simply housing the organisations they contained. Good examples of these are the monolithic buildings created by Victorian insurance companies in a number of UK cities which broadcast clear messages about stability, prosperity and trustworthiness to potential customers and investors.

As organisations grow and mature, they also tend to use property in different ways with a single building being replaced by a number of buildings with specific functions (Figure 8.1).

Developments in communications technology have facilitated this move towards more dispersed property portfolios and triggered the development of global corporations which can take advantage of differences in labour rates and property costs around the world to minimise production and distribution costs.

THE CHANGING RELATIONSHIP BETWEEN ORGANISATIONS, BUILDINGS AND INFORMATION TECHNOLOGY

As the business environment has become more competitive during recent years, and organisations have been forced to look very closely at how they do business, major 'downsizing' exercises have resulted in the disposal of many surplus buildings or the relocation of many parts of the organisation to less expensive space away from the main cities. For a while, the corporate HQ stood somewhat apart from the rest of the property portfolio and its symbolic value far outweighed the practical significance of the location. However, as organisations strive to make themselves more cost-effective, even the HQ building has been scrutinised to see how it is contributing to overall business effectiveness. In many cases this has led to the HQ being downsized, with back office functions dispersed across the city, region or country and all units being linked together by wide area networks, electronic mail and other corporate information systems.

What remains of the corporations in city centre locations is often just the public function of organisation, with the building acting as a 'shop window', hinting at a structure and products that are located in other buildings in other places. Even the public function of the office building's role is being challenged by technology. One could argue that the corporate home-page on the Internet has taken over many of the functions which buildings formerly carried out by, displaying organisational structure, providing information about products and services, and communicating between staff and customers.

The major advantage of the homepage is that it is accessible globally and can be constantly updated to reflect current organisational needs.

Taken to the extreme, these trends may lead to the development of *virtual corporations* which are able to thrive by networking between dispersed organisations and individuals, servicing global clients without ever needing to meet them face-to-face.

INTELLIGENT BUILDINGS

The 1992 DEGW/Teknibank research project, *The Intelligent Building in Europe (IBE)*, examined the changing relationships between organisations, buildings and information technology (IT). The IBE model of building intelligence focuses on the building's occupants and the tasks they are trying to carry out inside the building rather than on the computer systems inside it. Information technology is one of the ways in which the building can help or hinder the occupants, but it is not the reason for the building's existence.

An intelligent building was defined as any building which: '... *provides a responsive, effective and supportive intelligent environment within which the organisation can achieve its business objectives.*'

The model (Figure 8.2) states that the three main goals of an organisation occupying a building are:

- **Building management** – the management of the building's physical environment using both human systems (facility management) and computer systems (building automation systems).
- **Space management** – the management of the building's internal space over time. The overall goals of effective space management are the management of change and the minimisation of operating costs.
- **Business management** – the management of the organisation's core business activities. In most cases, this can be characterised as a combination of the processing, storage, presentation and communication of information.

Successful intelligent buildings rely on the provision of three layers of inter-related solutions:

1 Providing effective building shells which can absorb information technology and allow the organisation to grow and change.
2 Applications of IT to reduce costs and improve performance in building, space and business management.
3 Provision of integrating technologies and services which allow disparate organisations, systems, data and personnel to focus on the common goal of increased business effectiveness.

Each of the key organisational goals can be translated into a number of key tasks such as environmental control of the building, user access to environmental systems, the management of change, the minimisation of operating costs and the processing, storage, presentation and communication of information. Any organisation can use these headings to develop a demand profile that describes what is required from a building for it to function effectively and thrive.

While the technologies in each of these areas can help to create a 'responsive, effective and supportive intelligent environment', they can also be used to explore different models of organisational growth and development which are not so spatially linked.

Computer Integrated Building

One of the key technology trends within intelligent buildings is integration, both for building control and IT systems. In the IBE study, the move towards an integrated building is described in the 'Integration Pyramid' model developed by Teknibank (Figure 8.3).

Over time, increasing integration will occur in both building automation and communications. This will ultimately result in the computer integrated building where all systems are interconnected and integrated into a single building system.

While this model is a useful guide to what is happening within a building, it does not include the links between buildings and other locations which offer so many opportunities for progressing organisations. With building management, for example, the focus at present is on getting incompatible systems to function together and share data effectively within a single building. However, wide area communications technology also allows for geographically separate pieces of space to be brought together under a single building management system and managed as though they were all parts of a single building. In other words, a 'virtual intelligent building' can be created out of separate pieces of space, thereby facilitating better management and control of occupation costs.

Similarly, with space management, the use of integral CAD systems, databases and wide area communications should allow organisations to manage more effectively the space they occupy, wherever it is. For example, the space manager's role, supported by computer database systems, will be to ensure that spaces are available and serviced to allow staff to work in a variety of locations over more varied periods of time.

While innovative use of IT in both building and space management may produce valuable efficiency savings, most of the opportunities for organisations to increase their effectiveness lie within business management. In most cases this can be described in terms of a range of information tasks.

Information technology is playing a vital role in allowing organisations to rethink how they operate and how they use space (Figure 8.4). Structured cabling, and portable computers and telephones, for example, are crucial to the success of hot-desking or space intensification exercises. In the near future, wireless data communications within the building will also help to remove the last umbilical ties between the occupants and fixed work locations.

The cellular phone is having a major impact on how people work outside the building. Within the last five years, cellular phones have moved from being a rarity to becoming an essential work tool which allows work to continue while in, or travelling to, other locations throughout the world.

Improved communication networks allow businesses to make the best use of time and space through organising work in different ways. Advanced technologies in all three areas are moving organisations way past the physical envelope of the building into a range of locations and work settings. Building and information technologies are facilitating major organisational change.

Intelligent organisational networks

The Integration Pyramid, discussed previously, challenges the notion of the Computer Integrated Building as the ultimate intelligent building. The same advances in information and building technology which would allow the development of a CIB will also allow organisations to completely rethink how they use both space and time. CIBs may well render themselves unnecessary and the focus will instead move to intelligent areas, cities or regions (Figure 8.4). The CIB will be a key node on the intelligent organisational network.

There are still a number of barriers which prevent the development of intelligent organisational networks and the virtual corporation. They are:

- **There are still very large 'gaps' in the technologies.** Integration within building automation has yet to be achieved, let alone integration between building automation and information technology. The communications problems that result from this make any form of integrated management approach very difficult to achieve.
- **Data communications are still relatively rudimentary.** Current modem technology, the multitude of communications protocols and the vagaries of the Internet all combine to make wide area data communications problematic for many users. Data communications need to be as transparent to users as a standard voice telephone call if the virtual corporation is to thrive.
- **Bandwidth limitations.** As IT applications have become more complex, the bandwidth needed for data communications has increased very rapidly. Cable and network specifications have improved to cope with this demand and data speeds over 100 megabytes per second can be handled comfortably with optical fibre or, increasingly, high specification twisted pair cable.

Difficulties will arise, however, as wireless data communications are increasingly demanded both within buildings and for wide area communications. The radio spectrum will not be able to cope with bandwidth demands unless there is a complete reorganisation of how the spectrum is allocated. Terrestrial television services will need to be moved to cable delivery. This will allow the range of services to be exponentially increased to include multimedia and other interactive entertainment services. The range of interest groups involved in the communications industry, with competing interests and priorities, makes it likely that agreement on this reorganisation would be a lengthy process.

- **Conflict between data security and seamless voice and data communications.** Many organisations are very concerned about the security of their corporate information systems and the protection of their computer and voice systems for unauthorised access or eavesdropping. However, isolating a building to provide protection will prevent the use of cellular telephones and other mobile communications, systems which will be needed by employees and visitors to function effectively.

- **Management structures to manage work in many locations.** Data communication allows people to work either from home or a wide range of other locations, accessing the corporate information systems by modem or direct line. However, very few organisations have modified their management procedures to make this change work effectively.

  - How can staff be supervised effectively when they only come into the office occasionally?
  - How can an organisation ensure that the working conditions in these other work locations are safe and satisfactory?
  - How are the social needs of employees met if they are very seldom in the office?

These and many other questions must be addressed if the virtual corporation is to manage its employees effectively.

TOWARDS THE DISTRIBUTED WORKPLACE

As described above, the 1990s saw major changes in the way that space and time were used in leading organisations. New ways of working have allowed many organisations to integrate the physical work environment into the business process, to increase density of occupation within office buildings while at the same time creating effective work environments that encourage interaction and communications.

The current decade will see even greater challenges both at the level of the individual trying to use the scarce resource of time more effectively and at the level of the organisation trying to manage a dispersed workforce while creating the spirit and teamwork necessary for organisations to continue to generate new ideas and thrive. Increasingly, organisations will move outside the physical container of their own buildings into larger organisational networks across cities, countries, the region or the world.

Once again, information technology has played an essential role in the transformation, allowing forward-thinking organisations to integrate a wider range of urban work settings into their corporate workspace. The need for building or space ownership becomes less significant as space is purchased on demand, on an hourly, daily, or monthly basis, or as non-owned spaces such as hotels, airport lounges and clubs become a standard part of the working week. The city is the office.

As discussed elsewhere in this book, the office environment has not been immune to change. One of the most significant trends has been the dramatic rise of the serviced office in virtually every part of the world. The concept is not new – for decades it has been common practice for organisations entering new markets to start off in serviced office space allowing them to start up quickly with the central provision of administrative and IT services. Interestingly, in developing markets, these serviced office spaces were often associated with hotels or serviced apartment complexes – an early precedent for today's blurring of the boundaries between living and working.

The serviced offices on offer have become extremely sophisticated with companies such as Regus HQ providing global networks of 'on demand' offices with sophisticated IT and telecommunications services able to link the spaces back to the parent organisations. The use of these spaces is becoming common practice for organisations setting up project teams for limited periods of time rather than taking on long-term space commitments that may not be required in a few months time.

As organisations use this type of 'flex space' more and more, there is likely to be greater impact on the leasing structure of more traditional office space, particularly in the United Kingdom, as organisations become unwilling to take on long-term commitments apart from, perhaps, core headquarters space.

The continued rise of the serviced office is likely to be followed by the growth in more informal types of 'on-demand' work environments. The airport lounge is already a regular part of many people's working week but this will be supplemented by urban equivalents, linked to train stations, historic town centres, cultural centres or other amenities.

The Internet Café is the precursor to a new type of informal work environment. The Internet Café in its current form is likely to be a relatively short-lived phenomenon given the cost of internet access and the state of technology (internet access *via* mobile telephony or digital television is still in its early stages of development). But the Internet Café is likely to evolve into a work environment combining the IT and communications services of the café with access to sophisticated peripheral technologies such as video conferencing, plotters or CD mixing facilities with 'softer' business services such as the provision of meeting rooms, business catering and perhaps training or career counselling.

The new café office will be a place for meeting and interaction as well as for concentrated individual work. Its extended hours of operation will help bring life to the 24-hour city and will be a key part of the urban experience for many people. Historical models for the café office of the future are plentiful. From the medieval Guild Halls to Lloyd's coffee shop in the eighteenth century to the Victorian Clubs of England and Empire, shared ownership of business space and the provision of services on demand to members have been standard practice.

The future will be about options; about choice for individuals. It will be about constructing and managing one's personal and professional life out of a potentially bewildering set of options. It will be about using the city in new ways to make the most effective use of limited time or resources.

The challenge for the future will be to design a wide range of physical environments that can effectively incorporate working in diverse ways at any time of the day or week, and designing information and communication technology applications that will support this type of distributed working.

SUSTAINABLE ACCOMMODATION FOR THE NEW ECONOMY (SANE)[*]

The implications of the distributed workplace were explored in detail during the SANE project. SANE was a two-year research project, partially funded by the European Commission, that considered the combined impact of these changing factors on people, process, place and technology, with the intention of identifying new ways of accommodating work. Its focus was on the creation of sustainable, collaborative workplaces for knowledge workers across Europe, encompassing both virtual and physical spaces.

Work in the new economy involves more challenges and possibilities than ever before: new technologies enable greater mobility; divisions between work and home life are shifting, and business is undergoing fundamental change in delivery and production methods. Together, these factors are creating new possibilities for the way we work and fresh opportunities for those creating working environments.

The Distributed Workplace Model

The distributed workplace model, developed by DEGW during the SANE project, assumes radical changes in both the supply and demand sides of the building procurement model. In the supply side of the equation, developers will increasingly realise that increased profits will result from thinking of buildings more in terms of providing the opportunity to deliver high value-added services on a global basis to a customer base, rather than as simple, passive investment vehicles.

From the users' perspective, there is increasing interest in the provision of global solutions that provide flexibility and break down the old barriers between real estate provisions, building operation and the provision of business services. For global organisations, it is also becoming more important to reduce the number of providers of work environments to maximise the economies of scale they can achieve.

The distributed workplace model also tries to incorporate the increasing congruence between physical and virtual work environments,

*SANE (Sustainable Accommodation for the New Economy) project funded by the European Commission, under Framework V ("New Ways of Working", contract nr. IST-2000-25257) with partners from DEGW (London), Ove Arup (London'), RHUL (London), Telenor (Oslo), IAT (Stuttgart), Institut Cerda (Barcelona) und FAW (Ulm).

acknowledging the impact that information and communications technologies are having on the work processes of most individuals and organisations.

The organisational or social role that buildings are playing in many organisations is also changing. Historically, buildings have often provided a way of demonstrating organisational wealth, power and stability. The solid nineteenth century bank and insurance headquarters buildings in the UK, and the twentieth century drive for taller and taller office buildings, often in the absence of a sound financial or real estate case for them, are both demonstrations of this.

With distributed workforces only accessing buildings periodically, the role of buildings is shifting dramatically. Work can take place anywhere, so why should anyone ever come to the office? The office is seen as an opportunity to express the culture and to reinforce the values and beliefs of an organisation. The physical work environment and the opportunities it provides for interaction and collaboration aid knowledge transfer and communication and will form the infrastructure for learning organisations.

The model also incorporates the increasing congruence between physical and virtual work environments, acknowledging the impact that information and communications technologies have had on the work process of most individuals and organisations. In addition, the model examines the continuum between public and private space and produces novel solutions to their integration into workplaces. The workplace is divided into three conceptual categories according to the degree of privacy and accessibility they offer (Figure 8.1). The three categories of place used in the model are 'public', 'privileged' and 'private'.

Each of these 'places' is composed of a number of different types of work settings, the relative proportion of each forming the *character* of the space. *Public space* is predominately suited for informal interaction and touchdown working for relatively short periods of time. *Privileged space* supports collaborative project team and meeting spaces as well as providing space for concentrated individual work. *Private space* also contains both individual and collaborative work settings but with a greater emphasis on privacy and confidentiality, with defined space boundaries and security.

Each of the physical work environments has a parallel virtual environment that shares some of the same characteristics. The virtual equivalent of the public workplace is the *Internet* where access is open to all and behaviour

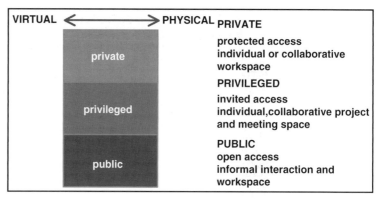

▲ 8.1   Physical and virtual workplaces

is relatively 'unmanaged'. The equivalents of the privileged workplace are *extranets* where communities of interest use the Internet to communicate through a form of information resource membership.

There are restrictions to entry into a knowledge community (such as registration or membership by invitation only) and membership has obligations and responsibilities attached, perhaps in terms of contributing material or communicating with other members. The virtual equivalents of the private workplace are *intranets*; the private knowledge systems belonging to an individual organisation that contain the organisation's intellectual property. Access to such Intranets is restricted to members of the organisation and the value of the organisation is related to the contents of this virtual space – the customer databases, the descriptions of processes and project histories.

When designing accommodation strategies, organisations will increasingly need to consider how the virtual work environments will be able to support distributed physical environments: how, for instance, virtual environments can contribute to the development of organisational culture and a sense of community when the staff spend little or no time in 'owned' facilities.

An organisation could choose to locate the Public, Privileged and Private workplaces within a single building and location. In many ways, the rich mix of work settings provided in New Ways of Working implementations could be said to already do this. In Figure 8.2, this type of combined work environment is referred to as '*Office is the City*'. All workspace is owned by the organisation and is occupied solely by it. Zoning within the building is often used to reinforce culture and community, and urban metaphors such as 'neighbourhood', 'village' and 'street' may be used to describe these zones.

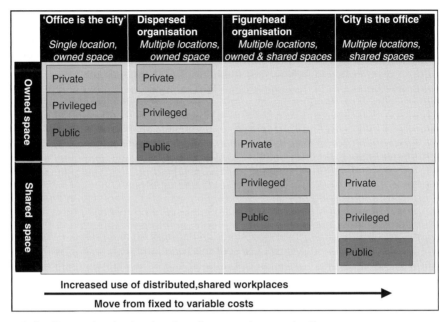

	'Office is the city' *Single location, owned space*	Dispersed organisation *Multiple locations, owned space*	Figurehead organisation *Multiple locations, owned & shared spaces*	'City is the office' *Multiple locations, shared spaces*
Owned space	Private Privileged Public	Private Privileged Public	Private	
Shared space			Privileged Public	Private Privileged Public

Increased use of distributed, shared workplaces

Move from fixed to variable costs

▲ **8.2**   Property strategies for dispersed organisations

As the level of remote working increases in an organisation, it may not be desirable to house all types of workplace in the same location. Distributing workplaces around the city may allow staff to reduce the amount of commuting they need to do and allow the organisation to start using the attributes of the city to reinforce organisational culture and community. For example, an organisation that wants to be thought of as innovative and trendy could choose to locate drop-in work centres in downtown retail/leisure areas such as Soho in London or Chelsea in New York, while the bulk of their workplace could be in more traditional business locations. In Figure 8.2, this property strategy is described as 'dispersed'.

As mentioned previously, organisations are increasingly incorporating semi-public spaces such as hotels, serviced office centres, airport lounges and cafés into their work environments. It is possible that this trend will continue to the point where the only spaces actually owned by the organisation are the Private Workplaces, including such facilities as Headquarters Buildings, Training and IT Centres. All other space could be provided by outside organisations on a flexible, 'as used' basis, along with many of the business support services. This type of real estate strategy is described as 'figurehead' in Figure 8.2.

If this move away from owned organisational space is taken to its extreme, it is possible to envisage an organisation where virtual work environments are used to house the organisation's knowledge and information resources whilst all physical work takes place in either individually owned space (for example, staff working at home) or in shared work environments booked on an 'as-needed' basis. In Figure 8.2, this is described as *'City is the Office'*. If this strategy is adopted by an organisation, issues related to training and knowledge transfer, use of ICT to support the work process, management of distributed work teams and informal interaction and team building will need to be carefully thought through.

The introduction of a distributed workplace strategy potentially has both efficiency and effectiveness benefits that can work at the level of the individual, the organisation and the city. The Space Environment Model suggests that workspace in the future will be broken down into smaller units distributed across the city, including both suburban (close to home) and urban (close to clients) space.

Smaller units of space can more easily be incorporated into the existing city fabric and, when combined with new methods of delivering both voice and data communications, these smaller units may be accommodated within old or previously obsolete buildings in downtown areas. Opportunities are therefore provided for regenerating existing city districts to provide homes for New Economy companies. An example of this is the re-use of obsolete office buildings in Wall Street in New York (Silicon Alley) that have been wired up for high bandwidth communications and now act as incubator space for dot com companies who occupy the space on a 'space for equity' basis.

The re-use of buildings contributes to sustainability by avoiding the construction of new buildings and the consequent use of materials and energy, and in the maintenance and support of existing communities. Remote working, whether at home or at neighbourhood work centres (using café/club type space) aids sustainability by improving the quality of life for individuals (by, for example, reducing commuting time) and by the reduction in energy consumption.

The increased use of shared space has economic implications for the organisations concerned. Buying space on an 'as-needed' basis rather than committing to long-term leases allows organisations to move from a fixed cost structure to a more variable use of freed-up capital to be invested in developing the business rather than just housing the existing business.

As well as providing re-use and regeneration opportunities across the whole city, a distributed work strategy also offers opportunities for specific cultural and historic facilities and areas that can attract organisations who want to use these cultural facilities to reinforce their organisational culture in the absence of their own buildings. Museums, historic buildings, art galleries, universities and even department stores could all earn extra revenue from providing café or club-type office services centres.

At the level of the individual, distributed working allows more control over the use of time, with reduced commuting and increased ability to match the work environment to the tasks required. It enables individuals to use visits to the office to meet with colleagues and to work with project teams, whilst using a range of other locations for concentrated individual work, away from interruptions and distractions.

Sharing workspace with other organisations also provides opportunities for interaction with people from other professions, which may lead to the development of new business ideas or projects as well as opportunities for career development and networking.

The Space Environment Model can be applied in many different ways to meet the needs of a specific organisation. One of the key purposes of the set of diagnostic tools being developed to support the Space Environment Model is to help organisations develop appropriate solutions to meet the requirements of their business process and the needs of their employees.

However, to further develop the model and evaluate its implications for the design and management of the workplace, we are developing models of a number of generic real estate components that together could form the elements of a distributed strategy for organisations of various sizes, appropriate for a range of countries and market sectors.

These generic components can be described in terms of whether they are public or private, in terms of shared access by other individuals or other organisations, and whether they are localised (close to the homes of the people using the components), or centralised (close to commercial or city centres).

The four generic real estate components (Figures 8.3 and 8.4) have been identified as:

- Personal Centre;
- Project Centre;
- Corporate Centre;
- Operations Centre.

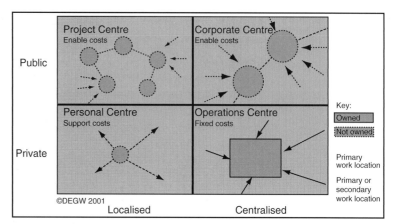

▲ **8.3**   Generic real estate components for the distributed workplace

The *Personal Centre*, or home office, may be the primary work location for some people working as freelancers or in roles that can be entirely undertaken from home using technology (such as distributed call centre employees). For the majority of knowledge workers, however, home will be a secondary work location that is used for individual concentrated working or to carry out routine tasks that do not require the physical involvement of other people for their completion (such as dealing with emails, expenses or standard reports). Working from home for part of the week may provide individuals with significant work/life benefits in terms of avoiding long commutes, or flexibility in dealing with family or other responsibilities.

For some people, working at home is not appropriate either because of technology limitations, family or other distractions, or because the home is not sufficiently large to allow the setting up of an effective home work environment. *Project centres*, located in suburban and other areas near where the employees live, for example as part of neighbourhood shopping and commercial centres, will still allow individuals to achieve many of the same work/life benefits (such as reduced commuting time).

These centres could be shared by a number of organisations or they could be completely open to the public. As well as providing a location for individuals wanting to work near home, these centres could also be used to provide longer term project spaces for teams collaborating on a specific project. Such teams could be from different parts of a single organisation or they could involve people from a number of different organisations.

A wider range of work settings and services will be provided in the *Corporate Centres* which are likely to be housed in more expensive space in central business districts close to where the organisations' clients are likely to be located. The Corporate Centres will also contain both individual work settings that can be used by 'drop in' visitors as well as longer term project space. In addition, the Corporate Centres may also contain a wider mix of meeting and other client facilities such as presentation rooms and private dining facilities.

It will also be possible for Corporate Centres to be shared by a number of organisations with project and client areas being branded for specific events or projects if appropriate.

The *Operations Centre* will primarily house business functions that are not directly client facing. These are likely to be located in less expensive space outside the central business district and may include functions such as Finance, Human Resources, Information Technology and Training. The Operations Centres may also house representatives of the service partners who will be supporting the Project and Corporate Centre networks. The populations of the Operations Centres are likely to be more resident and predictable than in the other types of Centres. While there may be relatively low external mobility there may be high internal mobility, requiring a rich mix of work settings to support the work processes being undertaken, including call centre space to provide administrative and service support to users of the other Centres.

It is also likely that the Operations Centres will continue to be leased or owned by individual organisations rather than shared by a number of organisations. This is because of the more stable populations in the Operations Centres, the nature of the work being undertaken there and the lower real estate costs in the more fringe locations where these are likely to be located.

From these descriptions, one can predict two key types of work locations, Project Centres and Corporate Centres, will in the future be shared facilities. In these centres, people from a number of organisations will share the same space and purchase a range of additional spaces and services from the suppliers of the workplace on an 'as-needed' basis.

If these shared workplaces are to succeed, they will have to be supported by a number of information appliances that allow the users to make sense of how the facility works, to order additional services and products on demand and to locate and interact with other people in physical and virtual space.

Public	**Project Centre** • Primary/secondary work location • Close to home • 24 x 7 flexible working • Itinerant workers (indiv/collaborative work) • Project teams • Training and development • Supported by high-speed network • Shared with other users • Lower cost space/suburban locations	**Corporate Centre** • Primary/secondary work location • Close to clients • 24 x 7 flexible working • Itinerant workers (indiv/collaborative work) • Project teams/Solution • Training and development • Supported by high-speed networks • Shared with other user • Higher cost space
Private	**Personal Centre** • Primary/secondary work location • Knowledge and service workers • Concentrated work, low face-to-face • Intermittent/continuous use • 24 x 7 flexible working • Distance learning • Supported by high-speed connection • Work/life balance issue • Privately owned space	**Operations Centre** • Primary work location • International/regional centre • Business support functions • Knowledge Centre • Resident/non-resident • Low external mobility, high internal mobility • Mix of settings including call centre • Flexible and shift working • Lower cost owned space
	Localised	Centralised

▲ **8.4**   Characteristics of the generic real estate components

The providers of Project and Corporate centres will seek to maximise their revenue from their centres by selling value-added services. Active directories around the Centres will ensure that users know what is available as a regular service and what special events and products are available at any particular time. If the Centres sell 'memberships' to users so that an accurate database of potential users exists, mobile telephones and PDAs can be used to broadcast this information outside the physical workplace to encourage members to use the space and facilities of the Centre.

These devices will also have a critical role to play in helping a mobile worker 'on the move' to find out what appropriate spaces and services are available at any given location, by accessing the global booking system of the workplace provider.

Information appliances located throughout the Centres will be used to display whether users have reserved rooms or work settings, the availability of the setting over time and perhaps even cost and other related information. These devices may also function as the interface through which to order audiovisual or IT resources and catering requirements.

With smaller scale shared workplaces, it may be relatively easy to determine who else is in the Centre and to locate colleagues from the same organisation. We envision that Corporate Centres could be very large, housing hundreds, or perhaps even thousands of workers from a number of organisations. Some of these people will be located in the Centre for a number of months or years, occupying a dedicated project space.

Others will be more transient, occupying a range of spaces and settings over time for the brief period that they are in residence at any one centre. We believe that there is a valuable role for some sort of 'office positioning' system within these Centres that can be used to accurately locate each individual user who wishes to be locatable. Obvious privacy issues will need to be addressed if any such appliance is to gain acceptance.

If each person had a unique identifier, they could be found within the centre by accessing a display screen on the Centre's intranet, or by viewing plasma screens located around the Centre. With appropriate access control, the system could be interrogated to locate all people from a particular organisation or all people with a particular set of skills that one needs. Personal profiles built into the system would also determine how willing, people were to be found or to interact with people from other organisations.

If the provider operates a number of Centres in different locations, the system should be able to be interrogated across all such locations, identifying where the person is and what resources are available at that site to facilitate communications. Virtual corridors between Centres – constant videoconference links – could then provide opportunities for people to meet informally to follow up on a phone call and perhaps share documents or other information.

If each person is wearing a unique identifier, whether or not it is set to be visible to the system displays, such a device could also be used as the primary vehicle for paying for goods and services while in the Centre. The contents of the information directories could also be dependent on the identifier of the person interacting with the device, proving company-specific, sector-specific or skill-dependent information based on the person's profile. This profile could be entered into the system or it could be developed by the system as choices and purchases are recorded over time. The information appliances will, in effect, have the ability to map the information networks onto physical space.

Shared workplaces have the potential to be large, anonymous workplaces where there is little interaction or sense of community – like an airline lounge on a large scale, with people arriving, working and moving on without any sort of meaningful social experience. Information appliances can help to ameliorate this by making sense of the space, providing access to the spaces, services and people who inhabit the Centre and acting as the catalyst for new types of interaction and communications between the occupants of the Centre. Information appliances will also act as the bridge back to the cultures and communities of the 'home' organisations of many of the users, and will help these workers to continue to feel part of the organisation regardless of where they are physically located.

We have concluded, with numerous other authors, that team- or project-based knowledge work will make important contributions to corporate success in the future. We have also identified above trends and models enabling a more distributed working strategy. But if the benefits of this move are to be realised, new and emerging technologies will have to be applied to the problem of supporting collaboration and interaction among teams of distributed co-workers. Existing groupware solutions contain many useful features but fall far short of reproducing the information-rich context that can be provided by the physical workplace. While many workplaces still fall short of this ideal, innovative designers such as DEGW, working with leading companies through the 1990s, have developed a very clear understanding of how interaction and collaboration can be maximised among co-located workers.

This last section of the chapter focuses on one of the core problems which the SANE project sets out to address: the problem of freeing knowledge workers from locational constraints.

As we have identified above, knowledge is the key to success, yet leveraging knowledge across an organisation is problematic. During the 1990s, many organisations made considerable investments in knowledge management systems with varying results. What we can say is that despite the best efforts of knowledge managers, knowledge documentation always runs behind acquisition: the latest and often the most relevant knowledge is in peoples' heads, not yet in their reports. The socialisation of knowledge – promoting the direct exchange of ideas through conversation and other interaction – speeds up the exchange of knowledge thus allowing organisations to get more value from it. However, this takes place most readily when people are located in the same physical environment.

From our research into interaction in the physical workplace, we have identified a number of factors that we believe are important for sustaining collaboration and knowledge exchange. Our experience suggests that spontaneous interaction and *ad hoc* meetings decrease as the distance between people increases – people rapidly become less likely to leave their worksetting to have informal discussions with colleagues. Teams dispersed within large organisations often recognise this consciously and create informal interaction time by meeting together for breakfast, for example. Such meetings are essentially social, yet provide an important forum for informal knowledge exchange.

Within the office environment, 'ambient' information also plays an important role in our interactions with others. We know, for instance, that there may be colleagues in the same room who may be able to help resolve a problem even though we may not be directly aware of them all the time. When we do need their help, we may also detect other information, such as the fact that one's colleague is on the phone, or deep in thought and thus unwilling to be disturbed.

Distributed workers have little or none of this information about their team mates and co-workers. Specifically, they have little or no information about the availability of co-workers and their willingness to be interrupted. The absence of this shared information-rich context acts as a barrier to spontaneous interaction and can lead to friction rather than enhanced collaboration.

While providing locational information to distributed workers does appear to provide benefits, it does also raise problems. Systems that provide this information are essentially tracking systems that can produce a record of people's movements. Some concerns have been voiced, although not by our users, about the privacy implications of these systems. Should organisations be able to track individuals' movements second-by-second throughout the day? While generations brought up with game shows such as Big Brother may not find this as disturbing, older generations may have reservations which may lead to serious privacy implications. If in-building monitoring systems were combined with external tracking, based perhaps on 3G, even more serious issues about the ownership and use of this information would have to be addressed.

Location awareness technologies are part of a broader trend towards what is known as Ambient Intelligence (AmI) where computers and other information and communications technologies cease to be artefacts on top of the desk or items of furniture within rooms but instead become integral parts of the architecture, objects and materials within the room. This trend is also sometimes referred to as a move towards 'the disappearing computer.'

This blending of the physical and the virtual within hybrid work and living environments is likely to have a profound impact in the future on the way we live. The 2003 report on future research priorities by The Advisory Group to the Information Society and Technology (IST) programme at the European Commission highlighted the future importance of AmI to the future prosperity of Europe.

AmI is seen by the Advisory Group as being central to the realisation of the strategic goal set by the Lisbon European Council in March 2000 where Europe is to become 'the most competitive and dynamic knowledge-based economy in the world capable of sustainable economic growth with more and better jobs and social cohesion.' The Advisory Group also acknowledged the difficult path that the introduction of AmI is likely to take. The technical realisation of the AmI vision is but part of the challenge. New regulatory frameworks and the social acceptance of AmI may take even longer than the development of the underlying technologies and infrastructures. Realisation of the AmI vision will also require a paradigm shift in how we organise labour and living involving much more flexible approaches to mobility and greater acceptance of new concepts such as portfolio careers and lifelong learning.

These paradigm shifts will result in new types of workplaces, new types of workplace and service providers and new types of technology and applications to support new types of organisations. The rapid workplace change of the last several decades will seem slow in comparison to what is coming during the next few years.

TECHNOLOGY FOR A NEW OFFICE

Philip Ross
CEO, Cordless Group

SUMMARY

In the next decade, new technologies are set to transform the workplace and the nature of work at a pace never witnessed before. Philip Ross, a leading consultant and commentator on the application of the new technology to improve the way we work, reflects on some of the technological opportunities that lie ahead and how they may influence in the future both how and where we work.

Radical advances in the power and performance of mobile devices, ubiquitous digital networks, 'the death of distance' as well as personal area networks are some of the technological trends that are already with us and which are impacting on the future workplace environment. New places are appearing, where traditional functions and perceptions of ownership are blurred, such as the Abbey/Costa high street centres; part coffee bar, part bank. In the future 'inefficient' space, which fosters chance encounters may be highly effective in stimulating ideas and generating knowledge.

DRIVERS OF CHANGE

For over a hundred and twenty years, the office has been dominated by fixed technology, from Bell's telephone in the 1880s to IBM's PC in the 1980s. But, many believe that we are now heading 'back' to a kind of mid-1800s, pre-IT era when the workplace had no such fixed technology at all – just clerks with pens working at simple desks or benches. The predominant model in the twenty-first century will be an under-engineered, technologically sparse workplace environment, at least in the eyes of the user or occupant.

Heavy desktop equipment has for a century tied the worker to his or her desk. As with the factory production line that influenced early offices, the white collar worker had to occupy a room or desk in order to 'produce'. Making telephone calls, typing or sending an e-mail has been the domain of the desktop.

Now, with the introduction of mobile, portable technology and the ability to communicate across distance at little or no cost, many of the fundamental rules of office life will be challenged.

The office of the future is always taken with a pinch of salt. Pundits predicting the end of the workplace or the rise of the teleworker have been a recurrent theme for the last 20 years. Various swings, from hot-desking to home working have threatened the demise of the desk. But ignoring the sensationalists, there is something significant happening to the nature of work, and the places created to house it in the twenty-first century.

THE TWENTY-FIRST CENTURY OFFICE

In the recent book, *The 21st Century Office* (co-authored with Jeremy Myerson[1]) we recognised four key trends for the workplace in the twenty-first century: narrative, nodal, neighbourly and nomadic. These four 'Ns' define the future workplace and they represent a radical departure from the containers that we have created for work in the past decades. There is no doubt that people will be working in different ways and in different physical environments, driven by changing management style and corporate culture, socioeconomic factors and new technology.

Four of the most basic features of the twentieth century office – its visual uniformity and banality, operational inflexibility, lack of human interaction and place-dependency – are now being subjected to a wide-ranging review. The narrative office, for example, represents a powerful reaction against the anonymous-looking, automated, over-engineered workplaces of the past 40 years. Nodal workplaces are responses to the inflexible, isolating culture of the twentieth-century headquarters, populated by sedentary workforces unable to share ideas with colleagues or clients as a result of a status-driven, departmental, static division of space.

The neighbourly office is a vibrant reaction against the command-and-control legacy of the twentieth century, which created suspicion and hostility between supervisors and staff, and undermined attempts to create social communities of purpose in the workplace. The earliest offices forbade conversation and frowned upon social contact, enshrining the work ethic in a dull, monotonous interior aesthetic.

Nomadic offices represent the logical conclusion of a technology-driven trend to liberate work from the workplace. For most of the twentieth century, the office was fixed in time, place and space. People commuted to and from the office buildings that were located in the urban 'business district'. The only way of communicating with a company was by physically connecting to its buildings.

▲9.1 Connectivity on the move means that people can work anywhere

Now, people can work anywhere, they are free to choose and the corporate 'address' no longer represents bricks and mortar. Call centres, e-mail and the internet have changed the rules as the 'death of distance' allows a reappraisal of where work takes place. This is a fundamental and psychological change to the way business is done and, in the future, the places where we will work.

Communications in today's building connect places, not people. Telephone switches in buildings put extension numbers on desks, and so to speak to 'Mr Jones,' you dial his desk. But that is an archaic way to connect people inside buildings and relies on an army of secretaries or the dreaded voice mail, because the facts and figures show that the average executive is not at his or her desk for the majority of the working day. Desks are not occupied, and so it will not be surprising to hear that 70 per cent of all inbound calls fail to reach the person to whom you want to speak.

DEATH OF THE PBX

So the very concept of a telephone switch inside buildings is now under threat. First, the growth of mobile phones in the past decade has led to a realisation and acceptance that people call people, not rooms and desks, and so there is an expectation of being able to communicate wherever and whenever you want. Furthermore, a new breed of technology born in the age of the internet is finally killing voice systems inside buildings. Voice over the Internet Protocol (VoIP, or IP Telephony as it is more commonly known) is the future, whereby all telephone calls are transmuted into data 'packets' and sent over data networks, both inside and outside buildings. This move from a 'circuit switched' world for voice, where we were charged for time spent on the 'phone, is giving way to a 'packet' technology where voice, in effect, becomes free and distance irrelevant.

IP Telephony is not just about a change in infrastructure, but heralds the death of the telephone itself. The rationale of purchasing a lump of moulded plastic is challenged in an IP age where, in effect, telephony becomes just another piece of software on a PC. Software telephones or softphones will kill the plastic telephone as all calls are made through computers, laptops or PDAs. Very soon your mobile phone will also double up as your internal wireless handset for the office as the first dual mode GSM/WiFi phones reach the market.

Not only is telephony becoming virtual; but also integrating with e-mail and facsimile to create a 'unified messaging' platform so that all your message types are presented in one 'in box' – e-mail, voice mail and fax – that can be accessed from anywhere in the world. Added to this are new types of messaging such as instant messaging (IM) and corporate presence systems. This means that your colleagues or boss can see if you are logged into the network – either in the office or at home, even in a hotel bedroom. Once they see your presence they can fire an instant message to you, and they know that you have seen it in 'real time'. Whereas with e-mail, people can ignore a message for a few hours, in a world with presence and IM, you can never switch off.

This has huge implications for work/life balance, privacy and stress. But like many technologies, such as the intrusive mobile phone, people have a habit of adopting and then accepting the consequences. The phenomenal rise of the Blackberry, a device made by Research in Motion for receiving e-mail on the move, is a testament to the competitive pressure people face to stay in touch.

As well as changing peoples' workstyle, the implications for buildings are fundamental. No more voice cabling means, a maximum of one cable per desk in the future, or none at all as both voice and data become wireless. Apart from saving on infrastructure costs, reducing staff costs and removing the costs of churn will also bring savings, as, less obviously, will the opportunity to have smaller communications and frame rooms, given the reduced heat gain and improved flexibility that these new systems bring.

WIRELESS MOBILITY

Over the past decade, mobile telephony has had a remarkable impact on work. From its early origins as a shaky analogue system, digital cordless telephony based on global standards such as DECT, GSM and CDMA has exploded. This has propelled the so-called second generation wireless (2G) into the hands of the vast majority of people. Now, we are witnessing a migration to third generation wireless or 3G where the phone becomes a smart communications device that provides data services as well as voice connectivity. Mobiles now also have built-in cameras, short range wireless technologies such as Bluetooth and WiFi, and will soon also have global positioning system (GPS). This ushers in a new era of personal communications that would have been deemed science fiction only a few decades ago. The next evolutionary step will see the phone becoming a 'personal mobile gateway' (PMG) through which a whole host of devices from cameras and messaging slates connect to the internet and beyond.

As telephones have dominated the desk for communication, so too have PCs for applications and documents. The rise of Microsoft's ubiquitous Office suite has led to a reliance on Word, Excel and Powerpoint for most office workers, and the communications interface of Outlook or Notes dominates our working lives as e-mails arrive incessantly during the working day.

But just as the phone call should not be routed to a desk, so the e-mail should be sent to a person and not a piece of furniture. Messaging in the twenty-first century will be person-centric, not office-centric. Instead of location, read 'locate'. The humble PC, as well as the 'phone, is thus giving way to a world in which we are free to connect from anywhere, either from portable devices or shared terminals.

First-phase mobility has been with us for some time. Laptop computers now pack the same punch as their desktop cousins, but offer the user the freedom and flexibility to work wherever they want, so long as they are near an Ethernet data port. Corporate life for most laptop-carrying executives, certainly in social spaces, was off line. Next came personal digital assistants (PDAs) that provided pocket-sized devices with calendars, databases and Office applications. Now with a new generation of devices, powered by Intel's Centrino processor, we are both mobile and wireless. Every new generation laptop has built-in wireless Ethernet (WiFi) and so people are equipped to connect. But wireless laptops require a wireless infrastructure inside buildings, and so structured cabling at high level (for example, in the ceiling void) will become a feature of future infrastructure requirements. This may dictate construction materials as well as floor plate typology.

Once the building has been wireless-enabled, and people are carrying wireless devices, a whole new paradigm emerges. We are truly free to create spaces for work without the constraints of cabled technology, and this will usher in a whole new era of workplace innovation.

Other new technology will also accelerate change. Bluetooth, one of a range of standards that refer to personal area networks (or PANs) will allow the *ad hoc* connections and temporary 'peer-to-peer' networks between people and their devices that articulate the future of collaborative work. Bluetooth's younger brother, ZigBee, will bring radio frequency tracking and logistics to buildings as inventory and people are managed in real time. And in the future, technologies such as Ultrawide Band, IrisNet and Motes promise to create intelligent 'sensor' networks in buildings.

▲9.2   Birth of the corridor warrior. Location aware building-based networks and sensors will change the places people work and connect

NIL BY MOUSE

New technologies for input and control of data will change the ergonomics of work. Tablet computers are the leading contender here, where, with Microsoft's new Office 2003, people can use a stylus and screen to input and annotate documents directly in Word, Excel and Powerpoint. As well as reintroducing the pen and handwriting back into work, tablets challenge the ergonomics of computer work and the predominance of the keyboard and mouse as the input and control mechanisms of the digital age. Here, as well as handwriting, voice is emerging as a powerful player in the control of computers and input and manipulation of test. Voice recognition is improving dramatically and Microsoft's Longhorn operating system (that is due to replace XP by 2007) should see significant improvements in the use of voice with computing.

Now tablets are joined by the first digital pens that remember what they have written or drawn on paper and then transfer these notes or images back to a computer wirelessly through Bluetooth or *via*

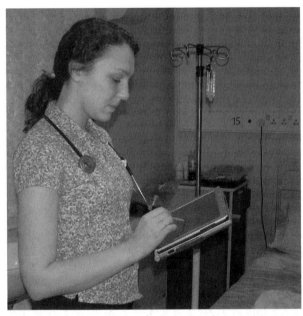

▲**9.3** Tablet computing brings back 'pen and handwriting' in the digital age and encourages work away from desks

a digital inkwell. Who would have thought that inkwells would make a reappearance in the twenty-first century office?

These technologies, and many more, are challenging the *status quo*. They demolish the assumptions that work has to take place behind a desk staring at a screen, and free the user from incessantly tapping on a keyboard to being able to revert to the more human interfaces of 'pen and paper'. But they also bring new challenges. When you can be contacted in the back of a taxi by 'phone or e-mail and asked to give instant opinions or advice, you then need instant access to your corporate knowledge – through an intranet.

This 'always on', constantly connected world is clearly leading to the slow death of paper, as more and more professionals realise that they need to be able to access their documents from anywhere. And this requires electronic document solutions, filed in virtual files that are housed in virtual deal rooms. Work 'on the pause' has to be the result of an holistic view by the corporation of how, where and why work is done.

Once the devices (mobile phones or personal digital assistants that are connected wirelessly to or from anywhere), and the applications to deliver telephony, messaging and access to corporate networks, have become commonplace, then most of our assumptions about how 'work' is defined will need to be reappraised.

IMPACT ON THE CITY

People now have the choice of tens of thousands of wireless internet hotspots and Starbucks, working with operator T-Mobile, is amongst the leaders with over 3000 wireless broadband connections in their coffee shops. Once you are wireless in the workplace, you then have a choice of thousands of other wirelessly-enabled venues in which to work, for the price of a cappuccino.

The wireless revolution goes further than just allowing people internet access from a café table. The next move will be to cover whole cities or urban areas with wireless domes or canopies. Already a number of cities, ranging from Cardiff to San Francisco have urban wireless zones that are 'individually financed' by people who want to challenge the *status quo*. These so-called 'guerrilla' networks have sprung up in all sorts of places.

Now in the UK, the first 'state-sponsored' wireless urban digital net-works are being launched in Bristol, Cardiff, London's Soho and other centres where ubiquitous WiFi coverage – a hotzone – allows people to connect to the internet at broadband speed from anywhere; a park bench, café or the town hall. Local authorities see this as a central part of their vision for connected communities and regeneration.

THE WORKPLACE OF TOMORROW

The technology will challenge more than just the office building. The mix that is the city will be challenged as people, frustrated with commuting and strained transportation infrastructures, choose new destinations for work, from the home to high street hotspot.

But, as well as being a liberating technology, these *ad hoc* networks encourage people to work and play in an *ad hoc* way, and while today that may mean working on a laptop from the park bench or the beach, tomorrow it will challenge urban planners and architects to create real places for work and inspiration that are a part of the townscape. Researchers often find that people have their most creative ideas anywhere but inside the office, and these realities have to be translated into a new paradigm for the city.

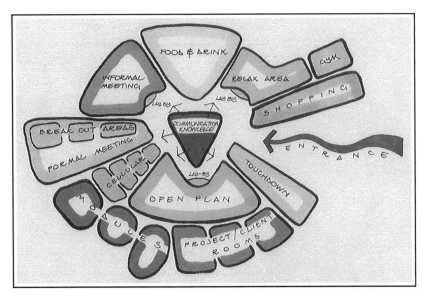

▲9.4   The Unitel – A cross between a university as a place of knowledge sharing and a hotel as a place of temporary residence – is the model for a future conected, digital workspace

Places for people to meet, to be stimulated, to have informal and formal meetings and to socialise, flirt, read and review, should be a part of the urban landscape of the future. Just as the market square articulated the nodal point of commerce and trade for a district in medieval times, so the digital market square needs to bring white collar workers together in an era of bit and bytes.

But what of buildings themselves? Well for many, the buildings of today do not serve the needs of tomorrow's firm. Whereas in the past hierarchy fitted predictable, efficient, rectilinear grids, tomorrow flattened pyramids will demand a new type of topology.

The 'freeway' office with its straight lines and narrow corridors designed to 'maximise efficiency' will give way to the 'medieval town plan' where journeys are less predictable and where the unplanned, unexpected, encounters that engender creativity and innovation thrive. Ikea revolutionised retail business by taking people on a journey round their stores, through settings that inspired, in contrast to the linear nature of most other stores. Their success is testament that the journey matters, and that surprise and juxtaposition make for successful experiences. Most firms strive for the serendipitous encounters through which innovation thrives, and yet all too often buildings are designed to keep people apart.

British Telecom, in their Workstyle 2000 study, found that inside an average building, people working for the same organisation, but in different departments on different floors have only a 1 per cent chance of bumping into each other on any given day. Architects plan buildings by 'adjacencies' where people who need to work together sit together, and so walking the corporate floorplate is kept to a minimum. Future planning should use 'disadjacencies' where people are encouraged to move around.

In the future, the occupiers of office space may well be different. The corporation has been the predominant economic model for the past century, but its foundations are built on the efficiencies that come from minimising 'interaction costs' and these are being challenged. One of the crucial issues will be whether corporates will still require and lease large quantities of office space in the future. The signals are mixed. Banks are still building monumental headquarters – for example, HSBC at Canary Wharf – but at the same time there is shifting geography, where once all financial institutions had to be in the 'Square Mile', now we find them at either end of London.

There have been examples of space reduction; Interpolis, the Dutch insurer, shaved 10 per cent from their real estate requirement when planning and building their new headquarters in Tilburg for 2000 people. By re-engineering processes and introducing new workstyles, they managed to save space. But this is by no means the rule.

CHANGING UTILISATION OF SPACE

Many corporates, rather than reducing space, see these trends as a driver to redistribute space. All too often in the corporate office, there are never enough meeting rooms or social spaces and this creates bottle-necks in the corporate process. And where such spaces are provided, all too often they are the wrong size, neutral and bland. They do not contribute to the creative process.

Now there is a realisation that the public: private space ratio has to be revisited. Already we have seen Manhattan high rise space where primary circulation is at the perimeter – where once the VPs offices would have been located, now everyone shares the best views down Park Avenue. But reallocation goes much further than this. Social spaces, libraries, pitch or war rooms, and team rooms are all part of a new land-scape that does not represent necessarily space reduction, but space redefinition.

But what was evident in the case studies in *The 21st Century Office* book was how many companies occupied 'unconventional' buildings. Low ceiling heights with the monotony of suspended ceiling tiles and strip lights were not features of future workplaces. Instead, warehouse-style volumes created multiple levels and interesting vistas, open spaces with easy circulation. 'Verticality', where buildings are planned in both dimensions rather than today's linear, horizontal approach to life, will become the norm and these will create new challenges for developers and their architects.

Buildings in the future will be constructed with a wireless infrastructure just as electrics and plumbing are installed today. But future systems will be radio agnostic, which means that any radio signal from mobile phones and pagers to emergency services communications will be picked up by the building's fibre optic cells and channelled through its backbone. The Sears building in Chicago is one of the first to adopt this approach, partly in response to the lessons learned from 9/11.

But just what proportion of the white collar workforce does this apply to? It is easy to predict these changes for the proportion of

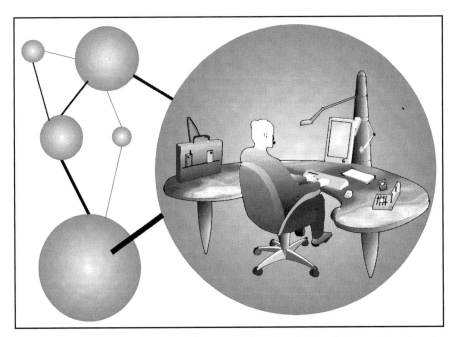

▲**9.5**   Peter's PAN – a personal area network – is the future of technology connectivity, linking people's 'bubbles' together in an unplanned, spontaneous, 'peer-to-peer' network

people that are mobile for a part of their working day; the management accountants, lawyers and advertising account executives have been early adopters. But in reality does an order entry clerk or administrator have any articulation with these trends? In all likelihood, any job function that does not involve some aspect of mobility (either inside or outside buildings) will not exist in its current form in ten years time. Those that are left will require the fluidity and real time connectivity that this vision of work entails.

The future office will be different, but with the long timescales and inertia that is endemic within the property industry, it will take time for new building forms to emerge. But the pressures of globalisation will accelerate change. Once call centres and IT support move en mass to Mumbai or Johannesburg and as China and other 'dragons' become the data processing centres of the future, then what is left for the high-cost real estate cities of Europe is financial, business and creative services that rely on cognitive skill rather than repetitive task. Places for people and not paper will be the challenges for tomorrow.

SECTION IV
MANAGEMENT
RESPONSES

Change needs to be managed. The literature on new ways of working has many examples of innovative ideas which have been initiated by bright consultants or far-seeing chief executives, but there is not very much information on how successfully projects have been adapted and whether or not they have delivered long-term business success.

Since the first edition of this book, in the field of real estate, there has been a significant shift in methods of delivery. Outsourcing of facility services, such as security, cleaning and office support services, combined with the growth of public–private partnerships, has begun to move towards long-term property partnerships that provide not only the entire portfolio of space, but also added-value services. The first chapter in this section reviews the performance of such providers from the perspective of a world class corporate customer and identifies opportunities for improvement and innovation.

The other two contributions show that successful schemes require sensitive management. If long-term success is to accrue, three imperatives should be met. First, the need for change should be thoroughly tested by assessing requirements, identifying resources available, reviewing alternative options, and preparing a business plan which meets both the company's objectives and with which management and key personnel feel happy. Second, once a project team has been appointed, proposals should be continuously reviewed against objectives and performance measures to ensure that proposals meet user expectations. As proposals are developed, solutions and requirements should be adjusted to maximise the outcome. Third, plans should aim to not only improve business performance, but should also propose a caring strategy for people and buildings made redundant by change.

The overriding message from all three contributions is to recognise the need to manage the process whilst monitoring the integration of organisational, spatial, and information technology solutions. From a business perspective a new building construction project, whilst large and disruptive, is simply a part of the wider project of delivering business success.

10 DELIVERING THE OPERATIONAL WORKPLACE

Barry Varcoe and John Hinks
Royal Bank of Scotland

SUMMARY

In the first edition of this book John Connor, then a member of Procord/Johnson Controls, explained why corporations at that time were concentrating on what they did best, leaving non-core activities to others. From the perspective of Procord, a facilities company that grew out of IBM, he painted a vision of a global facilities manager whose role was to manage flexibly a variety of worksettings in many locations – an animateur or concierge. Today, the new corporate real estate challenge is to improve business performance, not just to provide office space.

Barry Varcoe, head of facilities at the Royal Bank of Scotland, and his colleague, John Hinks, describes a new landscape where many major changes have occurred since the mid-1990s. IT companies, such as IBM, now act as total solutions providers. Established property companies also provide building and support services over a thirty-year period. But, from the perspective of the consumer, is the offer being delivered? The chapter identifies a gap between reality and the ideal of perfect service in what the authors provocatively term a '90 per cent Industry'. The construction industry, from which many of the new players came, focused on delivering at cost, on time, attributes which in any other sector would be taken for granted. A 10 per cent failure could mean a reduction in performance across 10 per cent of the business, a significant factor for businesses chasing ever slimmer margins. The challenge as the industry moves forward will be to develop measures which relate property to business improvement and use feedback to achieve continuous improvement and innovation. The partnership model must be able to share gains and losses. As we move forward into the twenty-first century, responding to changing business needs will be high on most corporate agendas providing four-star service at three-star cost.

DELIVERING WORLD CLASS SERVICE

Successfully delivering operational workplaces is often considered to be a Cinderella role within the workplace and property industry. It is what is left once the deals have been struck, the project is finished and attention has moved on to the next opportunity. But in reality, delivery of operational workplaces is the very reason why the deal was struck and the project was undertaken in the first place – to provide the organisation with an operational platform for its processes and activities, successful delivery is the most important role of all. Depending upon how well it is done, the workplace can be a major inhibitor (or enhancer) of organisational performance. This chapter therefore sets out some of the key challenges and opportunities facing operational workplace managers today as they seek to meet the organisation's expectations of tomorrow. It uses as its reference point the aspiration to provide 'world class' standards, not necessarily in absolute terms (providing six-star service), but perhaps more realistically in terms of overall value terms (four-star service for three-star cost).

A 90 PER CENT INDUSTRY

Whether called Estates Management, Facilities Management, Real Estate Operations or anything else of a similar nature, the management of operational workplaces has undoubtedly come a long way over the last 15 years. Over that period, a new industry sector has emerged within the broad property canopy, increasingly international in reach and outlook. Whilst the industry has undoubtedly come a long way in terms of its size and presence, it is perhaps more relevant to question how far it has developed in terms of capability. What the leading Facilities Management suppliers in the UK say about themselves is revealing. Taking the top 40, as identified by i-FM.net, the most frequently cited value propositions and future strategic objectives they promote are illustrated in Figure 10.1.

These are all the benefits that are easy to claim but harder to realise. Let us take a critical look at each of them starting with the least frequently mentioned.

- Since effective IT is arguably a prerequisite for any successful business operations in the twenty-first century, it is surprising to see this claim;

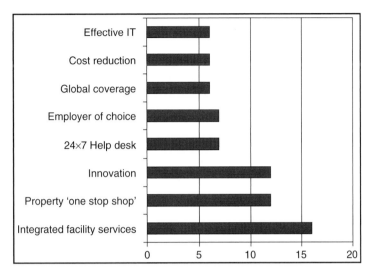

▲ 10.1   UK 'FM' Company Claimed Differentiators

- Cost reduction has been a big success story for the industry over the last decade but its comparatively low ranking reflects its status now as a 'must-have' characteristic and as such it is no longer a significant differentiation. Indeed, for many it has led to a vicious spiral of ever reducing cost, profit and service standards that ultimately leads to a distressed business model and unhappy customers;
- Global coverage is an aspiration for a number of suppliers following the increasing integration of operations across international boundaries within large multi-national businesses. Currently, however, emphasis is on coverage rather than operational integration with those that have the opportunity for deploying international solutions implementing what are in effect 'serial-national' operational models;
- 'Employer of choice' is clearly important within an industry that is short of talent. Chasing this accolade often takes the form of demonstrating evidence of sustained investment in people development such as achieving Investors in People accreditation;
- A 24-hour help desk is, like cost reduction, something of a commodity item now for those who need it most;
- Innovation is one of the hardest differentiators to achieve on this list. Without doubt many aspire for it, but few can claim genuinely to achieve innovation consistently. More often, advances in practice and capability are the result of responses to tactical operational pressures rather than a considered and structured approach to sustained

innovation. Not that anyone should be surprised at this, given the often wafer thin margins achieved by businesses in this sector of the economy. They simply do not have the investment headroom to make such commitments;

- Property 'one stop shops' are perhaps the single most significant development in the industry over the last few years bringing together all the capital and operational aspects of a building or portfolio into one long-term 'total cost of occupancy' lease arrangement. The current profile of these deals, however, while suiting the funding agenda of the public sector, tends to give them limited appeal in the corporate market;
- Integrated facility services is another 'one stop shop' proposition, but few have really addressed the true integration of services, more often to provide an operational management veneer over siloed service delivery (such as maintenance, cleaning and the like). There is still a long way to go before the truly integrated service appears such as one might enjoy from the cabin staff on a long-haul flight.

The biggest differentiator that could currently be sold is missing from this list, not unsurprisingly since it cannot readily be admitted. A service provider who could guarantee 100 per cent delivery of what the customer has bought (especially across any significant scale of operation) would, at the present time, be unique. The workplace operations sector whether delivered by an in-house team, an outsourced provider or a hybrid of both, is very much at best a 90–95 per cent industry. Achievement of excellence is usually set at this standard, beyond it is often considered to be worthy of a financial bonus. Let us consider what that 5–10 per cent that is not getting delivered on time might be:

- 5–10 branches out of a 100 location retail operation not being cleaned properly every day;
- Staff not being moved on time or not having everything ready for them when they arrive for work and thereby losing a morning's work;
- Buildings too stuffy and too hot in the summer because of chiller failures;
- Long queues at photocopiers or, more likely, the wasted time of staff wandering around looking for one that works;
- Key assets being lost or stolen due to an inattentive or missing security.

The point being that no one knows the exact consequence of the 5–10 per cent that is not provided until after the event, if at all. However, it is still an inescapable fact that every 5 minutes of work someone loses each day through an ineffective workplace is 1 per cent of their productivity gone forever. One of the big challenges of the workplace of the future is clearly therefore very fundamental – to get everything 100 per cent right first time. No easy task, especially with the increasing complexity and rate of change in organisations today.

KEY CHALLENGES

What are those responsible for operational workplace management doing about the challenges presented by occupiers and the workplace industry? At the leading edge, they are advancing practice on a number of important fronts.

Alignment with core business needs

Most people recognise the need to align what they do with the objectives of the organisation they serve but this overall priority only gains real relevance when the matter is given active thought and becomes the base for setting their own objectives. Once established, such alignments become an ongoing dynamic activity. Changes in the organisation's overall priorities and needs are continually matched by realignment within the workplace operations model. Over time, it may indeed be possible to introduce an element of pre-emptive planning so that solutions to match a number of likely outcomes can be made available for deployment as required. Such strategic modelling not only gives the workplace management team clarity in terms of its direction and purpose but it also provides a framework for performance measurement. This should ideally have four layers, two of which (business objectives and workplace objectives) have already been mentioned. Each workplace objective should have between four and seven critical measures identified that encapsulate desired outcomes from a business (not a property) perspective. This is the third layer which is used to demonstrate to the organisation the overall value provided by the workplace operation team. The fourth layer is made up of all the detailed operational measures that support each of the identified tier three outcome measures. These should be kept off of the business radar, being important for the workplace management team but of limited relevance outside that arena.

Continuous improvement

Service organisations are now looking at the quality and continuous improvement disciplines that have been developed in manufacturing environments to discover techniques that will improve workplace efficiency and effectiveness. One such technique is 'lean manufacturing', the tenet that simultaneous improvement in quality and efficiency is not a one-off objective, but continuous pursuit that delivers lasting benefits in terms of both processes and outputs. Lean manufacturing has four main characteristics, each of which has major relevance to the challenges of reliable service delivery to workplaces:

- Continuous quality assurance so that quality assurance is built into every step of the 'production' or service delivery process, rather than being achieved by post-delivery checking, reworking identified faults;
- Just in time, so that resource is provided at the point of need and at the time of need, and not before it is needed or afterwards. This greatly improves flexibility and minimises inventory. Time-managed workspace provision is a good example of this;
- Level production whereby peaks and troughs are minimised to optimise capacity utilisation. Portfolio-wide life cycle asset management planning is an example of workplace managers using these techniques;
- Waste reduction in this context means not just the removal of rubbish, but rather the elimination of redundant resources that arise from issues overproduction, excess inventory, inefficient proximity, repairs, and waiting time. A combination of the last two factors would be the eight-to-ten-week period it can easily take to fix a basic fault with a lift due to the lead time for obtaining the correct replacement components.

An example of a manufacturing inspired quality improvement technique that is gaining in popularity is Six Sigma^{TM}.

Innovation

As discussed earlier, the workplace industry has been less than industrious when it comes to sustained innovation particularly compared to other industries that have emerged over the last few decades such as in New Technology and life sciences. There have been however, a number of good examples of teams innovating to meet specific operational needs such as the winners of the CoreNet Global Innovators Award

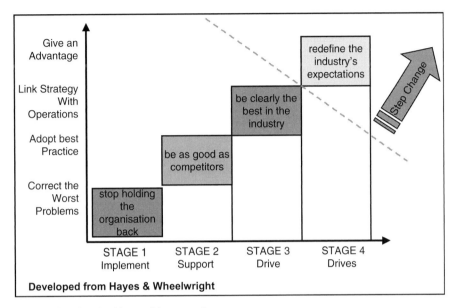

Developed from Hayes & Wheelwright

▲ **10.2**   Strategic Use of Innovation

(www.corenetglobal.org). To make significant advances in the future, however, a shift in the approach to innovation will be required from the opportunistic to the strategically planned and continuous. A model for this is illustrated in Figure 10.2. The insights achieved from organisational alignment and performance improvement priorities lead a portfolio of innovative improvement that takes due regard of how far up the outcome hierarchy each priority needs to climb. In addition, a step-by-step approach can be taken that may be more evolutionary in execution, more affordable, and thereby more palatable to the organisation as a whole.

Operational models

The conventional operational model for workplace management is usually simple – put a facility manager in each significant building and give him or her responsibility for any smaller buildings that are nearby. If there are enough buildings and people, a regional management hierarchy is often employed. For many years, this approach was effective providing each building with a direct point of responsibility. As portfolios have expanded and user needs have grown more sophisticated this model has, however, increasingly displayed significant shortcomings including:

- Dependency on generalists who also represent single points of risk;
- A lack of specialist skills available across the portfolio;
- An emphasis solely on local operations, with a limited portfolio-wide perspective, especially with respect to information, performance reporting and decision-making generally;
- A lack of process consistency with each individual manager or local team doing things their own way leading to variable practice, loose standards and no common focus for improvement;
- A lack of supply-chain leverage, because of a myriad of local arrangements. Conversely, if national or regional supply arrangements are put in place the management team can be in a weaker position from a knowledge perspective as suppliers can have a stronger pan-portfolio view;
- A lack of flexibility, because it is often difficult to realign resources to changing portfolio configurations.

Matrix organisations are beginning to address these problems. One example is that used by the Royal Bank of Scotland (RBS), as illustrated in Figure 10.3

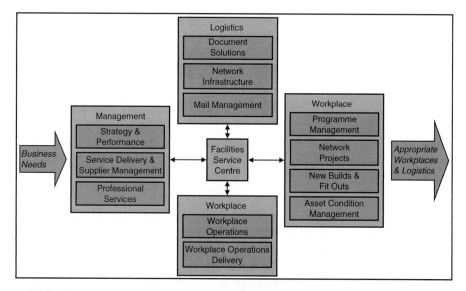

▲ 10.3   Royal Bank of Scotland Workplace Operations Model

The key difference in this type of model is the creation of a team dedicated to a portfolio-wide space management in RBS called the Management Solutions team which supports field-based operations. In so doing, these teams simplify the role of the workplace managers taking away daily distractions, thus allowing them focus on critical areas of quality service delivery (from suppliers) and consumer/customer (i.e. occupier) satisfaction. Central capability including analytical, service sector and functional specialists allows the operational team to have a much richer mix of skills and capabilities. Establishing area workplace management teams responsible for a large number and mix of facilities, rather than specifically aligning individuals to specific properties, achieves much greater flexibility. Each area team is a carefully blended mix of people with complementary skills and backgrounds so that they have a greater strength and capability, a team rather than a collection of individuals.

Project integration

A recurring complaint from operational workplace teams is that their views are often not taken into account during the design and construction of new or refurbished buildings. This is a common oversight and would not be countenanced in other industries. Who these days designs and builds a car without drivers and passengers in mind? The property industry manages to make things more complex by tolerating parties who all consider themselves customers (e.g. the building owner/landlord, the tenant organisation, the senior executives of the occupier who hold the operating budgets, the workplace management team, and the users or consumers of the workplace). There is no excuse for not considering these different needs from the outset. One way of achieving this goal is to introduce an operating statement and operating budget alongside the building design and capital budget throughout a construction project. This is illustrated in Figure 10.4.

The construction design drives both the project capital budget and also the operating statement for the finished facility. This in turn generates an operating budget which needs to be viewed in context with the capital budget to determine overall value for money. As each project proceeds and changes are considered, they can be evaluated from both the capital cost perspective as well as from operating impact and revenue budget consequences. In this way, there is some defence

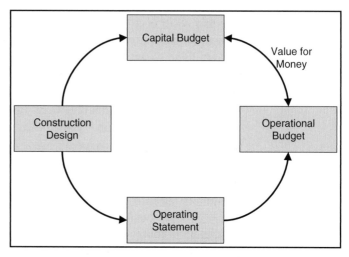

▲ **10.4**   Aligning Projects and Operations

against expedient short-term decisions being taken, which can prejudice operational use of the facility.

Supply-Chain Management

Supply-chain strategy is a vexed issue for workplace managers. In the past, outsourcing has been seen as a way of removing problems but has rebounded. In most cases, Supply-Chain Management has led to a reduction in cost particularly in the initial years of such relationships. But as has already been identified, the panacea of cost reduction tends to have a finite life once the minimum acceptable level of service has been reached. Without the engine of innovation to drive new solutions and value propositions advancement can stagnate and become stale. Corporate managers therefore need to be more sophisticated in terms of how they approach the supplier market both in terms of making the most of what is currently on offer and in seeking ways of moving forward.

Before commencing on a supplier-sourced solution, it is vital to know and to clearly understand the outcome that is required. This will in many cases drive the level at which the outsourcing relationship is pursued. For example, if a primary objective is to achieve cost savings or to improve reliability, then out-tasking service delivery functions may be all that is required. If, on the other hand, enhanced business value through flexible solutions involving risk transfer is desired, then operations management, process control and strategy will need to be transferred to the supplier in what may become a partnering arrangement. There is no 'one-size-fits-all' answer. Just as importantly, there needs to be a full understanding of the 'question' being answered in the first place. Each relationship needs to be tailored to circumstances if it is to have a chance of maximising its potential value for both parties.

Another important factor is the commercial model that will be used which must be fit for purpose and should give due regard to the information that is available. Where a significant amount of risk transfer is intended, perhaps embracing a risk/reward type incentivisation contract, complete information needs to be both available and transparent. If these two conditions are lacking, suppliers entering such an arrangement are putting themselves at considerable financial and possibly, reputational risk. Conversely, where a corporate organisation has complete knowledge of what is needed and conveys this to the supplier, but enters a cost-plus type arrangement, then they are putting themselves at risk and putting the supplier in a strong position to take advantage from the perspective of profit. Indeed, such cost-plus arrangements can also provide an inherent disincentive for improvement, and certainly cost reduction, as often in so doing the supplier loses business volume and growth. Cost-plus arrangements do, however, have a valid role to play where knowledge of what is required is significantly deficient, removing unreasonable risk for both parties until that knowledge gap is closed.

A lot of workplace operations sourcing arrangements can safely fall into a 'fixed price' type of arrangement. Increased maturity over the years on behalf of both the supplier community and corporate workplace managers should increasingly mean that there is a common understanding as to what is required. There are usually also a number of suppliers able to meet such needs, thus turning the requirement into a 'commodity' purchase. Where this situation prevails, there has been an increasing use of e-auctioning as a procurement technique. Used properly, this can be of great benefit to both parties. E-auctioning uses the same process as a normal 'request for tender/quotation', the only major difference being that the price submitted with the technical response is treated as an opening bid in an online auction that subsequently completes the process. Before suppliers are invited to the auction, prospective customers assure themselves that the technical solutions are appropriate and meet their needs—in other words, they are prepared to buy them. Thus there, no 'low-ball' supplier is allowed into the auction with a below-par solution to drive prices artificially low.

The auction itself allows all suppliers to see their own bid price against all others submitted by competitors (who nevertheless remain anonymous). During the period that the 'market' is open, suppliers can lower their price if they wish. Some choose not to whilst others can end up in something of a dog fight at the end to determine who ends up the lowest. The 'market' remains open until all activity is completed, there being no time 'guillotine' except through a lack of activity within predetermined parameters. From the suppliers' perspective, however, it is vital that they understand fully their value proposition and commercial model and know how much latitude there is within their opening bid for change. The e-auction is an excellent way of achieving transparency in the market, and for determining the market rate for the requirement.

Once the auction is over, the customer requires the suppliers in whom they are still interested to resubmit their commercial solutions recalibrated so that they are consistent with their final bids. They then have to decide which supplier has the best overall value proposition for them to buy—often not the lowest price. This technique, used properly, can save buyers a lot of money, often between 25 per cent and 35 per cent. But at the same time, because the specifications are very clear and the commercial model thoroughly thought-through, suppliers know what is required of them and how they will make their required profit. A customer who buys a solution where there is clearly inadequate or no profit for the supplier, or a demonstrable lack of resource, is possibly only one step away from being as short-sighted as the supplier who bid for it, for they cannot hope to have a successful long-term relationship that consistently delivers 100 per cent of what has been bought. Indeed, they will be lucky to get anywhere near the 90 per cent that is the norm today.

E-auctioning has a lot of merit if used in the right circumstances but is dangerous if it is used for requirements that embrace significant intangibles. Auctioning 'architectural flair' if you want to have an internationally renowned landmark building is less likely to be successful, for example, as is any requirement for genuine innovation. Indeed, outsourcing anything that demands a clear and sustained differentiation is perhaps dubious, but if you need to be no worse than your peers and perhaps a little bit better than most, it can be very successful.

Workplace capital

Successfully managing world class operational workplaces is a complex undertaking and will become more so in the future. There are a number of new approaches that can be deployed to address the shortcomings of the past and provide readiness for the future. All can be drawn together into a common theme of intellectual capital. Managing the workplaces of today and tomorrow requires far more than it did in the past. Aspects such as the skill and knowledge of the workplace designers and managers (human capital), the processes and use of evidence to manage optimisation and adaptation of the workplaces in a reactive or pro-active manner (structural capital), and the understanding of the nature of workplace usage by the business (customer capital) are increasingly important. This is without doubt a serious investment that should mean that competitive advantages are not dissipated or replicated across competitors and can be built upon in a serial and sustainable manner. The resulting workplace capital is the vehicle that takes the discipline of workplace operations to a new future, one where it consistently enhances the intangible value of the organisation.

11

SUPPORTING ORGANISATIONAL CHANGE

Tony Thomson
DEGW plc

SUMMARY

The history of office layout design has reflected changing fashions in work process design and organisational development. The freeform, seemingly chaotic, layout forms of Bürolandschaft were in reality the outcome of careful analysis of data flows and organisational relationships. The absorption of information and communications technology during the 1980s resulted in the superimposing of new technology on traditional ways of organising, managing and accommodating office functions. In the 1990s, the automation of the office opened the opportunity to re-evaluate the processes of work and reinvent the workplace.

In this chapter, Tony Thomson, Director of DEGW, describes a consultancy approach that is designed to help us to understand, in addition to the more familiar components of time and space, the management of time and place. Thomson argues that real gains at the workplace depend on fundamental organisational change as well as the redesign of the work environment. He proposes that redesign must develop from within, be founded on a top-down vision and be implemented with the involvement of all constituencies.

INTRODUCTION

The reinvention of the workplace is more than a simple planning or design exercise. In reality, it is a co-ordinated response to changing organisational needs that arise from the pressure to be more effective in business. Effectiveness in business relates to added value and productivity, in addition to, but distinct from, efficiency which relates to cost minimisation.

There are a growing number of examples of fully reinvented workplaces. This chapter attempts to place in context what has and is being done by leading-edge organisations whilst at the same time identifying where many projects have fallen short of the full potential available and in some cases, have been considered failures. The reinvented workplace is not an off-the-shelf solution and, like all advanced management solutions, should not be blindly copied. This chapter sets out to achieve an appreciation of the concepts involved and of some of the processes that can be used to effect organisational change and to introduce new ways of working through business driven reinvention of the workplace.

THE KEY DIRECTIONS OF CHANGE

In *The Responsible Workplace*[1] Duffy, Laing and Crisp argued that the conventional stereotypes of the office building (in North America and Northern Europe) are incapable of offering organisations the capacity to both *add value* through ways of working and to *minimise* costs. Alternative models for offices are required.

The demand to add value to organisational performance means that the office is not merely a place of information and control. As routine operations are automated, the office becomes a place for stimulating intellect and creativity. The office has to provide high quality and attractive features to meet the demands of knowledge workers. But this has to be achieved alongside the pressure to drive down occupancy costs and in ways that use space more efficiently. Moreover, such offices also have to respond to the demands for healthy and environmentally responsible buildings. What are the devices by which such value adding and cost-effective offices can be achieved?

A key feature of strategies which add value and minimise costs are initiatives that take better advantage of the use of space over time.

When the actual use of space over time is measured by observation in conventional offices it is found that many desks are totally or temporarily

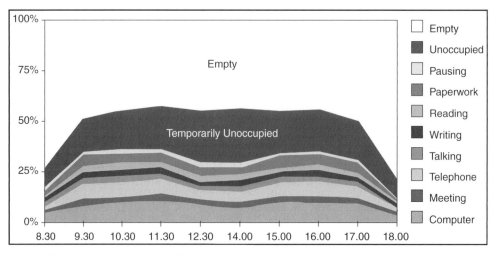

▲ 11.1   Typical office time utilisation of allocated workstations

unoccupied for much of the available time (see Figure 11.1). They are under-occupied because many people are spending time away from their desks, either interacting with colleagues within the building or working elsewhere outside the building – either with clients or in transit or at home. Once recognised, organisations are eager to capture this under-utilised space and use it more efficiently. The way in which any new office design solution captures and utilises this spare capacity is at the heart of environments that support new ways of working.

Duffy[2] asks whether the electronic office means the end of the desk and the rediscovery of the 'Club' – full of public rooms, meeting places and social facilities used occasionally, as needed.

The power of information technology encourages questioning the very idea of the place of work. The 'workplace' may be an information network that can be accessed from multiple places at any time. Organisations can choose to manage work across time zones and in multiple sites. Work may become nomadic across *real* places and occur in *cyberspace* on the networks. The office then becomes more of a focus for social activities (meetings, conferences, group and team work) or for occasional concentrated individual work, perhaps using special equipment and facilities that are not available elsewhere.

These influences have developed the concept of *The Distributed Workplace* described in a publication[3] of the same name where the principles of workplaces that are in more than one location within a city, country or

Objective	Improve		Innovations in work process relationship
Driver	Cost Minimisation	←————————————————→	Added Value
Impact	Existing design layouts – new operations		Re-design of working environment
Place	no change	change	high change
Process	change	increasing change	high change
People	change	increasing change	high change

▲ 11.2 Adding value *versus* minimising costs

region – depending on the work process and work life preferences of individuals and organisations – are explained and expanded.

The spectrum of impacts of workplace solutions that either minimise costs or add value is illustrated in Figure 11.2.

RESPONDING TO NEW PATTERNS OF WORK

Organisations which are working in new, unconventional ways, have historically been ahead of designers and suppliers in thinking about the nature of the office. Naturally, over time, the design and supply side of the market catches up with perceived thinking. However, care needs to be exercised to ensure that supply-side solutions are not inappropriately implemented.

We need to understand that leading organisations are developing different and more refined expectations (Figure 11.3) for:

- How they work;
- Where they work;
- Their control of time and place;
- The quality of the work environment.

There are still relatively few offices that have been successfully designed to support new ways of working, their associated technologies and emerging patterns of work.

What are the implications for the design and use patterns of the office in the future? These 'demand' factors create a brave new world of office design, use and management. The solutions to these challenges are more about a journey of discovery for each and every organisation that utilises

Office organisations have changed *how they work*:

From	To
routine processes	creative knowledge work
individual tasks	groups, teams, projects
alone	interactive

where they work:

From	To
places	networks
central	dispersed
transport	communication
office	multiple locations including the home

They are *using space over time in new ways*:

From	To
one desk per person	multiple shared group work settings
hierarchical space standards	diverse task-based space
nine to five at one place	anywhere anytime
under-occupancy	varied patterns of high-density use
owned	shared

▲ 11.3   Changing organisational expectations

components from the supply side to create an integrated workplace strategy that supports real business needs.

HOW DO YOU REINVENT THE WORKPLACE?

Once a decision has been made to implement organisational change, an opportunity arises for a contribution to be made by redesigning the workplace. The key to this reinvention is that it must arise from within, ideally founded on a top-down vision, but fulfilled by a bottom-up involvement and contribution. This involvement is the key to successful implementation. Without it, solutions become imposed and, in all but the most exceptional circumstances, have been proved to fail.

The implication of such a process with a high degree of user participation is that there are no real short cuts and, as every department of an organisation considers itself different from every other one, the time-scales involved could become unrealistic and related costs would increase. To some extent there is no real solution to this conundrum and it is important to realise that in the end, a full process may be required for each and every project. Undoubtedly, as more successful projects appear within the market place, or even better within the organisation itself, a snowball effect will ease the process to some degree.

The approach set out below proposes the development of a menu of work settings that can be used to create the workplace strategy for any department of an organisation. This means pre-defined settings can be arranged in terms of number and relational groupings to create environments that meet corporate, departmental and individual needs.

However, as well as the above, the aim is also to provide an integrated workplace strategy that will help rationalise existing and future spatial requirements. The two principal drivers are:

- Space efficiency;

  Making the optimum use of space consistent with the configuration and infrastructure of available or replacement buildings and commensurate with business needs.

- Organisational change;

  Changing work patterns.
  Changing business priorities.

There are also a number of other initiatives that lead to change in the demand for space and change in occupancy patterns. These include extending the use of properties through flexible working hours, home-working, new ways of working and the introduction of more information technology. Furniture and storage policies are also subject to review, particularly for the development of new working environments.

The method

The key to all successful projects that involve significant change is that they must be based on an agreed, visible and clear business case. Naturally the business case should be developed before such workplace projects are undertaken. Unfortunately, too many projects begin before the business case has been established.

The objective of any project is to satisfy business demand. This is achieved by establishing the projected organisational demand and to propose appropriate building forms and layout solutions to satisfy that demand. There are five main stages to the method:

1 Data capture
2 Analysis and refinement
3 Development of proposals (alternative workplace strategies)
4 Management and implementation of change
5 Feedback and review

DATA CAPTURE

Four principal areas of initial investigation are required:

(a) Organisational data

The collection and compilation of the current population and structure and the impact of change in:

- Headcount;
- Business priorities;
- Ways of doing business.

The prime method of data collection in this area will be through interviews with senior managers who have responsibility for key departments in the organisation. They should be aware of future business trends and the impact that these are likely to have on headcount, the need for space and working practices. In many instances, interviews are also combined with an information gathering workshop.

Discussions will also be needed with key functional support departments such as Information Technology/Communications to understand any 'infrastructural' changes that are planned.

(b) Existing space use

The measurement and analysis of current space usage and in particular data regarding:

- Current floor areas (net occupiable and net lettable areas and net to gross efficiencies);
- Existing densities of occupation;
- Existing patterns of space use (actual space standards, open to cellular ratios, ancillary and support space use);
- Interpretation of potential use activities (collaborative areas, interaction/network areas, formal and informal meeting areas);
- Tenure and investment criteria.

Conventional space auditing techniques should be utilised. It is essential to ensure that the appropriate amount of data required for the development of a facilities strategy is gathered. The objective is to be able to describe space use in the form of a current use model that will provide a base line for any future comparisons. Data should be available from the facilities department using at least the current base of building drawings and, if available, databases of supporting information.

(c) Time utilisation studies

There is no substitute for objective data on space utilisation, most people feel very proprietorial about their personal or team space. Most managers also believe they are unique and have little to learn from other space users due to differences in operations. However, experience suggests that cultural similarities lead to a degree of confluence in activity patterns. Time utilisation studies (TUS) provide evidence of such similarities.

There are many ways that time utilisation studies can be carried out. All systems require the setting out beforehand of what activities are being observed and a repeatable circuit for the observations to be taken. The observation system can be a simple paper recording system, analysed with the help of a spreadsheet. However, fully automated data collection systems enable direct entry into a database for handling the analysis.

The key to understand such surveys is that they record information about the use of defined spaces not about the people using them. In fact, great care needs to be taken in the use of TUSs, particularly where they are used to evaluate the success of new ways of working. If the workspace is truly innovative, it is likely to contain a number of dis-tributed work settings both within and outside the workspace. As the data collected is about spaces and *not* people, understanding real utilisation can become quite complex and could easily lead to misinter-pretation. However, as a means of opening minds to the problems associated with conventional office allocation and planning, the TUS is invaluable.

The findings from this stage of the work influence the concept recom-mendations and provide material for challenging assumptions.

(d) User questionnaire

An important part of understanding current space use is to appreciate how current users think the workplace performs. To attempt to provide some objective reference, the questions are not only about performance but also how important specific aspects of space are in carrying out their work. This ensures that no time is wasted on aspects that perform poorly but are not important at all. An on-line survey is developed and the resulting questionnaire is delivered to all staff *via* their networked computers.

Using DEGW's proprietary questionnaire (The Workplace Performance Survey) a survey can be completed in 15 minutes or less. With senior management sponsorship, a 60 per cent return rate is often achieved. A database is developed from the returns and, subsequently statistically robust findings are derived from evaluation of the data. This information is used to support interview findings and to stimulate discussion at user group workshops. The questionnaire can be used to substantiate the strength of feelings about the various elements of the workspace (such as the work surface area of desks or meeting facilities) across all levels of staff. The questionnaire also highlights opportunities for improvement and can include the collection of information about individual's patterns of work. This allows a picture to be created of the whole range of work-styles in the organisation.

The amount of data collection required has to be determined by the time available, existing company information and databases, and the appropriate statistical rigour.

ANALYSIS AND REFINEMENT

The analysis of data provides information that will be utilised in the development of the required workplace strategy. Optional planning and design approaches can be considered at this stage and these will depend, for example on such factors as recent projects with a high degree of user participation. While the research programme may be adapted to suit any particular organisation, it would be normal to conduct the analysis of data in two stages:

(a) Establishing facilities and spatial mores

Understanding current customs and practices in different departments and workgroups is essential. Comparisons across functions highlight differences. Measuring the effectiveness of current standards and their implementation in practice supports future proposals for change.

Several techniques are at our disposal. Their use depends upon each situation. However, it is not uncommon to utilise the data for modelling different scenarios that modify key elements. For example, a proposed filing programme could modify storage requirements. Sensitivity analysis provides outputs that enable decisions to be made based on a grasp of likely outcome.

(b) User group facilitation

The more the users that can be involved in the design of their working environment, the more successful will be the solutions. User workshops are the key to avoiding impractical wish lists and achieving buy-in.

Each user group should be taken through three stages that, ideally, are reflected in the agenda of three workshops:

- Seeking views and opinions (dumping);
- Building on ideas about the future (consensus building);
- Presenting resulting concepts (understanding and buy-in).

In practice, the time pressure of projects often necessitates the three workshops being compressed into two (which is workable) or even one (which can be sub-optional). The more time that can be given in this important area, the more successful a project is likely to be. Where more than one workshop is being held per group, the first session can be included as part of the overall data collection.

One purpose of the user workshops is to validate and interpret the collated information. Groups will be asked to prioritise the issues raised in questionnaire responses. Users may be asked for observation and analyses between meetings, but while this should not take more than 15–20 minutes, it certainly helps to build greater awareness of the issues involved.

DEVELOPING PROPOSALS

At the end of the analysis phase, we are in a position to:

1 State the ranges of current and projected demands for space;
2 Articulate work processes that require new work settings – geared to increase effectiveness;
3 Quantify the capacity of the buildings or spaces to meet organisational demands.

The key to this phase is communication and continuing involvement. Design development may take many different courses depending upon client and the project. However, we would expect to carry out two following exercises:

(a) Executive presentation

An executive workshop is essential to ensure continuity commitment. A good time for this workshop is when proposed spatial concepts are developed and when options have been developed. The methods for data collection are important in providing the best platform from which concepts can spring. User group workshops and interviews play an important part in explaining data and pointing the way to possible alternatives.

The central objective is to respond to all these inputs while using space as effectively as possible at minimum cost within an environment that can cope with change and actively encourages increased productivity.

The executive presentation should include the following:

- Confirmation of vision and links with the business case;
- Summary of data analysed;
- Key issues arising from data analysis;
- Concept options;
- Facility management issues;
- Impact of options on future business strategies.

Appropriate attendees for this presentation should be determined during the course of the project and should include managers whose environments are most likely to be affected.

Attendees should review proposals and influence preferences. This is the most effective time for them to be briefed on the findings of the study. There is considerable benefit in bringing the data from all the areas of collection together, at this stage, to enable attendees to understand the principles that underpin workplace strategies.

(b) Concept development

The purpose of this stage is to respond to the demand profiles developed above into:

- Concept plans showing how space might be used;
- Space budgets detailing all space requirements including sharing ratios and overlapped utilisation;
- Description of the work involved in setting the type and quantity of space required to meet the organisational demand;
- An indication of new management policies required to enable effective space management;
- Reference to relevant technology, required, to support new ways of working.

Never forget that the study may conclude that only very limited changes in working practice are possible or acceptable.

MANAGING THE IMPLEMENTATION OF CHANGE

As projects become more complex and demanding and as there is ever increasing change, there is a real need to manage change.

Workplace change requires more attention than most managers are willing to accept. As Laurie Coots from Chiat/Day has said:

> 'You need the diplomacy of Gandhi, the negotiating skills of Kissinger, and the patience of Mother Theresa.'

The key is to be aware that dealing with pilot projects or rollout implementation projects are not like traditional fit-out projects: Due to the human element they are likely to be an order of magnitude more difficult. *So why do it?* The rewards are likely to be an order of magnitude greater then conventional projects.

FEEDBACK AND REVIEW

Continual reassessment of the success and failure of implemented environments is necessary if the process is to be complete. As Roger Bricknell of General Electric said:

> 'If you teach a bear to dance, you'd better be prepared to keep on dancing till the bear wants to stop.'

A good way of performing such reviews (often called post occupancy evaluations (POEs)) is to re-run the user questionnaire carried out in the data capture phase. Not only will the questions be familiar but they will provide the opportunity to monitor *before* and *after* changes and look for trends in user reactions to the new environments.

SUMMARY OF METHODOLOGY

The methodology set out above must respond to the particular requirements of each and every organisation. However, the fundamentals are now well established and are unlikely to change significantly. New techniques will of course continue to be developed and the process has proved to be a dynamic one. In the early work that DEGW carried out with Steelcase some simple checklists were developed. These are still applicable and are shown here to act as an *aide memoir* for anyone embarking on a project that is seeking to 'reinvent the workplace'.

Keep asking these key questions:

1 *Have we studied* our clients' processes: Do we really understand the nature of their work?
2 *Are we basing* our plans on what we need to support, work processes or on outmoded traditions of status and rank?
3 *Are we building* streets, villages and colleges or yet another outmoded white collar factory?
4 *Are we supporting* the work wherever it is performed?
5 *Are we giving* groups and teams, as well as individuals, the settings they need to work effectively?
6 *Have we involved* all the people in the planning process? Are we ready to train them to use their new workplaces more effectively?
7 *What messages* are we sending to our internal and external customers in the ways we plan and furnish offices?
8 *Is our ultimate goal,* cost-cutting or the working effectiveness of the company?

Remember the rules have changed:

- What *you do* is more important than who you are;
- You do not have to *go to work* to work;
- You will not *sit in one place* very long;
- *No longer* one person, one chair;
- Group and team settings *are increasing*;
- There are *multiple models* for workplaces (street, village, college);
- We are moving from efficiency to *effectiveness* and should now embrace *expression*.

12 MAKING CHANGE WORK

Adryan Bell
DEGW plc

SUMMARY

'Change has a considerable psychological impact on the human mind. To the fearful it is threatening because it means that things may get worse. To the hopeful it is encouraging because things may get better. To the confident it is inspiring because the challenge exists to make things better'.

King Whitney Jr.

'The art of progress is to preserve order amid change'.

N. Whitehead

Contributors have already set out the implications of information technology for the organisation of and the settings for work. Adryan Bell reflects on fifteen years of experience as a workplace change management consultant within the Civil Service and subsequently with us at DEGW. Since the first edition of this book, the role of managing and moderating the change precipitated by relocation has been elevated from simply administering the move in and preparing welcome packs to managing the integrating process of renewing buildings, and simultaneously rethinking work processes and technologies to support business success. In today's frenetic world, we may embrace change but, as Bell tellingly points out, 'people are changed not by coercion or intimidation but by example'.

From his experience of having masterminded workplace change processes for major organisations in both public and private sectors, Bell draws lessons from the Scottish Enterprise Workplace of the Future project (1995) which became the pilot for Scottish Enterprise's move to Atlantic Quay and informed the subsequent moves at HM Treasury, the MOD and the Home Office. Uppermost in his menu for success are leadership, the importance of giving the project identity and meaning and effective two-way communications. Linking the change process with initial briefing and later space planning ensures that staff recognise the purpose of the move, that continuous evaluation and learning are established, and that organisational innovation is embedded in subsequent building adaptations. He argues that workplace change should be seen as a journey which has no precise beginning or end but, when implemented effectively, can have lasting impact on the well-being of staff and business success.

MANAGING WORKPLACE-RELATED CHANGE

It is entirely fitting in a book about the evolving workplace to explore the topics of *change and change management*. Indeed, many change experts see the workplace as one of the most *difficult*, yet most *important* areas of change to deal with.

Difficult because of the often emotional attachment that people apply to their personal work space – be it an office, desk or filing cabinet – and their reluctance to allow change or to give anything up no matter how outdated or ineffective. Physical elements are often viewed as a personal right by many office workers and as such can be regarded as a no-go area for any radical organisational intervention. Also, in a world of constant business, technological and organisational change, over which such workers generally have little control, their immediate working environment can become their only haven of stability and security to which they, perhaps understandably, cling to.

Important because a change in workplace – whether a refurbishment, redesign, redevelopment, new build and/or relocation – can often be the perfect catalyst for wider business, organisational or cultural change. Quite simply, a new environment provides an ideal platform or backdrop for implementing and accelerating change – influencing and impacting attitudes, morale, behaviours, habits and so on. Through workplace change, much wider opportunities and improvements can typically be achieved. It is an opportunity to embrace new ideas and leave behind old reminders and 'baggage' – not unlike how we often treat a house move or relocation in our personal lives as a new start.

In the context of designing and delivering effective and successful workplaces, it is therefore worth exploring some of the theory, application and outcomes of properly managing change for the people involved.

WORKPLACE SUCCESS

'People – the key to your success or the reason for your failure.'
Adryan Bell, Transforming your Workplace, 2000

Clearly, paying proper attention to physical design, appropriate fit-out and supporting technologies based on sound analysis, plays a vital role in creating an effective working environment. However, in many respects, it is people who are the most important workplace ingredient. The workplace has considerably less value without their intervention.

And this can so often be overlooked in the quest to complete the physical project and get the aesthetics right.

Indeed, the success or failure of any workplace transformation project depends entirely on how well its users understand, embrace and exploit the new facilities and opportunities being provided. Many project managers have found to their detriment that ignoring, or inappropriately responding to, the needs of the intended users of new workspace, is a dangerous strategy. And because of the sensitivities already outlined for many office workers, the tendency for the communication and support around these issues to be handled badly, mistimed or avoided, is unfortunately all too commonplace.

However, the good news is that increasingly the need to 'prepare the people for the workplace, as well as to prepare the workplace for the people' is being recognised by project and business managers. In addition, the need to recognise this early, so as to influence the project objectives, scope, approach and outcomes, is also acknowledged as being extremely important to the success of the overall process.

Skilful tactics and well-planned and effective change and communication programmes are enabling workplace innovation to not only take, place but also to really work in practice. They are allowing the changes to be sustainable and to deliver real business benefits, linking to, and helping the realisation of, other important organisational or business initiatives.

THE PRINCIPLES OF MANAGING CHANGE

Before exploring these approaches in more detail, it is worth looking at some of the basic principles of change management in a general sense. We can then better understand the relevance and application to the workplace context.

We all embrace change in our everyday lives – job changes, house moves, holidays, marriage, change of car and so on. Sometimes the change is welcome, sometimes less so. In the latter case, as long as we understand and accept why the change is needed, we are usually prepared to take it on.

In addition to understanding and accepting the rationale for change, other factors that can support the positive embracing of such generic change include:

- The ability to have some choice or influence (even if limited);
- The opportunity to do some forward thinking, research, planning and/or preparation;

- The provision of support, guidance and advice;
- The sharing of the change with others, enabling peer support and understanding;
- The scope for personal benefits to be achieved, enhancing personal motivation.

Rationale and motivation are two key elements that help drive positive change of any nature, and certainly apply in the workplace concept. It is said that people do not resist change, so much as resist *being* changed – suggesting that the way change is handled – introduced, communicated and managed – is as important as the change itself in terms of getting a positive and effective outcome. All of this is logical, even intuitive, in the sphere of personal change but, like many other things, it often does not seem to translate well into the context of the corporate environment.

Nobody likes having things imposed on them, with little or no choice. However, it is clearly impractical to give office workers free choice on the design of a new workspace – if only because their ideas about what is, or is not possible, may be stifled by their limited experience or the specific perspective of the organisation. Additionally everybody, of course, will have an individual and sometimes contrarian view on design, layout and furnishing considerations – fuelled by increasing media attention to and coverage of these topics. Such dilemmas have the potential to create a mass of unmanageable and conflicting individual expectations that can dilute the original organisation-level vision. So a sensitive approach and skilful tactics are very important here.

Scale and appropriateness

Where office change is limited to simple 'churn' moves (i.e. physical re-alignments to support organisational changes and growth) and minor updates, cultural change is probably not a consideration, although some basic staff communication, often overlooked, is still important. It usually takes a more significant workplace development to present the sort of opportunities where a structured change management and communications approach is desirable, even essential. This will enable the goals and objectives of such projects, which are becoming increasingly ambitious, to be fully realised, whilst avoiding related business operations being detrimentally affected during the change process.

In considering the need, scope and resourcing of such change-support for people, the cost of doing nothing should be remembered: the negative potential for staff confusion, demotivation, productivity losses and wasted investment and opportunity, is considerable. A good business case for investment in workplace change management can, arguably, be secured on this basis alone. Add to this the scope for new business opportunities and benefits to be achieved by suitably enlightened and motivated staff and the case for change management becomes unarguable!

Vision and leadership

'People are changed, not by coercion or intimidation, but by example'.

Source unknown

A strong project vision, championed at a senior level, is always essential for any organisational or business change. This will provide direction, consistency and confidence in the process.

In simple terms, change management could be viewed as an exercise in eliminating or minimising resistance to change and increasing or maximising the appetite and positive energy or motivation to embrace change. And this is achieved through well-informed, well-planned and, most importantly, *well-led* tactical communications and interventions.

Leadership comes not only from senior managers/executives, but also from anyone with influence and respect such as a secretary, line managers or a long-serving member of staff. So, it is important to understand who your allies are and how to use their influence.

Without doubt, the skilled change manager will employ tactics to facilitate the most effective change process, recognising the particular situation, context, culture, strength and weaknesses of the organisation and people involved as well as making best use of motivations and incentives for organisation and individuals at that particular time.

Consultation

The balance between imposing and agreeing change is a delicate one. Clearly, staff consultation should happen in some way, typically facilitated through the use of team representatives or champions who act as conduits for communication between the project and local teams, but it needs to be the right sort of consultation.

Rather than asking what people want, workplace project briefing increasingly focuses on what people do and what will add value to the business processes. The emphasis of change-related consultation beyond this needs to focus on ensuring that:

- Workers understand the rationale for the new concepts and practices being introduced;
- Expectations are appropriately managed;
- Those involved are supported in making the changes work for them and the organisation.

Care needs to be taken to recognise different communication and consultation needs in terms of appropriateness, preferences, timing and purpose. Where a large number of people are involved, it is particularly important that communications and involvement is targeted and timed appropriately.

Communications strategy and techniques

'Successful change communications is about saying the right things, in the right way, at the right time, with the right people – it's as simple and as complicated as that'.

Tim Allen, DEGW

The development of a communications strategy to underpin any change management plan or programme is essential – and this can often be preceded by a stakeholder analysis to better understand who needs to be involved and what the different interests and needs are.

Two considerations here are, first, the audiences and, second, the timing. In addition, the interest and needs of the audiences may vary over time. Most organisations are prone to subjecting their workers to information overload and even initiative fatigue. Consequently, ensuring that communication, support and/or interventions are relevant and appropriately timed and targeted is very important.

Initially, high level strategic or contextual headlines are required to aid understanding and acceptance – typically of the rationale for change and the related big picture or business strategy and the desired benefits.

At later stages, more detail can be imparted to aid practical preparation and adjustment activities, including detail of technology requirements, new work practices, workspace layout and facilities, filing and storage arrangements.

Too much detail too early can be overwhelming and will be ignored. Conversely, detailed information without context or rationale will be challenged or cause unnecessary confusion. The communications programme must recognise the typical stages of change that people go through – often expressed through 'the change curve'.

An alternative representation of this is provided in Figure 12.1 below, which also indicates the emphasis of the supporting actions and desired outcomes required to enable progress.

Figure 12.2 provides a very simple framework for considering the purpose and method of communications and the responses and actions required, if any. In other words, deciding what you want from people will help you decide to whom you need to communicate, and how. This can be helpful in ensuring that messages and involvement are appropriately targeted.

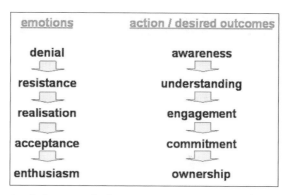

▲ 12.1   Typical stages of change process – Bell 2000

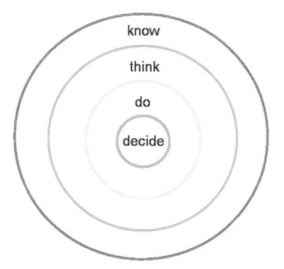

▲ 12.2   Targeting communication and involvement based on desired outcomes – Bell 2001

In most cases, it might be necessary simply to inform people. In other cases, you may want particular individuals to think, act or even make decisions. This also helps you think about the media used to communicate – and typically a range of media should be employed to aid the process and ensure everybody can be accessed and engaged, recognising that people have different communication preferences.

It is also important that the style of communication is consistent with the vision of the project – for example, reflecting a change from paper and push style communications (like desk-dropped newsletters) to electronic pull-style communications (such as intranets).

Where it is important that staff are engaged in the process and, where relevant, that information is to be understood and accepted (as well as just being received in order to trigger action, input or decisions), then two-way, face-to-face communication (such as meetings or workshops) become valuable. One-way, blanket communication – such as presentations, video or e-mail – are highly appropriate when imparting information, usually to large numbers of people, at the outset of a project, for example.

Branding

Communication strategies, often include the consideration of an identity or branding for the workplace project. This will help distinguish the project from other initiatives (of which there can be many) as well as to link different aspects of the project together so staff are able to see connections and the 'big picture' in a clear and consistent way.

If the workplace change programme is supporting a wider organisational or business change programme, then it is good to achieve linkages through project identity, for example, by using similar colour schemes, imagery or signs. This can also help raise the profile and relevance of the project.

Figure 12.3 shows the logo used on the recent DEGW-supported workplace change and communications project undertaken by the Ministry of Defence, to support their move to their redeveloped head office in Whitehall, London, occupied in the summer of 2004. A fictitious character was invented to show empathy and provide reassurance for staff – with the character going through the same emotions and actions as staff. This helped to make the programme relevant and accessible to staff. Adding a degree of fun to the process can also be a good thing!

Giving the workplace project a name or identity, can also help add consistency to communications. This has led to a whole plethora of

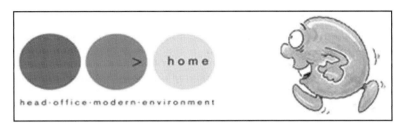

▲ **12.3**   Head office modern environment (>home) programme logo and character for MoD – Ministry of Defence/Crown Copyright 2004

catchy project names used by organisations. As long as the project has substance beyond such identities and is not just superficial spin, then such tactics can be extremely effective.

Figure 12.4 shows the name and logo used for one of the earliest pioneering workplace projects designed to support new ways of working – the award winning DEGW-designed Workplace of the Future for Scottish Enterprise (BIFM Small Office of the Year 1996). More detail and background about the Scottish Enterprise project can be found as a case study in Section V of this book.

Programme of Change

The use of structured workplace change management programmes underpinned by a multimedia communication strategy and plan as a means of appropriately informing, engaging, involving and supporting workers through change is now becoming common best practice.

Ideally, such programmes begin with a detailed cultural assessment and analysis of needs, as well as a pre-change benchmarking exercise. As part of this process, the benefits of the change should be identified and the means for 'tracking' and measuring progress towards the realisation of the intended benefits determined. This early diagnostic work is very important in ensuring that the most effective and relevant change interventions can be provided.

A phased framework, recognising the timing considerations already outlined, typically involves an initial information phase to aid understanding of rationale and context, an interactive phase to support discussion and acceptance of change, an action phase to initiate preparations and adjustments, a familiarisation phase to provide practical support and an aftercare or review phase to support the embedding of change in the new environment.

▲ **12.4**   Logo for Scottish Enterprise Workplace of the Future project – Bell 1995

A generic model for such a workplace change management project is provided in Figure 12.5.

Within each phase of the model, there is a host of activities that may be appropriate, such as presentations, exhibitions, workshops, newsletters, training, coaching, filing, clear-out events and so on. Such a programme may last months or even years. Much depends on the scale of the project and the complexity of the changes.

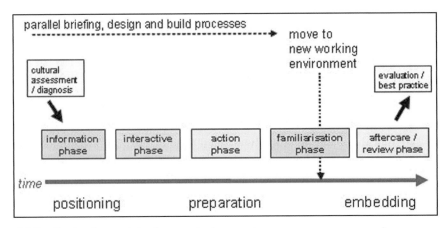

▲ **12.5**   Typical model of a workplace change management programme – Bell 2003

Importantly, these programmes can be used to integrate the various strands of change that are going on – for example, technology, work process and work practice changes that are accompanying the move to a new office environment. This helps to avoid confusion and further reinforces key project messages.

STORAGE, FILING, CLUTTER AND CLEAR DESKS

Without doubt, filing and storage levels, although often regarded as a dull topic, will need to be addressed with enthusiasm and commitment as this is often one of the most significant manifestations of the baggage of the past – another area where people are often reluctant to let go and embrace a change. Indeed, many a well-designed workspace has been stifled by inappropriate levels of storage or clutter.

Where the new work environment incorporates shared workspaces with concepts like hot desks, then particular attention to adhering to a clear desk policy, will be required. Once established, this is not as difficult as many people fear and it does not require people to work without any material or personalisation on their desks, but simply that the space is cleared after use or at the end of each day.

Aside from the practical aspects, the wider benefits of such developments are quite compelling, including their impact on issues like security, safety, flexibility, personal organisation and office aesthetics and appearance. Paying attention to the latter can, for instance, make all the difference between an office environment looking innovative and fresh or tired and dated.

TECHNOLOGY

Often a key ingredient of new working environments is new or enhanced technology – sometimes simply new kit like laptops or flat screens, sometimes new versions of software and sometimes new means of connectivity like wireless networks or roaming profiles. All these need to be taken into account as part of the preparation and support for the working environment, ideally as an integral part of the change management programme.

Technology may be a key enabler of desired new work processes and practices, such as hot-desking, home and remote working, knowledge and collaborative work and so on, so the key will be full understanding, acceptance and adoption of new opportunities. As this requires personal effort, adjustment and changes in routine, do not under-estimate the energy required to achieve it.

PROTOCOLS

One common activity within a typical process of workplace change management is the development of new protocols (behavioural guide-lines or ground rules) which help staff envisage and prepare for the new working environment.

They are often simply a refinement or extension of existing office etiquette or good practice and can help encourage desired behaviours and work practices. Where workplace change is fairly radical – such as involving a move from enclosed to open plan working or from dedicated desks to hot-desking – these protocols will play an important part in helping to ensure that the new working environment is effective and harmonious.

Much of this is about common sense and courtesy and it can embrace areas, such as noise levels, clearing spaces after use, telephone practices, meeting culture, handling visitors, booking facilities, dress code, eating food at desk policies and so on.

It is good for staff to get involved in developing these protocols thus increasing ownership and commitment and reducing any sense of imposition. Protocols can often be identified as a means of addressing staff concerns, so can easily be presented as a positive aspect of the change.

PILOTS

Workplace pilots are another feature of many workplace change management programmes and can be used to help staff to become more familiar with new workplace concepts and working practices. They also help staff to gain a better insight into the physical changes involved as well as a better understanding of the work practice adjust-ments required and the new opportunities which will become available.

Pilots typically provide an opportunity for a sample of staff (ideally a representative cross section) to experience the proposed future workplace concepts in practice and, in some cases, to influence their final design and detail.

As a relatively small group of people, occupants of pilot projects should be provided with ample support to help them to positively and effectively exploit the new opportunities, develop new protocols and procedures and assist in wider communication and influencing thus acting as 'ambassadors' of culture change.

It is also a good idea to create opportunities for non-pilot staff to visit and use the pilot workspace – such as inviting them to attend organised events, or to use new corporate facilities (such as a library or resource centre) or specialist equipment.

There is, of course, a risk that, if pilots are seen to fail for any reason, then the reputation and acceptance of the wider project can be damaged. The key to organising successful pilots is timing, planning, support and choosing the right sample of staff, as well as clear communications to clarify objectives and manage expectations. The risks can also be offset if it is understood that, where difficulties arise, these provide important and valuable learning tools for the future and the wider project. Conducting familiarisation visits around the actual new workspace shortly before staff move in can be a good way of further familiarising, preparing and reassuring staff.

Proper investment in a pilot is, however, probably the most important factor of all. Unless done well, there is a considerable danger of doing more harm than good.

LEARNING FROM OTHERS

Visits to other organisations, who have already undertaken similar projects can also be a helpful way of influencing and enlightening key staff and assisting decision-making, and can be used to help staff more generally, if you are unable to create a pilot.

Those organisations that have been successful in this field, whether in the private or public sector, are normally very proud of their achievements and willing to share their experiences and advice. Because such approaches to managing change are very much tailored to a particular organisation's culture and situation, it is more about sharing ideas and principles than precise detail which often overrides potential commercial or confidential sensitivities.

PERSONAL MOTIVATION – 'WHAT'S IN IT FOR ME?'

'Success is not about getting what you want, but wanting what you get'.

Anon

Change starts at an individual level influenced by a range of factors including leadership and example, but certainly also stimulated by personal incentive and benefit – the 'What's in it for me?' factor. It will be important that individuals see some direct or indirect benefit for themselves in the proposed changes beyond the benefits to the organisation. The change management process may need to help highlight this and swing the focus from any perceived negativity to positive elements of the change.

Of course, different things are important to different people. The change process has to be attractive in a number of ways, and at a number of levels to be truly successful.

Figure 12.6 shows some different mindset perspectives and approaches for embracing and facilitating change, based on what is important to that group or type of person – distinguished for ease of reference by colour.

There is no doubt that different people require different information, incentives or evidence before they are willing to embrace change. You may have to deal with a wide spectrum of viewpoints, so you must ensure that the approach and communications recognises these different needs, preferences and motivators and do not alienate anyone or any group.

What colour are you in terms of your viewpoint on change? What predominant colour is your organisation? Have you ever employed an approach or tactics that was aimed at the wrong colour? Such questions

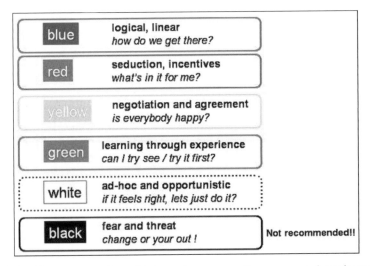

▲12.6   Six approaches / interest perspectives around embracing change – Bell / Twynstra Gudde 2003

can give you a sense of how this sort of consideration can be helpful in taking the right approach to achieve the impact and outcome desired.

Organisational tactics

Another important tactic is in dealing with large numbers of people – for example, a whole organisation. With limited resources and time, it is impossible to give everyone the ideal level of attention and support in taking on board desired changes. And not everyone will need the same level or even the same kind of attention.

However, a high level analysis of the organisation can typically allow you to split the organisation into the people and teams who are negative or positive to the change to some degree or other as well as those who may or may not be influential. These can be plotted on a grid as suggested in Figure 12.7 which helps to understand the make-up of the organisation and how to best target your efforts.

You certainly need to work with all those with influence – deal differently with those who are positive (your champions whom you need to support and encourage) than with those who are negative (whom you need to win over). It is worth recognising that senior management (those with hats in the diagram below) may well fall into both positive and negative camps.

The remaining people may require less personal attention as they can be influenced, hopefully through others although everybody needs to be involved in the process and communications in some way. However, such tactics can help you focus your energy on those who will enable the biggest impact to be achieved.

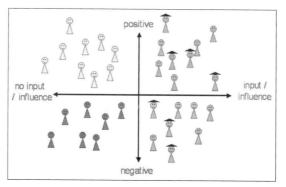

▲12.7   Grid analysing positive/negative/influential/non-influential perspectives around embracing change – Bell 2003

Creating a change community

Another obvious tactic is not to try and implement complex workplace change management projects entirely on your own. It is always a good idea to enlist the support of external expertise – those who have ready experience of similar projects – avoid re-inventing the wheel, as well as the pain often associated with such challenges and to speed up the process of planning and implementing the change support programme.

You can also make use of internal resources, colleagues and specialists, to support your project. Indeed, it will be essential to do so to help support the all important internal ownership and responsibility needed to facilitate and embed sustained change. Figure 12.8 shows an example project set up with various input and support channels to aid decision-making and communications.

Aftercare and review

It could be argued that workplace change management is never finished as every new workplace will, and should, be an evolving entity. Certainly, as the model in Figure 12.5 implies, it is important that the change programme continues after the move to help embed changes in working practices, process and behaviours.

The immediate post-change period is a critical stage which, without adequate support and guidance, might well see staff reverting to old ways especially if there are teething problems. Unfortunately, many major workplace projects are programmed to complete just after the physical conclusion of the project (perhaps three months after move in) taking focus and resources away from the task of embedding

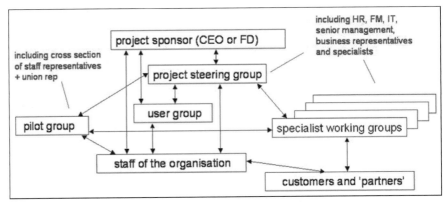

▲ **12.8**   Creating a supporting project infrastructure – Bell 2003

the cultural change required, to ensure the long-lasting success of the new workplace.

The need for an on-going champion or guardian for the new workplace is increasingly recognised and it is worth building this function into the business case and planning of future projects.

Formal and informal reviews are also important to understand the progress, learning and benefits achieved. This also helps the new workspace or working practices to be adjusted, if required; and highlights where additional areas of support or guidance may be required.

THE JOURNEY OF CHANGE

'More than seven miles of internal walls were removed as part of the Treasury redevelopment project. This physical change was symbolic of much deeper cultural, business and technology transformation within the Treasury, where numerous time-bound organisational barriers were removed to support the more agile and dynamic organisation that is evolving today'.
Paul Pegler, Her Majesty's Treasury from Working without Walls – DEGW/OGC 2004

Rather than a destination in itself, thinking about workplace change, or indeed any organisational change, as a journey is a good way of acknowledging the reality and full potential of the situation. It is not always possible to achieve everything or win over everybody before a move and indeed, it is sometimes best not to plan to do so. Equally, you should not be disappointed if ambitious change is not achieved at the first attempt.

Much can be done afterwards, using the new working environment as a platform for further progress. Indeed, in many respects, the implementation of a new workplace should be considered the start of the journey – the point from which new opportunities and benefits can at last start to be achieved. Organisations which plan their change programme with this in mind will achieve the greater goals.

Successful change does take time, patience and commitment. Figure 12.9 demonstrates how change takes time to become embedded, typically the result of a number of initiatives and projects, using a series of quick wins to confirm and stabilise progress.

Organisations serious about achieving lasting business, organisational and workplace change need to be in it for the long haul. But the rewards are many and extremely worthwhile. The organisation and individuals involved can normally learn and benefit as much from the

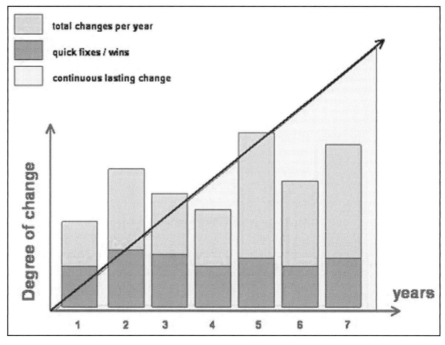

▲ **12.9**   Embedding change over time – Bell 2003

process itself as from the eventual outcome. Indeed, this is where the real value and impact of change lies – ask anyone, who has embarked on travelling the world as a personal or professional project. The following quotation provides an apt conclusion to the discussion in this chapter.

> 'The future is not a result of choices among alternative paths offered by the present, but a place that is created – created first in the mind and will, created next in activity. The future is not some place we are going to but one we are creating. The paths are not to be found but made and the activity of making them changes both the maker and the destination'.
>
> *John Schaar, futurist*

SECTION V
WORKING SOLUTIONS

Being a world class corporation is more than ever a matter of continuous appraisal and acceptance of change. For many businesses, this has meant the need to address competition in new markets as well as changing technologies, improving performance and reducing overheads through eliminating bureaucracy and harnessing the value-adding potential of creative professionals. For real estate providers, changing ways of working and the rise of the intelligent consumer have triggered the somewhat reluctant property industry into reappraising what their offer stands for and how it can support changing business demands more effectively.

Lora Nicolaou, in her study on the context of distributed working argues that more important than answering the question, 'what sort of building will an organisation require in the future?' is to provide appropriate portfolios of accommodation, an offer embracing space, tenure arrangements, facilities management services and neighbourhood amenities. As technology allows us to be ever more footloose, fixed locations with strong identities and sense of place will paradoxically become much more important as secure havens in a sea of change. The focus is moving from the single buildings housing single organisations to dynamic neighbourhoods, with a diversity of firms and space types, forming clusters of functions symbiotically supporting each other.

Calder and Laing in their contributions provide an overview of workplace provision in Asia Pacific and North America, respectively. In North America, after the false dawn of e-business and the early, much publicised, experiments of innovative media firms, the predominant office building typology continues to be a sealed, deep plan boxes with central cores and aisles of screened cubes within. In Asia Pacific, the speed of development has been phenomenal but imaginative innovation, disappointing. North American Building typologies have been repro-duced with scant concern for how local culture and ways of working may impact on the building form and local neighbourhoods. Over the next two decades, India and China seem destined to become significant locations for global manufactur-ing and producer services. The challenge will be to invent a genuinely Asian Pacific model that build on outstanding examples of cost-efficient, highly effective workplaces that add significant value to the people and organisations that work within them.

The Scottish Enterprise case study, responding to the theme that the buildings are containers to support business success, describes the process of managing the relocation of a government agency so that the building supports the evolving aspirations of the organisation and has organisational infrastructure that can sustain change.

New-style, non-hierarchical, ideas-focused, networked corporations have changed their attitudes towards buildings. Gone is the demand for a corporate icon to house the board of directors. Buildings now provide the business support facilities and act as meeting places for flexible 'just in time' organisations. Glimmers are emerging of new property offers that could match the opportunities afforded by the changing ways of working. The challenge for the property industry and their design teams will be to be prepared to set a new agenda and match the inventiveness of their clients.

13 EMERGING BUILDING FORMS AND ACCOMMODATION SOLUTIONS: NEW BUILDING TYPOLOGIES OR DISTINCTIVE PLACE-MAKING

Lora Nicolaou
DEGW Urban Strategies

SUMMARY

In the first edition of Reinventing the Workplace, the chapter on emerging building forms focused on the design of simple, correctly configured floorplates, with considerable capacity for servicing. The character of the building, it was argued, resulted from the level of service provision, entrances, handling of the skin, location of cores, depth and configuration of floorplates and sub-sequent fit out.

Less than ten years later we have seen a fundamental shift from building specification to the exploration of wider 'accommodation' offerings. Lora Nicolaou, an architect and urbanist, argues that with the agility afforded by advances in information and communications technology (ICT), organisations in future will be less about a matter of building specification, but rather an interest in 'accommodation', i.e. office space, plus tenure, value-added management services and local amenities. Generic building shells within which uses can change and a wide range of activity settings accommodated will afford the flexibility required by most fast changing organisations. Identity is less about each building shouting 'look at me', and more about the character of the area and specific setting designed within the shell to meet changing organisational needs.

To meet the planning demands for more sustainable environments there is a need to use space more intensively by overlapping functions and at the same time providing greater flexibility of usage within the same building form. Lora Nicolaou argues that within the existing space types, added flexibility required can be provided by combining existing typologies to make appropriate portfolios of space within larger developments, linked with greater flexibility of planning usage, tenure arrangements, and the appropriate supporting services and estate management. To support this approach, a methodology of tenancy profiles is proposed, reflecting the mix of functions, demographic profile and business culture of each organisation. As organisations become more distributed and networked across locations, accommodation solutions will be as much about urban context and local character as the functionality of building specification. In the future, the office may draw its value as much from the city as the building in which it is housed.

INTRODUCTION

Work and the ways in which it is accommodated are changing, resulting in a major impact on both building forms and urban settings. Information and communication technology, combined with new organisational thinking, result in work being distributed across locations, changing office processes and locational character. In parallel, planning policy is becoming increasingly proactive, driven by a strong sustainability agenda which, in turn, is impacting on infrastructure plans and the distribution of land use. These primary drivers generate the context within which work-places and work settings take shape and thus have become the basis of new accommodation solutions.

Over the last 100 years, we have seen fundamental changes in the structure of office functions, lifestyles and urban conditions whilst the office as a building type has hardly changed. Office work has moved from paper processing to generating ideas, cities from central, functionally zoned, defined entities to distributed metropolitan regions. The impact of information and communications technology (ICT) has been the driving force for change, challenging the logic of locational decisions and stimulating new ways of working. In the early 1980s, office buildings in high-value locations became vulnerable to obsolescence as they were found to be inadequate in meeting the demands of the emerging computing technology for cable distribution for cooling and for accom-modating additional equipment. By the mid-1990s, with miniaturisation and increased computing power, issues of heat gain were resolved, the spaghetti of wiring reduced, and we were confronted with new demands for more effective office environments. Hardware components, such as computers, their servicing and interior design settings become obsolete in relatively short period of time whereas software drivers, such as key management theories, concepts of urban planning and real estate practice are slower to change and have a longer impact.

In the context of the development of cities, the introduction of more effective movement and communications systems in the 1960s (people, goods, data and ideas) allowed extensive sub-urbanisation of both the workplace and housing. Zoning of functions became the predominant idea, promoting mono-functional environments in developments such as business and industrial parks which were structurally segregated from housing driven by a very different servicing and infrastructure and brand image requirements. Similarly, organisational theories shifted the emphasis from the building as a direct expression of the organisation to a more subtle concern for the environmental and cultural condition of work settings and their impact on users' performance. The focus on the individual and qualitative performance indicators gave rise to more complex office environments, expressed not only by the greater diversity of settings and support functions, but also by the use of the office as a metaphor for organisational values.

By the mid-1990s, the convergence of computing (wireless) and communications (visual) technologies supported by miniaturisation and mobility has resulted in a merging of physical and virtual work space. In parallel, new urban models suggested by the sustainable planning agenda implied different models for development characterised by greater intensity of use of space and time as well as a shift from mono-use to multi-functional and mixed use environments. To attract the best staff, companies are increasingly concerned with the quality, diversity, character and accessibility of buildings and locations. Where traditionally workplace design aimed at consolidating organisations into single headquarters buildings or campuses, business parks or corporate estates, twenty-first century accommodation strategies are based on a network of accomodation types each providing the most appropriate environment for a given function or corporate activity. The interdependence of physical and virtual space is changing the sense of appropriateness of building types as well as locations.

A NEW PARADIGM: THE WORKPLACE AS THE INTERFACE BETWEEN BUILDINGS AND THE CITY

In parallel with new technologies and modes of communication, the nature of work is also shifting away from information processing towards generating ideas. Effectiveness, particularly in the knowledge and creative industries, is directly associated with collaborative and interactive work patterns. New building settings are concerned primarily with informal contact and the encouragement of social interaction as the means of stimulating the generation of ideas. Physical places become important for:

- Communicating what organisations stand for (culture);
- Facilitating and increasing the effectiveness of face-to-face interaction;
- Building trust between co-workers and collaborators;
- Fostering relationships and generating the context for casual creative contact.

Personal knowledge and exchange of information expands well beyond the boundaries of organisations and day-to-day interactions. Learning, intelligence and information, as well as guidance within disciplinary

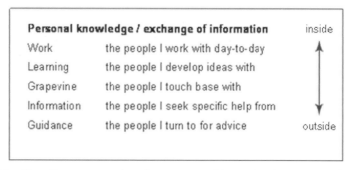

Personal knowledge / exchange of information		inside
Work	the people I work with day-to-day	
Learning	the people I develop ideas with	
Grapevine	the people I touch base with	
Information	the people I seek specific help from	
Guidance	the people I turn to for advice	outside

▲ 13.1   The Components of a personal knowledge network

frameworks, depend upon ever wider networks of contacts such as colleagues, professionals, publicity experts and mentors. (Figure 13.1)

While such networks are becoming increasingly virtual, the assimilation and processing of information (simple exchanges) into knowledge (complex exchanges) is more effectively supported by face-to-face inter-action. Formal and informal exchanges are taking place in a variety of settings, both public and private, with spaces between buildings becoming as important in support knowledge generation as the space within buildings:

- Semi-public spaces within buildings, and public spaces between buildings serve, as the front door and exchange spaces. The London School of Economics (LSE) campus in central London uses connecting streets as gathering spaces. Lecture spaces, such as the Peacock Theatre, are used for public performances outside teaching hours;
- Use of shared space (e.g. a public coffee shop within an office foyer);
- Collective socialising and project space within urban events spaces (e.g. training and conference centres, exhibitions and galleries).

Transportation hubs and their associated accommodation at airports and railway termini are becoming destination places, just in their own right. They are no longer places of transition, but increasingly provide a wide range of settings for meeting and working. The basic transport and movement infrastructure is becoming enriched by business centres, airline customer lounges and cafés.

Short-term leased workspace, hotels and conference centres associated with transport hubs are also becoming accepted as venues for business contact and for formal appointments. The new generation of workplace environments relies more on new urban typologies and outsourced networked amenities rather than on new building types.

Most current thinking on the new generation of solutions for office accommodation only engage with the implications of the new paradigm of the 'City as the office' at a relatively superficial level. Andrew Laing, in his review of North American practice (Chapter 15), suggests that there is a clear understanding by organisations that as 'work is becoming virtual and distributed over time and space, the value of the design of the physical office environment to express and communicate the values, messages, and ideology of the organisation becomes even more important'. However, he concludes that, despite this structural need, in reality the speed of change does not allow organisations to think of, or evaluate, the effectiveness of new workplace models which align business strategies with design. Similarly, at the city scale, where sustainable urban policy implies the fundamental restructuring of city services and infrastructure, there does not seem to be enough investment in the testing and piloting of urban design ideas. For example, there is very rarely funding for the development of infrastructure and delivery systems which would support mixed use and more complex urban models often advocated by planners.

ACCOMMODATING COMPLEX WORK STYLES IN SIMPLE SHELLS

The introduction of sophisticated technologies in the 1980s changed the configurational character and servicing demands of new office buildings, rendering many of their predecessors redundant. More recently, wireless technology and miniaturisation has reduced servicing demands and impacted on building specification and plan configuration (floor-plate size, floor-to-ceiling heights, core-to-perimeter depths, etc.). The option of decentralising large organisations to a number of locations is resulting in more distinctive localities reflecting the different functions and a wider variety of unit or building scales. The result is that the functional and organisational needs associated with the *efficiency* and the *effectiveness* of organisations depends less on particular building types and more on the flexibility of generic building forms combined with high-amenity local areas context. Similarly, the *expression* of culture and brand is increasingly communicated more through interior fit out, the technology infrastructure, or the choice of city 'neighbourhood', than by the design of the building itself. In theory a Georgian house, with its generic floor plan and interconnected spaces, could be used as well by a multinational as by a local professional firm.

In the absence of a decisive demand for specific space types, such as deep plan or specialist buildings, other conditions will determine building typologies and the scale of property offers. Climatic responses in building design (to achieve natural ventilation and reduce lighting levels) increasingly dictate such building characteristics like depth of plan, reverting to pre-1970s narrow building forms. Similarly, the demand for flexibility and shorter leases to suit the speed of change of organisations encourages a shift from purpose-designed, signature buildings towards universal, speculatively built forms and simple building typologies.

Whilst building types are becoming simpler and fewer, accommodation solutions and alternative business environments are becoming more diverse and part of a more highly differentiated urban structure.

Another key implication of the new trend towards diversification of demand is the increasing attractiveness of older buildings for new patterns of work. Conversion and reconfiguration of old buildings (for example, live/work, loft and workplace accommodation, industrial building conversions and so on) are becoming equally, if not more, valuable as real estate branding concepts in the inner city and some fringe locations (like London's Docklands). Disregarding for a moment, development economics, traditional medieval city quarters, under certain servicing conditions, could be equally appropriate as high-value corporate work environments.

The choice of office 'accommodation' type and location is broadening. The internationalisation of business is resulting in greater communality of approach to real estate between countries whilst the improved accessibility within and between regions is increasing locational opportunities. European regions which span political boundaries such as Oresend (Copenhagen, Malmo), or the Maastricht, Liege, Aachen, Lueven region, are becoming coherent economic drivers with shared objectives and resources. Such network geographies are providing increasingly competitive choices of appropriate places for work and living.

NEW AND 'HYBRID' ACCOMMODATION MODELS

Within this scenario of increased diversification of demand for not only space but also the way it is leased and managed, the market is beginning to respond by delivering alternative paradigms:

1 *A new generation of mono-use*, but multi-functional work environments in two distinctive models:

- The new generation speculative business parks, such as Paddington Central or Chiswick Park, developed at a higher density than their predecessors with a higher degree of associated services and external amenities.

- Large-scale, multifunctional, complex, purpose-built work environments for single organisations, such as British Airways Waterside at Heathrow, or Telenor's campus outside Oslo.

Both the models are based on increased densities and the incorporation of amenity and alternative support functions in a flexible manner within the overall building layout. These work environments include e-services; they have the flexibility to be subdivided, and, in the case of the more complex buildings, have elements which can be sub-let. Increased emphasis is placed on a collective spatial reference and on providing central interaction points for a relatively homogenous clientele. At Chiswick Park, a series of similar buildings are clustered around a landscaped water garden, with shared amenities within the ground floor of separate buildings (Figure 13.2). At the British Airways headquarters, Waterside, eight separate, but connected building blocks are organised along a common street (Figure 13.3).

CHISWICK PARK

- Suburban business park,
- Total Built Area:150,000 sqm (external gross area)
- Site previously used as a bus depot and maintenance facility
- 12 buildings 8,000 -16,000 sqm

- Population of 7000 -10,000
- 5 miles from Central London
- 5 local mainline and LU stations, bus service
- Development of Chiswick Park community through events and intranet

DEGW Amsterdam-Boston-Chicago-Glasgow-Hong Kong-London-Madrid-Melbourne-Milan-New York-Paris-Rome-Sydney

▲ 13.2   Chiswick Park

▲ **13.3** British Airways headquarters – Waterside, Heathrow

2 *Hybrid environments,* incorporating a variety of uses or functions within a single building.

- Dual use accommodation types, such as work/live, serviced hotels, learning centers, etc such as the World Trade Centre in South Amsterdam.
- Multi-purpose and multi-function environments, including alternative tenure workspaces within larger infrastructure projects which are often associated with transport (airports, stations, air-right developments) and major utilities, e.g. hospitals, higher education, leisure and shopping.

Such environments are becoming microcosms of the city using the principles of urban design rather than building configuration as their point of design reference. However, the few emerging examples of dual use buildings have not as yet triggered a new building typology. Work/live units have adopted the Georgian house or industrial loft as their model. New marketing concepts rely on the design of amenity, use management and tenure to differentiate the space on offer.

3 Space within *comprehensive area (re) development*, a diversity of work-space types within new Masterplans with mixed use and function, including housing, culture, leisure, learning and all associated services (i.e. Stratford, Media City – Dublin, Zuidas – South Amsterdam). Planning and urban design agendas dictate a mixed schedule of accommodation on all large-scale developments particularly in high accessibility locations.

Most plans inevitably begin with proposals for speculative and, there-fore, generic types of space appropriate for a wider section of the market. With the exception of the multi-function, mono-use, custom-built complexes for large organisations, the majority of new workplace developments are designed according to an assumption of user needs, rather than directly responding to specific user demands. The result is a small number of standard building types, which are then customised to specific market demands by providing:

- Appropriate support services within the development and amenities such as retailing, leisure, education, space for small businesses in the wider development;
- Intensive and extensive estate management;
- integrated, high-value, semi-public spaces;
- Options for a diversity of transport access.

Such facilities are only part of the amenities supplied by office neigh-bourhoods, the success of which relies not only on the composition of the individual development but also on attracting users from the wider surrounding catchment area. Significant added value relies on the whole area's potential for providing a broad mix of space and tenure types, good housing and social services (including education and health), casual meeting places, and external, quiet space in which to work.

The significant shift in emphasis from signature buildings to service experience and place branding is highlighted by comparisons between new and old generation developments of a similar type. Stockley Park and Chiswick Park are both designed as top of the market, mono-use employment environments, relevant to a very similar clientele but built

20 years apart. The differences of approach between the two represent the general change in development practices:

- While Stockley Park was marketed on the efficiency and effectiveness of the space, Chiswick Park is advertised as a total environment package, emphasising the workplace setting. This is reflected in Chiswick Park's very distinctive 'enjoy-work.com' logo.
- While Stockley Park was marketed on the signature architecture of individual buildings and intended for single occupancy, Chiswick Park relies on the individualisation of the central space (designed by West 8) which contrasts with the utilitarian architecture of the group of architecturally identical buildings by Richard Rogers Partnership.
- Chiswick Park offers a more diverse level of service and amenities with outsourcing and e-retail supporting wider demand. The proximity to Chiswick High Street is marketed as a key feature of the amenities on offer.
- Services and amenities in Chiswick Park are integrated into standard office buildings which have the flexibility to change scale according to demand. This is in direct contrast to Stockley Park, with its purpose-built, central amenity building.
- Chiswick Park's nett site density is significantly higher than Stockley Park's, with lower parking provision reflecting the multi-model access potential (private car and public transport) and a planning policy imposing restrictions on car users to meet demands for greater sustainability.

The management and servicing of accommodation, and its placement and integration within a wider city context is becoming increasingly important in the development of new workspace models.

MIXED FUNCTIONS RATHER THAN MIX OF USE

The exploration of the role of the building, in the context of new urban models, is relatively undeveloped and is compromised not only by supply industry conditions, but also by the tardiness of the professions to innovate. Working practices, design concepts, funding, planning use classifications and hierarchies derive their terminology from the old paradigm, where the building typology is selected from existing models, which are then finished in the latest fashionable style. A better paradigm would begin with a consideration of the way people actually use space followed by a review of appropriate settings for each activity. This information could then be used to compose the brief and make the design relevant to how places are utilised both within buildings and in the immediate space between buildings. At the outset of such an exploration it is necessary to establish a common understanding of terms and clarifications which facilitate the debate and form the basis of new conceptual and operational framework.

At present, three key notions are used to describe and prescribe space performance. They are used in an almost interchangeable manner:

> *Use* (housing, offices, leisure, industry) – a *planning* term borrowed from land use class orders, defined in planning systems.
> *Function* (employment, training, science and technology, marketing, etc.) – an *organisational* term, referring to operational classifications.
> *Activity* (meeting, contemplating, eating, etc.) – a *behavioural* term informed directly by and derived from physical settings and, therefore, suitable for describing or informing *design*.

Mixed use developments are much talked about and strived for, yet with limited understanding of what is expected. A clarification of terms, as set out above, could help to establish appropriate planning controls and help us rethink the new demands of working neighbourhoods.

Exploring user needs and space utilisation concepts with clients leads us to believe that new building types are more likely to emerge from the exploration of mixed operational functions, rather than mixed organisational components (use classes). Aspects such as building efficiency, a more complex specification for support and amenity space, the blurring of boundaries between organisational components, or the interface of buildings with their surroundings, can be more effectively described and understood within this new terminology. This shift would mean organisations rewriting their rules of space ownership to focus on functions and activities rather than a programme of uses in order to support contemporary needs. Multi-functional environments suitable for a diverse clientele, whilst potentially leading to space efficiencies, place greater emphasis on creating a diversity of appropriately serviced settings as well as a shift of investment from the building fabric to interior fit out.

The paradoxical demand for distinctive places and adaptable settings, results in the identification of core functions with high symbolic value which become the fixes around which functions can adapt and change. DEGW's proposals for Parkview Developments at Battersea redefine the space typologies required for creative firms by providing a matrix of different space types, both in plan and section, organised around squares with distinctive character between buildings and atria within.

The Battersea example shows that despite their multi-activity character, multi-functional buildings can correspond to single typologies and plan configurations.

Whereas mixed function buildings can maximise utilisation and effectiveness for different functions (such as education, marketing or administration) within the same use type (for example, the office), mixed use buildings, often encouraged by planning policy agendas, are problematic in a number of ways. Staking out areas for alternative uses (offices, housing, hotel, leisure and so on) might be valid for larger developments, such as tall buildings, or large, complex building shells, but mixed use buildings at conventional European scale tend to be overspecified with complicated shells and service arrangements. Considering the conditions they create — the inefficiencies of space utilisation, future maintenance and management complications, tenure agreements, funding arrangements and potential for redevelopment — buildings with a fixed mix of defined uses can be considered, in essence, unsustainable components of cities. If a mix of use is a priority for a given area, it is preferable to accommodate it at the street or neighbourhood level rather than in the design of each individual building.

The notion of design deriving from the exploration of multiple activity settings is equally relevant to outdoor spaces and cities. A mixed function employment environment, with all the associated amenities has the potential to fulfil a number of policy objectives such as reducing the need to travel, 18-hour use, support of shared amenities, improved safety and surveillance and place-making. Similarly, a residential neighbourhood, including amenities and associated user activities, is an environment which contains a set of different functions necessary for a self-sustainable place. With the increase in home working and new modes of business communication systems, the assumption that a city neighbourhood needs to consist of a mix of use classes may now be invalid. With greater planning flexibility, the same building typology (use type) can accommodate a variety of functions and activities to provide a vital and diverse neighbourhood.

Alternative understanding of multi-functional space settings and the potential for overlaps and synergies across activities can creatively inform new development models and are key to a more energy-efficient environmental future. A DEGW review of industrial space and its servicing conditions for Venlo Municipality in the Netherlands has explored the potential for more efficient land use in industrial, logistics and office park resulting from reformatting the space around shared functions rather than individual activities and land use. The reorganisation of function on the basis of compatibilities and conflicts (actual and perceived) had significant implications for the site density, layout and appropriateness of other uses. It clearly suggested new accommodation types and a different composition of 'places' within a single site.

The study of diversification of environments through the exploration of the notion of mixed function rather than mixed use, needs to be informed by a better understanding of how we use space and by the actual implications of how new technologies affect our behavioural patterns and choices. A natural starting point for arriving at this understanding is the identification of the users' and tenants' needs and behaviours. The idea of a mix of uses is primarily notional and, to an extent, operational, whereas a mix of tenancies implies a variety of actual aspects of habitation. It implies an examination of functions and activities – not only density but type of occupation, providing an economic, social and cultural base. Such a rich context responds to a diversity of operational modes and uncertainties that new environments need to accommodate and which brief writers and designers can use as a model to explore and test designs.

DEGW briefing for masterplanning increasingly draws on an understanding of potential tenancy profiles. A rich pallet of potential inhabitants and generic clientele relates to both existing populations and newcomers. The sketching of tenant profiles and research on users' urban and building needs directly informs scales of development and building types, as well as aspects of the detailed design of interior and exterior spaces. The resulting designs can then reflect in an informed manner such things as the behavioural codes, spending capacities and demographic profiles of future tenants and users. Another advantage of this type of briefing framework is its potential to define aspects or notions such as 'compatibility of use', 'flexibility', 'developmental change over time', 'interim conditions' and appropriate 'infrastructure recourse', taking into account not only their qualifications but also their qualitative characteristics (Figure 13.4).

Tenancy profiles can inform a design directly through the specification of building types and appropriate outdoor space settings: public and semi-public, or private. Underlying conditions, such as property economics, acceptability of servicing constraints (car parking) and management responsibilities, are all implied by the new prescriptive tool. However, one perceived shortcoming of such a framework is how far any underlying trend indicated by the tenancy profiles can be formalised into planning prescriptions that convey the degree of clarity, certainty and 'measurability', which is required by both formal planning systems and development practice.

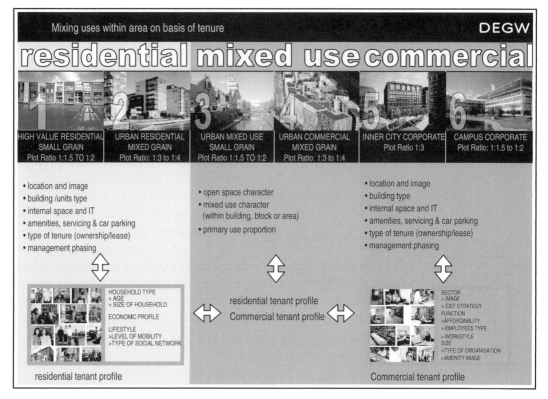

▲ **13.4**   Tenant Profiles

CONCLUSIONS

Will the distributed workplace and an increasing choice of lifestyles have an impact on the environment and the way it is designed? While the concept of the new urbanism is being increasingly debated, there is relatively little discussion about what the new generation of building types will be. Similarly, the new workplace is more concerned with identifying new accommodation solutions than new buildings' typologies. In this context:

- Buildings will become increasingly generic and simpler in type, with emphasis on environmental design and the ability to accommodate a wider range of functions;
- Existing shell typologies will combine to make new work places;

- The value of the working environment will increasingly rely on the quality of the place, with equal emphasis on internal and external spaces;
- Issues of management, maintenance and additional services will influence the overall design of places and new accommodation solutions;
- The success of employment locations will rely more and more on their network connectivity and their proximity to facilities in the surrounding area (housing, lifestyle amenities, social services, etc);
- Large, multi-functional, complex buildings will simulate urban settings and will rely on diversity of use at interchange points within the city.

In exploring these potential new models of accommodation, we need alternative paradigms and new tools and methodologies. Functional prescriptions, such as building use types are insufficient to describe the more complex dynamics of emerging work styles. Modelling behavioural patterns, and tenancy types, first introduced by DEGW in the 1970s is still valid as a basis for the exploration of new 'workplace accommodation' concepts. Modelling patterns of use, and allowing for a variety of activities within a building with a predominant allocated function, has the potential to increase the adaptability and diversity.

14 ASIA PACIFIC: A MELTING POT OF GLOBAL EXPERIENCE

James Calder
DEGW Asia Pacific

SUMMARY

In terms of economic development in the twenty-first century, all eyes are on Asia Pacific as the region of most rapid change. India and China, two economies that in sheer population dwarf all others, are developing at an astounding speed. China is becoming the workshop of the world and India has become the focus for service support and software development. Japan is recognising the value added to the basic product through knowledge generation, innovation and design. With such opportunities, how far is the real estate market reflecting these new opportunities? Is it still following the paradigms of design and real estate delivery of the Western economies?

James Calder, Managing Director of DEGW in Asia Pacific, with extensive experience of consulting throughout the region, reflects on the outcome to date. Overall progress has been patchy: the Asian workplace suffers from the unimaginative adaptation or imposition of foreign models. For many companies and investors, the US model is perceived to be the best and is the most fashionable. The North American model of office layout has been adopted and rolled out, albeit at twice the density. There are few examples where fundamental questions have been asked about the changing nature of work, the culture of people, the integration of new technologies and the value of the workplace to business. The office building is a parody of global models. It is no accident that the world's tallest buildings are in the region. Office buildings are seen either as symbols of power and success, or as investment vehicles rather than places for people and the achievement of business success.

Some innovative and successful work spaces and work places have been developed over the last decade, perhaps equal to the world's best. This chapter provides a series of case studies from around the region about work settings, buildings and business areas that are imaginative, thoughtful and have long-term value. As we look ahead, change is discernable in emerging centres such as Bangalore, Shanghai and Sydney. New work-place models suited to local conditions are appearing which reflect local aspirations and the new energy. The next decade should build on these pointers and create a new kind of specifically Asia Pacific Workplace that would lead the world.

INTRODUCTION

The reinvention of the workplace over the last decade in the Asia Pacific region has been patchy at best. Whilst some countries such as Australia and New Zealand have made significant advances in the design and design thinking of the workplace, others such as India and China normally use North American models. The typical workplace in the Asia Pacific region has changed little from the poor conditions and relentless monotony of the last decade of the twentieth century. However, today we now have a handful of examples of cost-efficient, highly effective workplaces that add significant value to the people and the organisations for which they work. These examples set new precedents and will help to make the region a highly innovative part of the office world in the next decade. In a few key fitouts, the remoteness from the control of corporate real estate head offices in the USA or Europe has actually helped to facilitate significant innovation and the development of some of the world's best workplaces.

The Asia Pacific office building is normally a North American imitation. The office buildings of leading European architects such as Norman Foster and Renzo Piano and US firms such as Kohn Pedersen Fox and Architectonica stand out, as do a few homegrown examples such as Denton Corker Marshall and Bligh Voller Nield from Australia, and Ken Yeang from Malaysia. There are, of course, exquisite buildings from a long list of Japanese architects such as Toyo Ito, Tadao Ando and Kengo Kuma but the workplaces within are often still grim and unimaginative. The basics of effective office building design, where more than facade and form are considered, is unusual in Asia. Aspects such as planning grids, depth of space and floorplate shape are rarely considered. The notion of designing from the inside out is still a radical idea and many of the world's best architects have enjoyed the patronage of a less-rigorous client and have thus got away with lazy concepts that would not be tolerated in their home country.

As we have seen in the 1990s in Europe, a handful of good workplaces such as SOL and British Airways can have enormous impact on reinventing the workplace. Examples equivalent in their ambitions now exist in the Asia Pacific and they will have an equally significant impact on raising expectations.

Examples of fitouts that have shown the way over the last decade are:

- Campus MLC, Sydney, (1999–2001) an innovative rejigging of an existing building;
- ARUP, Hong Kong, (2000) a relocation and organisational rethink;
- Maddocks Lawyers, Melbourne, (2001) open plan for knowledge sharing;
- Fuji Xerox Pilot, Japan, (2003) an environment for ideas creation and knowledge sharing;
- ANZ Bank, Property Group Laboratory, Melbourne, (2003+) a laboratory for new ways of working.

In terms of buildings, the following stand out:

- 126 Phillip Street, Sydney, 2005, by Foster Associates and Hassell;
- National@Docklands, Melbourne, 2004, by Bligh Voller Nield;
- Festival Walk, Kowloon, 2000, by Architectonica;
- JR Central Towers, Nagoya, 2000, by Kohn Pedersen Fox Associates;
- HKSB, Hong Kong, 1998, by Foster Associates;
- Dongbu Financial Centre, Seoul, 2003, Kohn Pedersen Fox Associates.

At the precinct scale, there have been many business districts that have been extended and re-planned, and business parks created. Most fail to create attractive places for people but the following are exceptions, or could become so over time:

- Corporate Avenue, Shanghai;
- Roppongi Hills, Tokyo;
- Melbourne Docklands, Melbourne;
- Dongbu, Seoul.

There are of course other workplaces which could be added, such as Sun Microsystems almost anywhere in the region, and Cisco in Singapore. However, these workplaces seem to be more about marketing, branding and sales. They have the functionality right but engagement of the client with the design and change process is lacking. Facilities for market leaders like Bloomberg and Nike are effectively accommodated but are not significantly different than what one would see in the US or Europe.

EMERGING WORKPLACE DESIGN CASE STUDIES

The five workplace case studies chosen share many characteristics yet at the same time, are very different. One of the endearing features has been the robustness of the original design to change.

For example, the MLC fitout has proven adept at handling density ranges of 10–14 square metres per person to accommodate short-term growth.

The shared characteristics include:

- A thorough analysis of workstyles before design development;
- Innovative design solutions;
- The desire of the client to readily embrace change;
- An understanding by management of the significance of the workplace to the business.

Australia has been a leader for workplace innovation in the region. The reason for this is probably a combination of the desire to be seen as world leaders and a healthy scepticism for imported models, particularly from North America. In addition, the relatively stable economic situation over the last ten years, and the predominance in the market of 5- to 10-year leases, has helped organisations to make longer term fitout decisions. This is not true of many countries in the region where the expenditure on new workplaces has been difficult to justify, with management averse to risk-taking, an acceptance of US head office workplace models and a tough economic climate.

Campus MLC, Sydney, 1999–2001

The refit of MLC's 1950s office building in North Sydney has become an outstanding example of the workplace reinvented. The combination of a CEO and executive team (especially HR and Finance) looking for significant commercial advantage and an effective place for their people, a talented architect (Bligh Voller Nield), the project management skills of Lend Lease, and the research and space planning experience of DEGW, has led to the development of a remarkable piece of corporate design for around 1500 people.

The starting point was the understanding of the dynamic nature of the teams and the challenging of the conventional wisdom of the right-angled workstation and relentless layouts of 'six-packs' of desks.

A key problem to solve was how to create a campus-style environment in a thirteen-floor office building – a vertical village. The solution to this problem was the insertion of a stair running from top to bottom and to spread the meeting rooms throughout the building with different themes (such as the Café, the Beach, The Table and the Zen Den) on each floor to encourage mobility and chance encounters.

The business benefits have been significant, with perhaps the best indicator being that the MLC personnel often bring in friends and family, in order to show off where they work.

Arup, Hong Kong, 2000

Arup is the world's leading engineering firm. Their Hong Kong office has been one of their outstanding successes, employing around 800 people. In an amazingly short period of time (13 weeks) and with a very tight budget, a completely new workplace concept was developed that enabled teams to work together and knowledge to be centralised for the first time. The large floorplates of around 5000 square metre, with an impressive central atrium and a bridge, was used to good effect to create a hub to encourage face-to-face interaction and knowledge-sharing.

The office is seen as one of Arup's best in the world and has won numerous awards. The design team was DEGW, who provided the strategic briefing and space planning concept with interior design by CL3 and project management by Arup itself. The success of the project highlights that it is often easier to innovate when time is short.

Maddocks Lawyers, Melbourne, 2001

Maddocks is a boutique law firm of around 300 people occupying one of Melbourne's best 1970s buildings, 140 William Street. They needed to expand to a new floor, and the decision was taken to investigate a more effective workplace than the conventional legal office model. The driver was not space-saving (the new, predominantly open plan floor has the same density and cost as the other more conventional floors), but to increase knowledge-sharing and learning, provide better customer service, and to support the team culture. The open space is not completely quiet but has a low hum, with adjacent noisy rooms where people can go to meet or to have loud conversations. It is however, far removed from the noisy, unproductive space one would normally associate with open plan.

An independent audit confirmed the success of the solution, with greatly improved learning by osmosis and effectiveness. Contrary to the common belief that lawyers do not like open plan, Maddocks has continued to grow and recruit lawyers who actually prefer the new space.

(The strategic briefing and space planning concept was by DEGW, interior design by Carr Design, and project management by Montlaur).

Fuji Xerox, KDI Studio, Tokyo, 2003

The Knowledge Dynamics Initiative (KDI) is co-ordinated by a small team of experts under the direction of Kaz Kikawada. The team and its collaborators are passionate about the importance of the role of place in knowledge management, so it makes sense that their own team should use some of the principles developed in their research. Whilst their space is modest at this stage at 120 square metre, their research is gaining wide acceptance in the corporate world of Japan, so we can expect this team concept to be expanded on by many organisations over the coming decade.

ANZ Bank, Property Group Laboratory, Melbourne, 2003+

The ANZ Bank is one of Australia and New Zealand's largest retail banks. Like many large corporates, the workplace is constantly evolving. The next evolution, the distributed workplace, where staff are increasingly mobile and space needs to be more flexible and intensively used, is something with which ANZ's property group had little experience and yet the beginnings of the user demand were being felt. The idea was to develop a laboratory to be used by the property people themselves so they could experience first hand what the new workplace model was about. The results have been a revelation to them – that the distributed workplace concept works, given a detailed understanding of the IT and paper issues, and the realisation that change management is critical. Space savings of around 20 per cent, a more effective workplace and a significantly better team culture have been the results. The laboratory will not be dismantled but will continuously evolve to enable the property group to be one step ahead of the business units.

It seems strange that given the millions of square metres of office space in the region, very few laboratories such as the ANZ exist. Whilst the prototyping of workstation furniture prior to a major purchase is common, it is rare for clients to create a proper pilot like this with actual workers using the space and equipment over a period of time, supported by a serious attempt at measurement and evaluation. This simple approach, if adopted more widely, would lead to a

▲ **14.1** ANZ Property Group Laboratory, Melbourne (Laptop Bench – 'Parking' and short-term work)

dramatic improvement in the quality and business value of new cworkplaces (Figure 14.1).

WORLD CLASS BUILDINGS

Office buildings that have challenged the conventional style and added significant value to their clients are even harder to find than innovative fitouts.

The good office buildings in the region all provide the opportunity for users to create highly effective workplaces, but in different ways: Festival Walk, for example, is a 'groundscraper' with 5000 square metre floorplates and an atrium and bridge, the Dongbu Financial Centre takes local handicraft forms yet creates effective side core space in a tower, and Aurora Place creates reasonably efficient space with naturally ventilated winter gardens in a tower of sculptural beauty. The 126 Phillip

Street tower is an outstanding example of new thinking, with a remote core and wide bridges to create the impossible – 360 degree views in 1450 square metre of rectangular space with no internal columns or core to act as an impediment. These buildings should also be useful for a long time. Foster's HKSB building, with its large, clear floorplates and excellent daylight is still a more useful building for people and business than most new buildings in Hong Kong (Figure 14.2–14.8).

It is much easier to find hundreds of examples to illustrate what is wrong with office buildings in the region. Office towers are mostly symbols of power and control and low-rise buildings are primarily driven by ruthless efficiency that is at best inhuman and at worst, as global corporates move office work where labour is cheap, the breeding grounds for future global conflict. Staff turnover rates of 25 per cent or more in call centres in India are an indicator of how poor the working conditions mostly are.

One aspect where there is greater user awareness is in leases, where terms of as little as 2–3 years for a new building are common in many parts of the region. The combination of cheap and reliable global communications, inexpensive and good-quality labour and flexible leases is an irresistible mix for many global corporates.

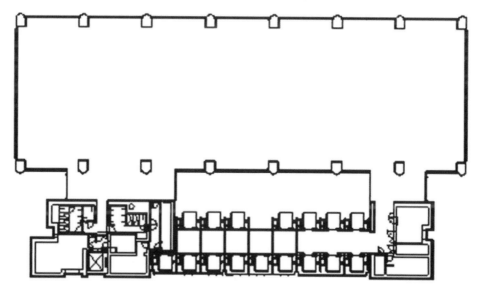

▲ 14.2 Typical floorplate of 126 Philip St, Sydney

▲ **14.3** 126 Phillip Street, Sydney, 2005, by Foster Associates and Hassell

14.4 National@Docklands, Melbourne, 2004, by Bligh Voller Nield

There is almost universally a disconnect between what developers provide, what property experts advise, and what users and business need. The industry is energetically conservative, with many developers thinking art deco is a new design philosophy. And, architects are queuing up with increasingly competitive fees to design new buildings and put their name on them. Serious questions facing the industry in other parts of the world such as productivity and sustainability are rarely an issue. If the client does take an interest, it is usually in the status or symbolic value of the building. It is bizarre to see the juxtaposition of capitalistic values and religious symbolism in buildings such as Cesar Pelli's Petronas Towers, which provide only average quality internal space with large central cores and heavily faceted facades. Why is it possible to mix these seemingly conflicting ideologies so convincingly in other building forms such as Kisho Kurokawa's wonderful Kuala Lumpur International Airport but not in office buildings?

▲ **14.5**   Festival Walk, Kowloon, 2000, by Architectonica

▲ **14.6**   JR central Towers, Nagoya, 2000, by Kohn Pedersen Fox Associates

▲ **14.7**   HKSB, Hong Kong, 1998, by Foster Associates

THE FUTURE

All too often it has been the corporate facility or property manager, living out of a suitcase, tasked with minimising cost at all costs, who has been the culprit for much that is wrong with the Asia Pacific workplace. This is quickly changing, with the internet providing immediate access to the world's best practice, and the growth of professional organisations such as IFMA (launched, for example, in India in 2003) and CoreNet (launched, for instance, in China in 2001) leading to a rapidly educated local client.

Certainly in Australia, innovation keeps coming. Recently completed office developments for the Lend Lease Corporation at The Bond

▲ **14.8** Dongbu Financial Centre, Seoul, 2003, by Kohn Pedersen Fox Associates

in Sydney will continue to raise standards, as will the soon-to-be completed Brisbane Square development for the Brisbane City Council and Suncorp, and Melbourne City Council's sustainable office building, both in the heart of their respective central business districts.

It has taken a decade to generate a handful of good workplace examples. The next decade should invent the first wave of truly Asia Pacific workplace models. The region has the creativity, energy and resources to provide the next generation of workplace environment innovation that could play a very big part in the continuous reinvention of the workplace globally.

▲ **14.9** Brisbane Square, Brisbane, 2006, by Denton Corker Marshall

▲ 14.10   Melbourne City Council CH2, Melbourne, 2006, by City of Melbourne and DesignInc Melbourne: architects in association for the project

15 NORTH AMERICAN OFFICE DESIGN AT THE START OF THE NEW MILLENNIUM

Andrew Laing
DEGW North America

SUMMARY

At the end of the twentieth century, there was a flurry of interest in North America in new ways of working. Franklin Becker at Cornell University, with his study tours of new office solutions around the world, had expanded perceptions of office design and organisation. This thinking had been reinforced by a series of reports published by the International Development Research Corporation (IDRC), which documented new approaches to innovation in the workplace and provided tools for implementation. Andrew Laing, a workplace strategist, who over the last eight years has been responsible for DEGW offices in North America, reviews the state of office design at the start of the new millennium and concludes that whilst innovation exists, mainly drawing on European experience, most corporate offices continue to be housed in air conditioned, introverted boxes, focused on cost reduction and paying little attention to long-term sustainability.

Laing begins his review with Duffy (DEGW) and Tanis's (Steelcase) 1993 article, which proposed that the real business returns are achieved by concentrating on both using resources more efficiently and improving staff performance (effectiveness). Whilst the basic typologies of office design had changed little over the last fifty years, the way that work is organised has changed dramatically. The thrust of the argument was that the opportunity for suppliers and designers was to rethink building and interiors to support organisational innovation and the resulting new working methods. During the mid-1990s, innovative workplace settings began to appear on the West Coast, for media firms (like Chiat Day) and in the electronics sector (Silicon Graphics). However, most innovations were short lived while the tyranny of Dilbert's office cubicle continues unchecked.

Over the last ten years, many corporations have moved toward greater interaction in their work processes, combined with greater individual autonomy. Organisations have changed faster in how they work than in how they are physically accommodated. In the case of those organisations at the leading edge of applying office technology, such as Accenture, the physical presence of the centralised headquarter office has been superseded by the virtual network of distributed workplaces. The dot-com crash of 2000, followed by the impact of 9/11, brought the feverish demand for offices virtually to a standstill, and a subsequent rethink, encompassing not just issues of escape and security, but wider concerns for location, staff satisfaction linked to performance and the implications of the mobility afforded by technology. The skyscraper, an icon of North American commercial architecture, is being reconsidered as innovative designs from European and Asian architects are changing the focus to access to daylight, natural ventilation, bringing nature into the heart of the building and mixed use localities. What is emerging is a new form of sustainable high rise.

The challenge ahead for the North American real estate and design community is to respond to rapidly changing organisational structures and invent meaningful building forms and property offers that match these emerging demands.

The end of the twentieth century had its appropriately *fin-de-siècle* air of excitement even in the world of work and the workplace. It seemed that a new age of 'new ways of working' in new kinds of environments would be possible. The astonishing offices of Digital and SOL in Finland had already showed in the early 1990s, how the combination of early primitive mobile phones combined with anti-hierarchical workplace planning would turn the world of office design upside down. Driving this optimism was a belief in the liberating power of technology to revolutionise how and where we work, to challenge the design of our buildings, and even to transform our lives.

The key questions posed at the end of the twentieth century were, even then, not really new, but they have had to be constantly repeated and answered in ever changing ways: how will the workplace respond to the opportunities of information technology that enable work to be re-designed? How should the workplace be designed to integrate changing organisational strategies?

The question posed by this chapter is perhaps less far reaching: were the high hopes expressed in the late 1990s for integrating the workplace with new organisational strategies realised, or not? More specifically, were they realised in the very particular context of North America?

A VISION OF THE NEW WORKPLACE

In 1993, Frank Duffy and Jack Tanis published 'A Vision of the New Workplace', a paper that insisted that new life should be breathed into office design — and that office architecture was in need of radical re-design.[1]

The starting point for the paper was the collapse in the property markets in North America during the late 1980s and early 1990s. This in turn switched the office furniture industry into a tailspin of falling sales. Duffy and Tanis' brave conclusion was to re-assert the importance of the design of the physical working environment for organisational success. Spending on the physical and technical environment of the workplace should be regarded as an essential catalyst for achieving and sustaining business success, especially for those industries creating ideas. This controversial position — spend more while your assets are declining in performance and value — was justified because most workplaces were still dominated by rigidly Taylorist assumptions about the nature of office work and needed to be fundamentally re-thought. The authors posited a major fracture between the supply-side dominated furniture and construction industries and the rapidly changing reality of business. Design innovation had become impossible. 'Never has organisation theory been so rich and inventive as in the 1990s. Never has innovation in office planning fallen so far behind'. The new business and organisational theories were shown to have direct implications for the re-design of the physical environment of work. Design should correspond to the highest levels of strategic management and could be used by corporations as a lever of organisational change.

The capital expenditure on the office had to be moved from a purely cost focus to one that is energised by the need to maximise performance of people and the work process. Revenue enhancement replaces cost reduction. Effectiveness augmented efficiency as a measure of workplace performance.

The call to action at the end of the paper was to develop new ways of closing the gaps between organisational design and the design of physical space – to bring users and suppliers together, to provide a richer array of models of the new office, and to energise office design with organisational strategy.

THE CHIMERA OF THE WEST COAST TECHNOLOGY WORKPLACE

Nowhere were the hopes of Duffy and Tanis for an energised office design raised more highly – and more cruelly dashed – than in the multiplying buildings and campuses of the technology sector in Silicon Valley, California.

As the so-called New Economy boomed in the mid-1990s, the idea that the design of the workplace could and should contribute to the organisational performance of knowledge workers became more prevalent. The new kinds of knowledge work described by Peter Drucker[2] as long ago as 1969 as characteristic of a New Economy, became the basis for enthusiastic new economic and business programs such as Kevin Kelly's *New Rules for the New Economy* (Figure 15.1) in 1997,[3] written, significantly enough, for *Wired* magazine.

A whole genre of business discourse arose around the new age networked economy, most brazenly articulated by *Fast Company* magazine. The editor, Polly LaBarre, was in fact one of the organisers and facilitators of the first 'Alt.Office' conference held in San Jose – ground zero of the digerati and boomtown of Silicon Valley. The conference, held between 14 and 16 August, 1997, was a landmark in workplace thinking.

Kevin Kelly's New Rules for the New Economy

1. Law of Connection: Embrace dumb power
2. Law of Plentitude: More gives more
3. Law of Exponential Value: Success in nonlinear
4. Law of Tipping Points: Significance precedes momentum
5. Law of Increasing Returns: Make virtuous circles
6. Law of Inverse Pricing: Anticipate the cheap
7. Law of Generosity: Follow the free
8. Law of Allegiance: Feed the web first
9. Law of Devolution: Let go at the top
10. Law of Displacement: The net wins
11. Law of Churn: Seek sustainable disequilibrium
12. Law of Inefficiencies: Don't solve problems

▲ **15.1**   The New Rules for the New Economy

It was an exciting event, bristling with the electric frisson of innovation. The conference was billed as the first conference and trade show dedicated to the emerging alternative office market. The 'alternative office' (who says that anymore?) was widely and loosely defined to include team offices, non-territorial offices, home offices, professional home offices, telecommuter offices, virtual offices and multi-site offices. The company site visits to high-tech firms that supplemented the conference included Genencor (showcasing increased office density with maximised shared multi-use space), Tandem Computers (showcasing cockpit offices), Hewlett Packard (showcasing highly collaborative group work spaces), Sun Microsystems (showcasing experimental space with private individual offices and open group work meeting areas), and Cisco Systems. The zeitgeist was that technology and technology investment had created an alternative world of work and of the workplace. Alt.Office appeared to say that the vision of Duffy and Tanis was already realised in Silicon Valley. But was it really?

Steelcase, working with DEGW and others, had meanwhile launched in 1995 a Workplace Envisioning software programme, (Figure 15.2) intended to integrate business thinking and workplace design. The software was designed to help users of offices and their business leaders engage directly with the suppliers of office furniture to programme their requirements for office design. The programme was intended to create a brief for the facility by capturing the high level strategic directions of the business as well as its detailed work process characteristics, and then to

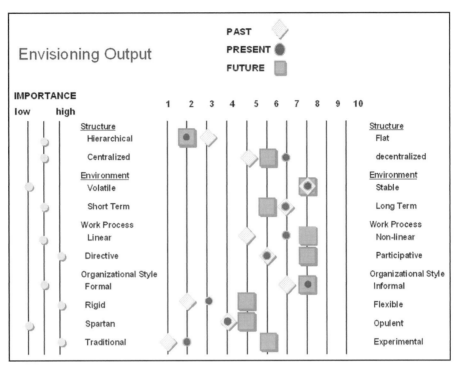

▲ 15.2   Typical workplace envisioning output software

correlate them with potential design and layout parameters. The Work-place Envisioning software was designed for use in facilitated focus groups with different levels of decision makers, and with representatives of different kinds of workers across the organisation.

The longer term intention of Steelcase was to train their dealers to use the software to programme solutions with their clients. It was paralleled by a broader interest by Steelcase and other furniture manufacturers to examine other ways in which they could provide office environments – in ways that were richer and more architectural in scope than the conventional market for desk and chair products. This led Steelcase into new directions for products that attempted to provide different levels of integrated services, scenery and settings for the office, particularly the Pathways products. The idea was to break down or re-connect the divorce between the building supply and the activity of office users. Behind this thinking was the recognition that, especially in North America, the building shell is designed and procured separately from the fit out of the interior – the services, scenery and settings of the workplace.

In its broadest sense, this mission of integration never fully achieved its brave aspirations. First, furniture dealers were not able, or even inclined, to become organisational consultants with the ability to translate business strategy into workplace design – with or without the envisioning software. Second, Steelcase, and the army of design consultants supporting them, were not able to challenge the fundamental market drivers of commercial real estate that in North America prescribe the design of the base building shell: big, deep, tall towers in downtown locations and big, deep, cheaply constructed low-rise buildings in suburban office parks.

Thus, the success of integrating work processes, business strategy and design was largely limited to internal space planning innovations. Within these constraints, the tool was a brilliant step towards integrating business thinking and the programme for the design of the workplace. Yet, the larger problems of the design of the base building or the broader integration of design across the spectrum of shell, services, scenery and settings in ways that were congruent, or aligned more fully, with the demands of business performance, was not accomplished. In both downtown high-rises and suburban business parks, this dis-connect remained intact.

The West Coast example is most telling here in that the booming technology businesses were the ideal candidates for re-thinking design in conjunction with business strategy. The Alt.Office conference was the most exuberant expression of this potential. The technology firms had funds, they were growing fast, they loved technology, they were not constrained by the conventions of the old businesses models. Yet, what was the New Economy workplace on the West Coast really like?

Beneath the Alt.Office jargon, the Silicon Valley technology business was typically accommodated in large, cheaply constructed, low-rise, deep-plan, suburban office park buildings that were constructed by developers with little regard for the intended office users and without regard for environmental sustainability of the building over the longer term. Efficiency (cost reduction) reigned over effectiveness (organisational performance adding value to user requirements). Even though the Northern California climate would have allowed for many alternatives to full year-round air conditioning, the buildings were usually sealed environments that were designed with little regard for daylight or for natural ventilation.

Visiting Sun Microsystems (Figure 15.3) new business campus at Menlo Park in 1995, (one of the case study sites of the Alt.Office conference), as part of the research for the *New Environments for Working* study (completed with the Building Research Establishment),[4] I was astonished

▲ 15.3   Sun Microsystems Business Campus at Menlo Park, 1995

to find that Sun's innovative combi-style office layout, with its tiny glass-doored cells for programmers and their associated local neighbourhood collaborative workspace (Figure 15.4), was innovative only within the context of the enormous depth of the office floor. Most of the individual and shared work spaces were far removed from daylight or views of the beautifully sunlit, landscaped courtyards and gardens that surrounded the large buildings.

By 2004, the world had changed. Sun Microsystems had re-thought its whole workplace strategy in terms of a large-scale regional distributed workplace, in which many of their employees worked in distributed locations and shared hotelled workplaces on Sun campuses – the so-called Sun I-work solution (the strategy was, and still is, also used to brand and sell Sun's technology).

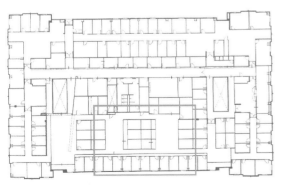
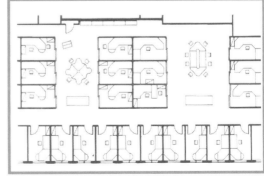

▲ 15.4   Sun Microsystems Floor Layout

The previous headquarters of Silicon Graphics (Figure 15.5) at Mountain View, California, also struck me as emblematic of the sea change in workplace thinking that had occurred even between 1997 and 2004. Their empty campus had now become the headquarters of a new business called Google. In re-fitting the campus for their own needs, Google was able to buy all of its furniture in the second hand furniture market, most barely used, left behind in the dot com collapse. Working on the brief for the design of Google's headquarters, I was reminded of the economist Schumpeter's concept of the creative destruction of capitalism.[5] Should we therefore be thinking of a theory of the creative destruction of the workplace, given that so many of the businesses in Silicon Valley had disappeared between 1997 and 2004?

Duffy and Tanis, themselves re-examined the case they had made for a vision of the new workplace in 1993, six years later in 1999[6] (Figure 15.6). They noted that many organisations had invested heavily in technology and in business process re-engineering in the 1990s, but had not integrated space and design into that process. The key problem for organisations was now seen to be the ability to attract and retain mobile, nomadic and demanding knowledge workers. The planning of offices should be focused on supporting the dynamic communication needs of knowledge workers as well as their needs for focused individual

▲ 15.5   Silicon Graphics at Mountain View, CA

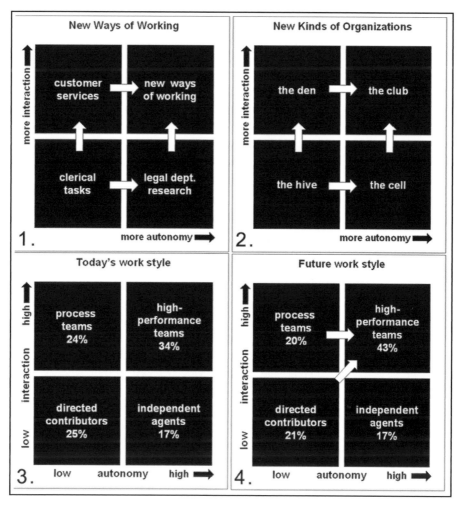

▲ **15.6** New Ways of Working, New Kinds of Organisations, Today/Future Work styles

concentration. The battle against simplistic universal planning and cost reductionism continued to be fought.

In the review of the actual organisational data collected through the Workplace Envisioning software, Duffy and Tanis were surprised and pleased to find that across their sample of 23 organisations in Europe and North America, more than half of their participants defined themselves as highly interactive/autonomous – active in process teams or in highly autonomous high-performance teams. In other words, organisations had moved ahead much faster in how they worked than in how they were physically accommodated in largely restrictive conventional office environments. They no longer had most of their people doing the routine of individual process work or isolated individual-concentrated work (the so-called Hive and Cell in DEGW's terminology) – a large proportion of their headcounts were already working in the more collaborative and autonomous Den and Club work styles. The change was expected to continue, with 43 per cent of all staff forecast to be in high-performance teams (highly interactive and autonomous – the so-called knowledge workers). The gap between emerging business needs and the existing office design had in fact widened. The call to battle now emphasised the need to track and measure the performance of the workplace much more systematically to prove the value and contribution of design.

THE ALLURE OF INTENSIFICATION

If, in the late 1990s, the white hot technology firms on the West Coast failed to deliver for themselves fundamental workplace design innovation, other organisations, using technologies or programs produced by those same firms, did undergo significant transformation of their workplace strategies. The evolving story of Arthur Andersen, Andersen Consulting and Accenture is perhaps the leading example of how many professional service firms were able to integrate technology into a systematic re-think of how the workplace would be procured, designed and used as part of fast changing global business strategies.

In the early 1990s, the combined firms of Arthur Andersen and Andersen Consulting, under the umbrella of Andersen Worldwide, had begun to research the policies of hotelling for their worldwide organisation. Andersen implemented global space and design guidelines that modelled the project delivery process and the high levels of space utilisation over time that could be achieved by incrementally adopting progressive hotelling policies for different grades of staff. High profile projects were used to showcase the real estate savings, the business benefits and the workplace performance gains that resulted. The Chicago headquarters of Andersen Worldwide (Figure 15.7) was re-designed in 1994–1995 by DEGW and SOM working with Steelcase as a major test case of this new kind of integration of workplace strategy and design (Figure 15.8).

This was followed by an even larger scale new office project for Andersen Consulting's own Metro Regional headquarters in Chicago at 161, North Clark Street in 1996–1997 (as Andersen Consulting separated

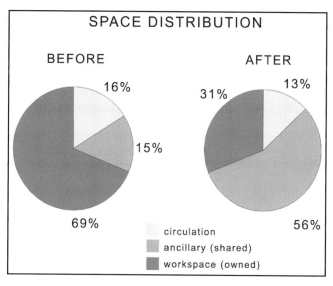

▲ 15.7   Andersen Worldwide Headquarters, Chicago – Space Distribution Chart

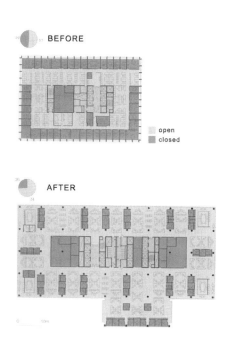

▲ 15.8   Andersen Worldwide Headquarters, Chicago

from Arthur Andersen). The downtown skyscraper hub was intended as the administrative and business centre for the more than 3000 resident and non-resident staff of Andersen Consulting in the region. Briefed by DEGW and designed by The Environments Group, the project was a major expression of Andersen Consulting's integrated innovations in business, technology and workplace strategy (Figure 15.9).

Following the Chicago project experience, Andersen Consulting's global workplace design guidelines were further developed, based on user research by DEGW that identified specific work patterns and linked them to a dynamic model of how different types of staff could be expected to make use of the workplace over time. The guidelines enabled worldwide offices to use consistent briefing and building assessment tools to support the design of local offices. High levels of intensification of space were built in, resulting in large reductions in real estate overhead as a percentage of revenue.

The design guidelines incorporated an enriched concept of hotelling, one that provided very high levels of servicing, technology and support to the end user. One of the major influences on this approach was Andersen Consulting's Paris office which opened in 1995, planned by Chadwick and Partners, where the building on the Champs Elysees

▲ **15.9**   Andersen Consulting Metro Regional Headquarters, Chicago

was branded as a highly serviced virtual office. Each floor was supported by Floor Attendants in chic uniforms. A concierge provided support for hotels, restaurants, theatre reservations and so on. Other support was provided for guest relations, reservations of work spaces, security, and technical support. The aspiration of the level of building services was to be as good as a five-star hotel. Hospitality personnel were recruited to support the new workplace in the worldwide locations that followed this example. Figure 15.10 illustrates an example of a guest satisfaction questionnaire.

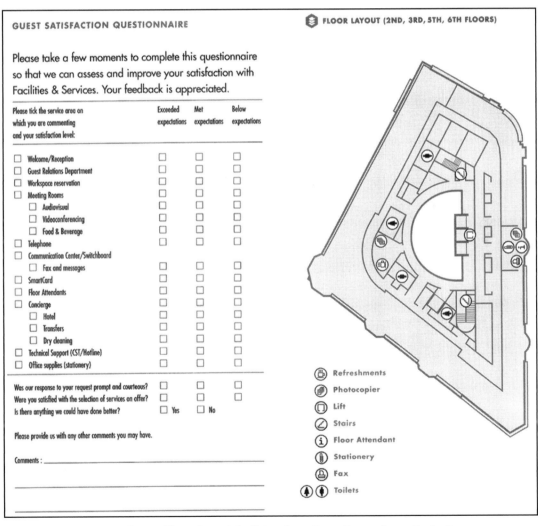

▲ 15.10   Andersen Consulting Guest Satisfaction Questionnaire – Paris, France

At last, it seemed that the vision of the office as a super highly utilised, highly serviced Club for knowledge workers had been realised and was being replicated all over the world – from Boston to Sydney. Yet, as Andersen Consulting became the publicly owned Accenture at the turn of the millennium, the concept of such highly serviced metropolitan Club offices radically changed direction. Perhaps this highly serviced vision of the office Club was not the end point of workplace and business strategy integration?

Several factors contributed to a change in workplace strategy at Accenture and other professional services firms that followed their lead: the global business went public and was re-focusing on much higher growth in off-shore lower cost locations; the economic downturn in the United States and other previously high revenue areas meant that the staffing projections for high intensity hotelling by highly leveraged consultants in expensive metropolitan centres were overly optimistic; and the assumption that if consultants were not working at client site they would be based in the office, was questioned. Driving these changes were new pressures to even further reduce overhead. At the same time, the research study in Europe referred to elsewhere in this book, SANE (Sustainable Accommodation for the New Economy), was articulating the conceptual framework for the idea of distributed working with the idea of the 'the office is the city'[7] (Figure 15.11).

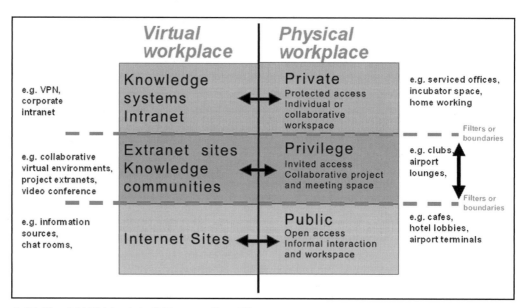

▲ 15.11   SANE Model, Office as the City

Accenture eagerly adopted the distributed workplace idea as a way of re-thinking where and how its global staff should be accommodated. In the evolving model, much more emphasis was placed on alternative locations of work outside the conventional office buildings or centres – including working from home, working from neighbourhood or satellite locations, as well as working in third party spaces such as universities, coffee shops and libraries. The distributed workplace could be supported by networks and often wireless resources and devices accessed from anywhere over the internet (Figure 15.12).

Thus, the grandiose Club offices of the mid- to late-1990s, were perhaps a false start of the new age of the office. The real innovation began when the very idea of the office was challenged and began to be replaced by the idea of a distributed workplace using multiple locations and resources.

The emerging model of the distributed workplace also coincided fortuitously with the devastating consequences of the terrorist attacks of 11 September, 2001. Suddenly, distributed working was not only more cost efficient, more effective for workplace performance, and made best use of technology, it was a strategy that was also highly resilient in terms of security and business continuity. The unprecedented impacts of 9/11 were superimposed on a North American economy that was already suffering from the dot com implosion and the worldwide recession. The effects of these interlinked economic and social disasters are of course still impacting the thinking of real estate executives, designers and city planners.

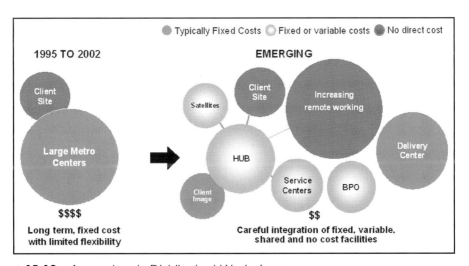

▲ 15.12 Accenture's Distributed Workplace

A last word about the allure of intensification: the concept of the Club office was expressed originally in terms of the coincidence of higher levels of autonomy and interaction in the ways in which people work in office organisations. This benign combination of organisational as well as individual demands, when supported by technologies that allowed work to occur in many locations, indicated the value of the intensification of the use of space over time in the workplace. This also fulfilled both *efficiency* drivers (cost reduction) and *effectiveness* drivers (business performance). In its implementation, it also highlighted a third performance driver that would become increasingly recognised and valued: the capacity of the workplace to *express* the values and meaning of the organisation. As work became increasingly virtual and distributed over time and space, the value of the design of the physical office environment to express and communicate the values, messages, and ideology of the organisation became even more important.

DOT-COM BOOM AND BUST, RECESSION, AND TERRORISM

What was the dot-com workplace? In reality, it never existed. While the Alt.Office conferences highlighted some alternative workplace models used by leading technology firms, the real dot com workplaces emerged in a thoughtless rush that provided a gloss of new economy aesthetics over routine and conventional workplace design. Most dot com work-places on the West or the East coast were produced at very high speed to cater for booming growth in staff numbers. Logistics drove everything. Some workplaces provided desks that could be moved on wheels or re-configured to allow for changing staff groups. There were new kinds of support spaces that provided for games and other 'fun stuff' mainly intended to look cool and acceptable to the demographic recruitment profile of young employees. A lot of attention was paid to colour and décor to enliven what would otherwise have been large areas of densely packed workstations.

The key driver was speed, speed and speed. There was no time to brief, measure, programme, or analyse the workplace performance. More space was needed more quickly in more locations to provide for what appeared to be endless growth – whether it was in Silicon Valley in California or Silicon Alley in New York – or the next sales office in Prague. Talking with one global technology workplace provider at this time (1997), I recall that she said that they did not have time to stop and measure whether any of their new workplaces were effective in any way – there was always the pressure to provide more of the same in new locations.

The crash of the dot com market and the technology sector in 2000 presaged the wider downturn of the economy in North America – the dot com became the dot gone. The economy was then further damaged by the terrorist attacks of 2001. The impact of 9/11 was so intense that most design and workplace activity and thinking was temporarily halted and then altered permanently. The outcome is still not clear.

A survey of the impact of 9/11 on the thinking of corporate real estate executives in North America (and later in the rest of the world), found that significant shifts in thinking had indeed occurred.[8] Aside from the expected much greater concern with means of escape from buildings and overall building security, the corporate real estate leaders were now re-thinking information technology, work practices, and the location of business. It seemed as if the demands for alternative ways of working, for the distributed workplace models we had been researching, were now being taken up with even greater enthusiasm as a result of the impact of the terrorist attacks. Security of information technology infrastructure and for business continuity became of much greater priority. There was greater interest in wireless and mobile technologies. Many corporate real estate leaders were now interested in strategies to support remote working, such as satellite offices, teleworking, and hotelling, combined with greater use of video conferencing and other virtual collaboration tools. There was a shift in preference away from downtown locations and towards the dispersal of core business activities. There was also a shift in preferences away from so-called high profile or highly branded buildings. Corporations now did not want to attract so much attention to themselves through their buildings.

INVASION OF THE EUROPEANS

While 9/11 temporarily halted much new activity in design and construction in late 2001 and 2002, there was nevertheless one spectacularly high profile site that by tragic necessity had to be planned and designed for – the World Trade Center in New York. The competition for the master plan held in 2002 for the World Trade Center site was won by architect Daniel Libeskind. The competition was significant in engaging enormous public interest in the urban and architectural problems of the site. Yet, the programme for the master plan competition made no attempt to re-think the nature of the office tower as a single use building type or to re-evaluate the wider urban purpose and functionality of such a downtown urban centre. The winning master plan scheme, while radical in superficial design characteristics and while creating an imposing memorial, did not depart in a major way from the standard shape of the deep plan towers driven by conventional commercial real estate thinking and the city zoning laws that have characterised North American downtown landscapes for decades.

Yet, the 2002 master plan competition for the World Trade Center did express a trend that had now become obvious: European and Asian architects were being commissioned on a significant scale to design major North American projects. (Libeskind himself, was born in Poland, worked for many years in Berlin, and became a U.S. citizen in 1965.) What was it that the Europeans brought to North America?

The most amazing illustration of what the European and Asian architects were bringing to North America, and to New York City, no less, was made very clear in an exhibition called Tall Buildings held at the Museum of Modern Art (in its temporary Queens location) in 2004.[9] Aside from the landmark museums, cultural, and educational institutions that had often looked abroad for major architectural talent, the Tall Buildings exhibition showed that non-American architects were innovating in the very design of the skyscraper! In New York itself, several startling new towers designed by Europeans could already be seen, such as the Christian de Portzamparc designed tower for the North American headquarters of Louis Vuitton (LVMH) on 57th street (Figure 15.13), as well as the proposed towers by Norman Foster for the Hearst Building (Figure 15.14) and by Renzo Piano for the New York Times building (Figure 15.15).

The Tall Buildings exhibition illustrated the exquisite irony of New Yorkers going to look at models of innovative skyscrapers designed for France, Germany, Korea, London, China and elsewhere. What is it that these innovative tall buildings offer that is new to North America? They bring with them a strong European and Asian concern for innovation in structure, care about occupants' access to daylight, natural ventilation and cooling, and a desire to bring nature into the heart of the building with internal and external gardens. The accumulation of these attributes, especially when they are thoughtfully integrated, is in fact a new kind of sustainable tall building. They express new ideas of living and working in the city. These architects also represent a much stronger interest in mixed use environments – living and working, offices, hotels, entertainment, and cultural activities in hybrid buildings. As such, some of these pioneering designs for tall buildings have re-captured the

▲ **15.13**   LVMH on 57th – New York City

▲ 15.14   Hearst Building, Normal Foster – New York City

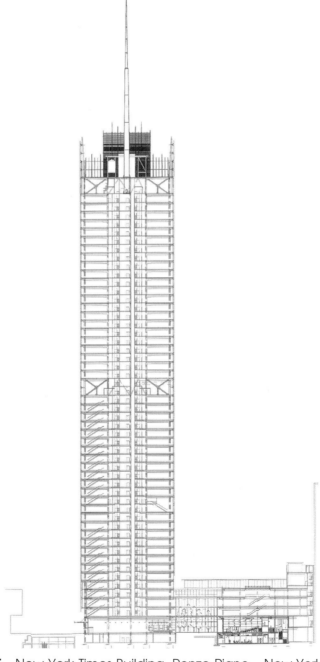

▲ 15.15   New York Times Building, Renzo Piano – New York City

high ground in expressing the relationship between the demands and aspirations of organisations and individuals in a new urban and technological context.

The partial loss of North American leadership in innovation in tall buildings is further exacerbated by the decline in quality of construction of large projects in North America. A recent New York Times article[10] noted that the United States has gained a reputation as being a shoddy builder reliant on outmoded construction practices. The singularity, craftsmanship and durability of European and Asian building traditions cannot be matched in North America. European and Asian architects such as Rem Koolhaas and Tadao Ando cannot achieve, in the USA, the quality of construction that they can achieve in their homelands, and have had to re-think how to construct their designs in North America.

Back in the 1980s and early 1990s, innovative British developers such as Sir Stuart Lipton studied best practices of North American construction and development. They brought ideas of American scale, speed, and efficiency to the overly craft-based British construction and development industry. Now, it seems the reverse is happening – the great European and Asian architects are bringing high levels of craft back to large-scale American projects.

SUSTAINABILITY: INTENSIFICATION AND DISTRIBUTION

So, is the recent story of North American office and workplace design only a tale of two worlds that have inverted their leadership and influence upon each other? I think it is rather a story of how fast-changing international thinking about the workplace and buildings is enabling us to re-imagine the cities in which we live and work, and their place in helping to secure the environmental sustainability of our world.

We are used to contrasting the North American speculative developer building with the North European user-focused and owner-occupied office building, a dichotomy that was richly examined by Frank Duffy and others at DEGW in the 1980s and 1990s. The large, deep, North American central core tower was contrasted with the organisationally specific, environmentally sensitive, shallow depth, low- to mid-rise, day-lit and naturally ventilated Northern European building.[11,12]

The research findings of *The Responsible Workplace* posited an alternative to, or an attempted resolution of, this dichotomy – of the cost efficiency of North America *versus* the user effectiveness of Northern Europe.

The alternative model suggested that the mission for organisations, architects and designers should be to achieve both: cost efficiency as well as organisational effectiveness — but how to do this without being excessively resource-hungry and expensive? The key innovation that *The Responsible Workplace* had outlined was that the opposition of reducing cost and adding value could be resolved, and in a sense radically overcome, through a new paradigm of office design and use: the intensification of the use of space over time. This was to be enabled by mobile technology, remote access to networks, and new ways of planning, designing and using space in a dynamic, shared, collaborative and intensive way over time. Time became the lever of innovation in workplace design, building design and even in urban design. The chronology and the nature of the use of space at every scale would be affected. It was this radical potential that Duffy and Tanis found so obviously lacking in workplace design thinking in 1993.

How has this radical potential fared since then? A partial view from North America suggests that workplace thinking has actually evolved very fast, faster perhaps than the clumsy jargon of workplace consultants might indicate (the litany of 'alternative workplace, new ways of working, hotelling, intensification, club offices'). Workplace thinking is inevitably forced to try and catch up with the always much faster pace of business and organisational change. But some real gains have indeed been made in closing the gap between innovation in business and the practice of the design of the workplace.

My recent North American perspective is that the technology workplace on the West Coast did not realise a proper integration of design and business strategy. Neither did the almost palatial luxury of the metropolitan office clubs designed for the professional service firms (Accenture, Deloitte & Touche, PriceWaterhouseCoopers,) realise the full potential of the new business models and associated advances in technologies.

By contrast, it is the idea of the distributed workplace that does seem to place the office fully into a complex web of social and technological networks that breaks our thinking of the office out of the building box into which it has been constrained. That is why some of the new international thinking and design practice for tall buildings seems so rich and compelling, as it positions the building in a context of social and environmental change. The distributed workplace challenges our idea of the office contained in the building, it challenges our conventional assumptions about cities and their downtowns, and it helps us to re-think the nature, quality and purpose of the city.

The idea of distributed workplace suggested by 'the city is the office' is rich because it also re-deploys our thinking on sustainability. The conventional idea of sustainability is overly technicised in its focus on energy used or materials consumed. A richer view of sustainability sees intensification (of the use of space over time) and distribution (of work and living across multiple locations and types of places) as two inter-dependent sides of the same coin.

Of course, the idea of the distributed workplace is not monolithic in its implications for design and use. The distributed workplace can be designed and used to very well support the high levels of individual autonomy and interaction needed by creative knowledge workers in a humane and sustainable way. It can equally well be used to accommo-date a footloose and fancy free capitalism that can roam the world and benefit the few.

Creative destruction! My North American experience tells me that the speed of change will not decelerate. As creators of workplaces, we will always have to fight to catch up with where organisations and tech-nologies are taking us. We will also have to continue to fight to create wonderful, humane, effective, supportive and sustainable workplaces.

16 THE DYNAMIC WORKPLACE: SCOTTISH ENTERPRISE HEADQUARTERS, GLASGOW

Adryan Bell, DEGW plc
Michelle Hynd, Scottish Enterprise
George Cairns, University of Essex

SUMMARY

This case study rather than focusing on the design and delivery of the building, presents through an in-depth analysis, how one organisation used the opportunity of moving to a new building to achieve its business objectives. Scottish Enterprise (the government agency responsible for economic development) used its new headquarters at Atlantic Quay to provide a physical representation of senior management's understanding that people are affected by their environment and that the environment is affected by the people. This two-way relationship is in stark contrast to the more commonly perceived viewpoint for either architectural or social determinism.

The case study outlines the important steps taken by Scottish Enterprise in planning the move in order to ensure and sustain success. Though the move to Atlantic Quay was undertaken in 2001, the story starts a decade earlier; providing a reminder that the pursuit of the optimal workplace takes time and commitment to realise. Building is a finite process with a clear beginning and an end. However, the life of a business is a continuing management project responding to continuous change. Scottish Enterprise's willingness to start the process of innovation in workplace design, well before moving to the new building, was a reflection of their understanding that whilst technically we can change physical surroundings overnight, it takes far longer to assimilate changes to behaviour and etiquette. The programme of pilot projects, started a decade before move in, allowed both the design of the settings and the working processes to be tested, developed and assimilated.

Underlying the case study are three themes which were critical to the workplace strategy and differentiated the project from many others. These are:

- Strong and consistent leadership, vision and commitment;
- A desire to identify and understand the most appropriate physical solutions to suit business requirements and to challenge conventional thinking;
- Paying proper attention to the social needs of staff, in terms of both their involvement and engagement in the change process, and a recognition of the diversity and dynamism of their evolving work styles and work practices.

Building Design Partnership's (BDP) building has been a fitting container for a thoughtful programme of office planning, and organisational innovation, welded together by a ten-year programme of change management. This chapter is a reminder that the new successful property solutions are more than bricks and mortar.

With its 100-foot high atrium providing view across the seven open-plan floorplates, its rich mix of worksettings that includes hot-desks, its glass elevators and open stairwell, its ground floor café and coffee shop with river view, and its contemporary reception area with running waterfall feature, Atlantic Quay (Figure 16.1) looks every square metre the perfect base for the modern, forward-thinking organisation. The work-anywhere, non-hierarchical philosophy adopted by its occupants further reinforces the high level of innovation in cultural as well as physical terms.

▲ 16.1 Atlantic Quay at night – BDP 2001

However, this is not the headquarters of some media or technology giant, but of Scottish Enterprise, the government agency responsible for economic development in lowland Scotland. Scottish Enterprise moved into its new headquarters in September 2001, following a decade of change and reform. Its journey of change is, of course, far from over, and Atlantic Quay provides the perfect base from which it can continue to evolve and excel in its business delivery.

Atlantic Quay is proof that an efficient and effective workplace that meets today's stringent government guidelines and aspirations does not have to be bland and boring. Recognising that people are influenced by their environment, attention to the design of the workplace and the development of working practices for those who use it has been essential to the success of this workplace, which has attracted world-wide interest and recognition from both the public and private sectors. But it was not always like this.

BEGINNINGS

Scottish Enterprise was initiated in April 2001 as an economic development agency through the merger of two organisations – the *Scottish Development Agency* (SDA) and lowland Scotland's *Training Agency*, formerly known as the *Manpower Services Commission*, and part of the mainstream Civil Service.

The two organisations' roles were different but complementary – the former dealing with trade and infrastructural development, and the latter with skills development. Not surprisingly, the culture of these two organisations were also very different.

A prime objective of the then Chief Executive was to create a single, fresh culture, and a common purpose for the organisation. This vision looked forward to the challenges and opportunities of the future, rather than looking back to the heritage of the past, and recognised the functional need of the headquarters to lead by example. However, initial progress was hampered by the office accommodation that was inherited – a number of buildings that said more about the past than the future. In common with other typical 1960s office buildings, the accommodation predominately comprised long corridors and rows of enclosed offices, with small areas of open-plan space, typically for occupation by administrative and secretarial staff, and reflecting a hierarchical and bureaucratic structure.

▲ 16.2   Working Café area, Atlantic Quay – BDP 2001

It was against this backdrop that the Chief Executive led, from
the top, on a journey of organisational and cultural change, which
has continued through his successors to this day. At the heart of the
development was the desire to create a new headquarters building
that would reflect the culture and values of the new organisation,
and that would enable staff to contribute to the development of these
elements. The new building was thus conceived both as a deterministic
driver of organisational change and as a physical setting for user-led
organic change.

FIRST STEPS

As outlined above, Atlantic Quay was the culmination of a series of
earlier developmental projects. Influenced by the private sector, Scottish
Enterprise had first introduced a pioneering (for the public sector) *new
ways of working* initiative in 1993, recognising new opportunities for

working across time and location. This was facilitated in particular by technology advances and was also driven by staff aspirations for a better work/life balance.

This initiative focused on the provision of management guidelines which empowered and informed managers to support how their teams might work in new ways that would be beneficial to the organisation, customers and staff. The initiative included options such as homeworking, remote working, flexitime, term-time working, condensed working weeks, annualised hours, sabbaticals and secondments. This initiative was well received, and taken up by staff and managers alike.

Two key areas of learning emerged from the *new ways of working* initiative:

- The need to better manage staff by outputs rather than inputs, through a more relevant performance management system;
- The need to have a working environment that better reflects the way staff are actually working – recognising greater diversity and mobility in work styles.

Two complementary programmes of action were initiated to address these needs. In response to the second area of learning, a period of research was put in place which led to an experimental pilot of the potential future working environment, aptly named the *Workplace of the Future* (WotF), and to the initiation of the business case for the new headquarters.

WORKPLACE OF THE FUTURE (WotF)

The WotF project was set up in 1995 with three key objectives:

- To further explore and evolve new ways of working and working practices;
- To further explore and exploit evolving support technologies;
- To test out a range of new worksettings and a new style of workplace.

All this was in the context of: Scottish Enterprise's role in supporting the Scottish business community and the need to lead by example, as well as being in response to the long-standing desire to create a new headquarters.

The design and functionality of WotF

The WotF was created in 1996, situated in 540 square metres of disused retail space on the ground floor of the existing main headquarters building, where it had a deliberately high profile from both an internal and external perspective. Its design, by DEGW, supported fully Scottish Enterprise's objectives of creating an experimental workspace that acted as a catalyst for change. Much of this was achieved through its bright, colourful, open and contemporary appearance, which contrasted starkly with the remaining dated and drab workspace.

The WotF pilot workspace provided a rich mixture of new worksettings, including hot-desks (with mobile extension tables), touchdowns, study booths, café space, project room, service area and a concierge (supporting a new role introduced to provide a hotel style of management and service for the new environment). More traditional settings, such as owned desks, meeting rooms, library and storage/filing area, were also factored into the design. Both mobile and static storage solutions were tested.

The volunteer teams who would work in the WotF pilot (initially around 70 staff rising to around 100) were selected to ensure that a relevant cross section of the organisation was involved – in terms of both functionality and grade – with one of the senior management team (Director of Strategy) directly participating. The space provided a setting which research suggested would support a diverse range of

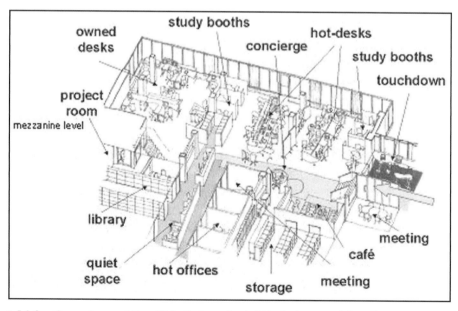

▲ 16.3   Overview of Scottish Enterprise's Workplace of the Future Pilot workspace – DEGW 1995

workstyles and work patterns. There was, intentionally, no direct user involvement in the design process – rather, these teams were asked to accept and try out a pre-defined generic new style of workspace. Beyond the participating staff members, others were encouraged to use the WotF facilities, in order that they too could experience the new concepts.

The space was designed to reflect different uses of time and space by staff, with more mobile and interactive work taking place near the entrance, and quieter zones provided deeper into the space. Those with permanent or assigned desks (typically those with non-operational/ external customer-focused roles) were assigned the best space environ- mentally. Two-thirds of the participating staff – predominantly executives and managers – were encouraged to hot-desk, supported by virtual telephony and roaming IT profiles. This arrangement was based on studies of the existing use of space, where underutilisation of desks reflected both absence from the office, as well as high mobility, inter- action and collaboration when office-based.

▲ 16.4   View across 'the workplace of the future' workspace – DEGW 1996

The WotF pilot attracted positive media attention during its five-year lifespan, and was visited by over 300 companies, schools and colleges, from all sectors and all parts of the world. It also won the coveted British Institute of Facilities Management (BIFM) Small Office of the Year Award in 1996 – putting Scottish Enterprise on the map for its workplace innovation.

After the initial group of volunteers settled in the WotF, new staff and teams were located there over time, as a result of ongoing organisational churn and change. The experience for some of these individuals was not always as positive as for the original volunteers. There were several potential reasons for this: perhaps they did not perceive themselves to be accepted members of the pilot, not having been part of the original high-profile volunteer group, or perhaps they had not dedicated so much time and resource in preparing for the move to the space as had the original volunteers. Continual change of personnel in the pilot was crucial to enable learning beyond the initial 'control' volunteer group. It seemed that there was a positive motivational effect within the volunteer group, possibly due to the special recognition they received, which may have influenced their feelings and tolerance towards the space. At the end of the WotF pilot, there was evidence of support for the concepts, but also some evidence of resistance. So, despite the high-profile and award-winning status, there was as yet no clear evidence that the new workplace environment would promote organisational effectiveness through some deterministic cause/effect outcome.

Change management and evaluation

A series of independent evaluations of WotF was undertaken by Hawthorn Consultants over a four-year period, to track progress and learning and to inform the developing business case for the new headquarters.

Some of the key learning from the WotF experience included:

- Successful reduction of space required with the new workplace concepts (the pilot participants occupied only one-third of their previous space);
- The improvements in morale, pride and productivity reported by staff as a result of the change in work environment and work practices (perceptions of personal productivity increases by up to 50 per cent were reported);

- The reduction in 'churn' costs (where despite various changes in the teams and personnel involved, no changes to the workspace was required – the only changes made being to support the experimentation of new concepts, ideas and learning).

In addition, from evaluation of the WotF project, two key issues were identified for taking forward into the hew headquarters project:

- *Change management* – recognising the continuous need to appropriately prepare and support staff in adapting to the new ways of working and workplace concepts so that they could positively embrace the changes and exploit new opportunities and benefits quickly; and
- *Workplace evaluation* – recognising the need to capture the learning from workplace implementations in order to develop the workspace (and concepts for the new headquarters) and good work practices.

Waiting for the new headquarters

A major challenge for Scottish Enterprise was to manage the interest and expectations of the wider organisation, following the implementation of WotF, until the new headquarters became a reality. In the lead up to ministerial approval to proceed with the procurement of a new headquarters, there was an ongoing requirement to evolve working practices and facilities of the organisation, and to embed developments into the current everyday operations.

These requirements were satisfied in two ways:

- The introduction of two further workplace pilots – FutureSpace and Skillspace – in 1997–98, to extend the organisational involvement, experience and learning in new workplace concepts;
- After formal approval was granted, the initiation of pre-move activities from 1999, to engage the whole organisation in a new focus towards the new proposed headquarters, and envisaged associated work practices and protocols.

A staff communication from Crawford Beveridge, CEO at this stage, set the scene and reinforced the vision:

> 'We are aiming to procure a new building that will reflect the dynamism that Scottish Enterprise represents and one that will support the creative, collaborative and intelligent workforce and workstyles that we need to practise to deliver our new strategy. We want to build on what we have learnt from projects such as the Workplace of the

Future, and create an office environment that is truly exemplary in the way it operates and is used – and in the way it supports its users.'

Planning and influencing

As indicated above, the brief for the new headquarters, to be designed by BDP, was driven by a desire for change and modernisation. However, despite the very high quality of physical design to be delivered, a positive impact on staff and on the organisation in support of these aspirations could not be assumed. In striving for a positive and effective transition to the new location, planning had to be undertaken well in advance. Concentrated relocation activities and interventions with staff began as early as two years before the move.

Four key elements of the preparations were:

- *A Space and Activity Study* – undertaken in 1999 as an objective investigation to understand the evolving workstyles and activities of all 700 staff, albeit framed and shaped by the existing physical environment. This study highlighted that only 43 per cent of the workspace was utilised on an average across the working day, reflecting evolving workstyles of staff, who were using a range of work locations both within and outside the office, including working at home. It also confirmed the mismatch with the current office environment in supporting needs. However, many staff members were not convinced that the findings provided a true reflection of their working lives. As often cited in situations of change, perceptions can differ from reality, and individuals can adopt a negative or denial attitude – and this was recognised as a natural reaction to preparations at this stage.
- *A Reality Check Workbook* – undertaken as a follow up in early 2001 with an emphasis on self-reporting and analysis of workstyles. The workbook was part questionnaire and part educational – helping staff to better understand and recognise their personal workstyles, use of space, and workplace needs. This initiative enabled a self-realisation and acceptance of what had been shown from the original space and activity study, since it closely mirrored the findings, with 45 per cent reported to be mobile and flexible. This was a significant step forward and, with this raised awareness amongst staff, the practical steps of planning the changes ahead were better informed, and the acceptance of designs and layouts better aligned with current and anticipated work styles.
- *Move Co-ordinators* – established from around November 2000 to represent each team and to act as local change agents, preparing

their teams for the move. One of their first tasks was to assist with the space planning of their team's requirements. Other activities included allocation of individual and team storage, driving reductions in filing, organising the clearance and rationalisation of stationery and so on. The appointment and involvement of move co-ordinators ensured that there was a local perspective, with an in-depth understanding of the relative team issues and sub-cultures. Most staff would relate to local team representatives appointed from within, who knew and understood their team. These people played a key and critical role in the move process.

- *Ambassadors* – also appointed at a senior level, with responsibility for dealing with senior management or matters that the move co-ordinators felt required upwards referral for resolution to ensure the continuance of project timelines.

Preparing for the move

Important as it was to prepare the building for staff to move into, it was equally important to prepare the staff to use the building and to ensure they could be as functionally effective as possible on the first day. To do this, it was vital that individuals began to imagine and visualise what would be different in the new office. There were a lot of changes ahead: a new address, new car parks and bus routes, a new security entrance system, the introduction of a cashless catering system, no desks for some staff, a desk booking system, a new IT/telephony system, new filing and storage solutions and much more.

In order to achieve as much learning/familiarisation as possible prior to the move, key interventions were planned:

- *Workshop events* were designed and delivered. These took the form of large familiarisation 'floor-by-floor' sessions, which brought together between 100 and 150 staff at a time, who would all be located together on the same floor in the new building. These events were compulsory and were purposefully designed to let people get to know and recognise each other in advance of their co-location. Leadership was important at these events and the most senior person responsible for each floor played an active supportive role. Speaking about the aspirations of the organisation and helping to articulate how organisational benefits could be gained through the process of the move and associated changes in behaviours and practices. Many of the staff were moving out of cellular offices into open flexible workspace and this was uncomfortable for some. It was helpful for individuals to see that these changes were being discussed and experienced at all levels, and that there was an understanding of the challenges that a non-hierarchically, traditionally symbolised space may bring, along with the need for new protocols.

- *An exhibition space* was set up, with a model of the new building and sketches of the new environment, to further assist staff in visualising and familiarising themselves.
- *Training sessions* – where specific and individually designed training was offered to staff regarding new ways of working and managing remote teams.
- *On-site induction* events were held for all staff in the new headquarters at Atlantic Quay just two weeks prior to the move which were also compulsory. These events equipped staff with information on how to access the building, associated security regimes, their floor location for the first day and directions to common/shared facilities such as the staff canteen. Staff were issued security access badges, hot-desk area or permanent desk, and filing cabinet number, along with their colour-coded removal stickers and instructions to be used in packing their belongings into crates for the move.
- *A guidebook* was created and issued to all staff to act as a reminder about the new facilities and layouts, as well as the new protocols and behavioural changes expected, to gain maximum return from the building design.

Physical dimensions of the new workplace

As a knowledge-based organisation, the objective was to design an environment in the new building which contained more flexible, shared workspace to support more nomadic work styles. Atlantic Quay was designed to support a greater degree of openness, interaction, sharing and mobility. New facilities, new worksettings and new technologies have been introduced – taking the learning from the workspace pilots fully into account. It is predominantly of an open-plan nature, with a balance and choice of both open and enclosed worksettings for all staff to use. It has been designed to maximise the external light and views, as well as to support internal visibility and interaction – with the atrium playing a key role in encouraging these connections.

The ground and first floor provide a range of corporate and visitor facilities, including a restaurant, café, conference centre, meeting room suite and innovation theatre (a flexible brainstorming facility).

▲ **16.5**   View across open floorplate at Atlantic Quay – BDP2001

The Atlantic Quay working environment has also been designed to support and encourage new ways of working and new ways of using office workspace. A range of work settings are available on each floor – designed to suit different workstyle needs and preferences. Each team has a dedicated team space, or neighbourhood. This area provides a certain level of shared team facilities, typically a mix of dedicated and bookable (hot) desks, carrels (study booths), touchdowns for short-stay working, bookable offices, project area, personal storage and an oasis area, where local printing, copying and vending facilities are provided.

To support a greater degree of sharing and flexibility, to maintain an acceptable office appearance and to recognise fire and security considerations, a tidy and clear desk policy exists for everyone, based on common sense and courtesy. Staff are encouraged to clear worksettings at the end of each day or after use, to ensure that they are always ready for use by others. And less cluttered workspace that is not over-personalised has brought much more flexibility in terms of the use and sharing of the workspace. An on-line booking system and concierge service further supports the effective operation of the workspace.

Social dimensions of the new workplace

There are many challenges inherent in a physical relocation or redesign of workspace – many of these are in aligning the social aspects of the organisation and this was particularly relevant for Scottish Enterprise, given its background and original vision. Social elements play a key role in the contribution of the physical environment to effective change. There is no simple cause and effect relationship between the elements of social, physical and organisational environments of work and no hierarchical ordering of social over physical. Rather, there should be an integrated conceptual consideration of all such elements together.

A key element of the social context of change is the users' perceptions of their level of involvement, which was found to be more significant than their real level of involvement. Effective and continual communication about what is being proposed, through participative and supportive leadership and management, is likely to be of greater significance than an actual involvement in generating ideas which may not be implemented. This was evidenced even where there was no user involvement in the design process itself. Intentions and actions, particularly of leaders and management, are important in influencing how staff will respond to their new work environment. Often, intentions and actions in relocation projects are explicit to some, such as management, but not to staff.

▲ 16.6   View of informal meeting space at Atlantic Quay – BDP 2001

In planning and influencing the move process, it is crucial to consider both the staff's understanding of current work practices and their understanding of new ways of working. This will be different for every organisation and the priorities, ordering and sequencing of interventions to drive change will be dependent upon such consideration.

Sustaining the change post move

On many large projects, involving a tightly managed relocation, the major focus of the team involved is on the successful delivery of the project plan within agreed timescales. Most resources are concentrated on the requirements up to and including the relocation but often the post occupancy requirements are neglected.

A full, independent post-occupancy evaluation of the new headquarters at Atlantic Quay was undertaken by DEGW, approximately six months after the move date (February 2002). This study was intended to set new benchmarks for future measurement, as well as to help the client understand the initial performance of the environment, and the impact on staff and business performance in line with stated project objectives. A range of activities was involved in the data-collecting process, including a further Space and Activity Study, staff and management interviews, staff workshops, a staff questionnaire and a visitor questionnaire.

The study highlighted that the take up and acceptance of new flexible working practices within the office, including open-plan working, hot-desking and non-ownership of offices, had been very effective. This reflected a very natural and positive transition and adaptation to the new environment and work practices for staff, a result of the extensive planning and preparation. In a substantial change from the legacy of the past, the vision articulated ten years earlier was very apparent in the reality that the findings demonstrated .

Some of the key statistics from the evaluation demonstrate the achievement of specific objectives as well as confirming the general improvements made in terms of efficiency and effectiveness. Examples include:

- Prior to the move, 30 per cent of the staff worked in dedicated offices. After the move, there were no dedicated offices. This removed visible status symbols and allowed hot offices to be booked by all staff;

- Prior to the move, 20 per cent of the staff formally worked flexibly, in terms of hot-desking practices, primarily through the pilot activities. At the time of the move, 55 per cent of the staff had opted to work flexibly in this way and these figures were confirmed in the post move evaluation;
- Prior to the move, with organised support and communications, internal document holdings were reduced by 70 per cent;
- The post occupancy evaluation revealed that the workspace in the new building was still only 75 per cent utilised at peak times, providing ample scope for growth and response to future organisational change. However, this was a clear improvement in the level of utilisation over previous work environments;
- In the evaluation, 85 per cent of the staff stated that the new building was a vast improvement on previous premises, 84 per cent stated that it was better than any other offices they had seen, or worked in;
- The new café area, designed to support and encourage informal meeting and interaction, showed a 96 per cent utilisation during the working day – reflecting its popularity as an alternative workspace and the importance of the social aspects of work;
- In the evaluation, staff also cited 'flexible working' as the best aspect of the new building. This demonstrates a blurring of the boundaries between what are perceived to be physical or social elements of the workplace. Flexible working is an intangible element with no dependency on the physical environment, yet it is perceived to have a direct cause and effect relationship with the relocation to the new building;
- In terms of the move process itself, 95 per cent of the staff stated that it exceeded their expectations;
- The number of visitors to the new headquarters had increased by 50 per cent in the first 6 months of occupation – some of this, no doubt, reflecting a certain curiosity.

The post occupancy evaluation also highlighted the areas of staff concern. Most of these were expected settling-in aspects, such as air temperature adjustments. However, it was found that whilst these hygiene factors were negatively affecting staff feelings towards their workplace, the physical environment overall was positively motivational, a positive contributor to productivity.

Awareness of the influences of the working environment on the well-being, social dynamics, motivation and productivity of its occupants has always been at the forefront of the Scottish Enterprise vision.

The following quote from the post occupancy evaluation is emblematic of the progress made in this respect:

'More open and more friendly – I know faces and people now that I had never seen in my previous two years in the organisation'.

LOOKING TO THE FUTURE

The post occupancy evaluation also highlighted some areas for further improvement, many of them cultural – emphasising the need for ongoing attention to ensure the long-term embedding of change. The emergence of some localised territorialism was reported, inhibiting the freedom for staff to work across floors in comfort, as intended, along with the breaking down of some of the booking protocols. These are not surprising responses to such radical changes and new procedures.

The Senior Management team at Scottish Enterprise gave serious consideration to the findings of the post occupancy evaluation and recognised that some key actions needed to be undertaken by respective internal departments such as the facilities, human resources, and internal communications teams. With the natural churn of staff and organisation initiatives, organisations can too quickly find themselves in a position where the original design philosophy, relocation project objectives and desired cultural or value changes can be forgotten. It is important that ongoing ownership and development of these are firmly rooted in the project plan from the outset. The move should be viewed as the first day from which continual development and beneficial returns from the building design can be realised, as the physical and social elements of the organisation combine to provide maximum effectiveness. Scottish Enterprise has tried hard to maintain this philosophy of supporting ongoing workplace change and learning.

At the time of writing, Scottish Enterprise has undergone further substantial structural change, including a formal alignment with the Careers Service in Scotland and the rationalisation and co-location of support services across its network. The design and philosophy of the building, and the work practices introduced have proven their flexibility in responding to these developments.

Despite the achievements to date the story is ongoing. The organisation will, without doubt, encounter new challenges and opportunities in the future. It is, however, now very well placed to embrace this future.

The expression, 'It's a journey, not a destination' is probably the most apt description of the case study of Scottish Enterprise and its headquarters project. And the learning and benefits achieved along the way, in operational and cultural terms, can arguably be regarded as being of much higher value than any eventual outcome.

FIGURE ACKNOWLEDGEMENTS

Figures 0.1–0.3	Source: DEGW
Figure 2.9	Source: Stone and Luchetti, 1985
Figure 2.13	Source: Duffy, Laing and Crisp, reproduced from *The Responsible Workplace*, Butterworth-Heinemann
Figure 3.4	Source: Nutt
Figures 4.9 and 4.10	Source: DEGW, 2004
Figure 6.2	Source: Francis Duffy (1997) The New Office. London: Conran Octopus Limited, p. 58.
Figure 8.1	Source: DEGW, 2002
Figure 8.2	Source: DEGW, 2001
Figure 8.2	Source: DEGW, 2001
Figure 9.1	Source: Plantronics
Figure 9.2	Source: workplaceinnovation.co.uk
Figure 9.3	Source: Microsoft
Figure 9.4	Source: workplaceinnovation.co.uk
Figure 9.5	Source: workplaceinnovation.co.uk
Figures 11.1 and 11.2	Source: DEGW
Figure 12.3	Crown copyright 2004
Figure 14.1	Source: Image by Peter Andrew, DEGW
Figure 14.2	Source: Foster and Partners
Figure 14.3	Copyright: Richard Glover

Figure 14.4	Source: Architect: Voller Nield; Photographer: John Gollings
Figure 14.5	Copyright: Ove Arup & Partners (HK) Ltd
Figure 14.6	Source: Image by Kohn Pedersen Fox
Figure 14.7	Copyright: Ian Lambot
Figure 14.8	Source: Image by Kohn Pedersen Fox
Figure 14.9	Source: Image by Denton Corker Marshall
Figure 14.10	Source: Image by DesignInc Melbourne
Figure 15.2	Source: DEGW, 1998
Figure 15.3	Source: Andrew Laing, Francis Duffy, Denice Jaunzens, Steve Willis, reproduced from *New Environments for Working*, E&F Spon, 1998
Figure 15.4	Source: DEGW
Figure 15.5	Source: http://www.jawed.com/pictures/sgi98/SGI/
Figures 15.6–15.9	Source: DEGW
Figure 15.10	Source: Andersen Consulting Visitor Guide for 55 Avenue George V
Figure 15.11	Source: DEGW, Ove Arup (London), RHUL (London), Telenor (Oslo), IAT (Stuttgart), Institut CERDA (Barcelona) and FAW (Ulm) (2002), reproduced from *Sustainable Accommodation for the New Economy* IST-2000-25257, European Commission, Brussels
Figure 15.12	Source: DEGW
Figure 15.13	Source: Photograph by Malcolm Brown
Figure 15.14	Source: Foster and Partners, London, UK, 2005
Figure 15.15	Source: Reproduced from *Tall Buildings*, Museum of Modern Art, 2004. Preface by Terence Riley. Department of Publications, The Museum of Modern Art, New York

REFERENCES

INTRODUCTION

1 Telecentre Association (1996) *The Teleworking Handbook*. London.
2 U. Hotopp (2002) *Teleworking in the UK*, Labour Market Trends. London.
3 US Department of Commerce (2004) *A Nation Online: Entering the Broadband Age*, September 2004.
4 J. Worthington (2001) Accommodating change – emerging real estate strategies. *Journal of Corporate Real Estate* 3(1): 81–95.
5 Blyth and Worthington (2000) *Managing the Brief for Better Design*. London. pp. 138–142. Case Study 'Briefing for adjustable use', Susan Stuebing.

CHAPTER 1

1 A. Leaman and W. Bordass (1996) Buildings in the age of paradox, Chapter 1. In A. Leaman (Ed), *Buildings in the Age of Paradox*, IoAAS. Heslington: University of York, pp. 3–14.
2 Surveys carried out by Building Use Studies Ltd and licensees 1987–2004.
3 A. Leaman and I. Borden (1993) User expectations, Chapter 2. In F. Duffy, A. Laing and V. Crisp *The Responsible Workplace: The redesign of Work and Offices*. London: Butterworth Architecture.
4 A. Brister May (1996) Returning 1960s buildings to profit. *Building Services Journal*, 12–13.
5 D. Jensen (1997) in conversation.
6 J. Whitelegg (1993) *Transport for a Sustainable Future, the Case for Europe*. London: Belhaven Press. For example, the list of 35 costs associated with car ownership, Figure 7.3, p. 138 (Source: Pollution Probe).
7 R. Rainbow (1994) Mobility, Shell.
8 F. Cairncross (1991) Making polluters pay, Chapter 5. In *Costing the Earth*. London: Business Books.
9 P. Hawken (1993) *The Ecology of Commerce*. Section on costs and prices, New York: Harper Collins, pp. 71–90.

10 TravelSmart encourages sustainable travel, especially by reforming journey to work and journey to school behaviour
www.travelsmart.vic.gov.au

11 N. Slack, S. Chambers, C. Harland, A. Harrison and R. Johnson (1995) *Operations Management*. London: Pitman Publishing.

12 MFI Fights to put its System Back on Track after Profit Warning, Computer Weekly (14 September 2004).

13 The Feedback Portfolios from the Usable Buildings Trust, are forerunners here
www.usablebuildings.co.uk

14 A. Leaman (1996) Space intensification and diversification, In A. Leaman (Ed), *Buildings in the Age of Paradox*, IoAAS. Heslington: University of York pp. 3–14.

15 R. Wynne-Jones (1996) *End of the Traffic Jam is Nigh*, Independent (14 April 1996) (Press report of Travel and the Superhighway which predicts a drop of 43% in work trips per week in the UK by the year 2010 from 328 million in 1996 to 186 million in 2010).

16 Teleworkers are people who work mainly from home (teleworker home-workers) or use their home as a base (home-based teleworkers) or work at home for at least one day a week (occasional teleworkers). Source: Teleworkers in the UK: who's doing it? Flexibility website, 2004; based on data from the UK Labour Force Survey.

17 Based on information from the Sustainable Teleworking report from the UK Centre for Economic and Environmental Development, July 2004
www.sustel.org

18 DEGW and BRE (1996) *New Environments for Working*, DEGW International.

19 University of York Development Plan Review, York, 1995.

20 William Bordass Associates (1996) *Mixed Mode Ventilation and Cooling Systems in Buildings*, Scoping study for the Building Research Establishment.

21 For example, the Higher Education Funding Council of England conducted a strategic review of university estates in 1994–1995. [2004; HEFCE now takes more pains to systematically review the performance of new buildings]

22 B. Clement (1996) *Unions warn of job losses as BA exports work to india*, Press report, The Independent, (12 June 1996). (2004: This has now become a feature of outsourcing)

Further background

1 R. Cole and R. Lorch (Eds) (2004) *Buildings, Culture and Environment: Informing Global and Local Practices*, Blackwell Publishing. Oxford.

2 G. Cooper (1998) *Air-conditioning America*, Johns Hopkins University Press. London.

3 P. Hawken, A. Lovins and H. Lovins (1999) *Natural Capitalism*; London: Earthscan Publications.

4 S. MacMillan (Ed) (2004) *Designing Better Buildings, Quality and Value in the Built Environment*. London: Spon Press.

5 M. Young (1988) *The Metronomic Society*. London: Thames & Hudson.

6 P. Schwartz (1996) *The Art of the Long View: Planning for the Future in an Uncertain World*. John Wiley.

7 T. Schnelling (1978) *Micromotives and Macrobehaviour* WW Norton and Co.

8 H. Simon (1969) *The Sciences of the Artificial*. Cambridge, MA: MIT Press

CHAPTER 2

1 F. Duffy (1992) *The Changing Workplace*. London, England: Phaidon.

2 F. Duffy and J. Tanis (1993) *A Vision of the New Workplace*, Industrial Development Section, April 1993.

3 ibid

4 L. Gatter (1982) *The Office an Analysis of the Evolution of a Workplace*. Master of Architecture Thesis. MIT.

5 Duffy and Tanis: op. cit

6 Gatter: op. cit

7 ibid.

8 F. Duffy (1966) *Office Landscaping - A New Approach to Office Planning*, ANBAR monograph. Re-printed in F. Duffy (1992) *The Changing Workplace*. London: Phaidon.

9 F. Duffy and C. Cave (1975) Bürolandschaft Revisited. *The Architects' Journal* (26 March 1975): 665–675, reprinted in F. Duffy (1992) *The Changing Workplace*. London: Phaidon.

10 F. Duffy (1992), op. cit

11 ibid

12 ibid

13 F. Duffy Building illustrated. *Centraal Beheer Offices, Apeldoorn, Holland The Architects' Journal* (29 October 1975): 893–904, reprinted in F. Dufy (1992) *The Changing Workplace*. London: Phaidon.

14 F. Duffy (1992) op. cit

15 P. J. Stone and R. Luchetti (1985) Your office is where you are. *Harvard Business Review* 63(2): 102–117.

16 F. Duffy, A. Laing, and V. Crisp. (1993) *The Responsible Workplace*, Oxford, England: Butterworth-Heinemann.

CHAPTER 3

1 E.L. Groshen and S. Potter (2003) Has structural change contributed to a jobless recovery? *Current Issues in Economics and Finance*. Federal Reserve Bank of New York 9(8): 1–7.

2 A. Parker (2004) *Two Speed Europe: Why 1 Million Jobs Will Move Offshore*. MA: Forrester Research Institute.
3 D. Coyle and D. Quah (2002) *Getting the Measure of the New Economy*. London: The Work Foundation.
4 B. Nutt (2000) Four trails to the future. In B. Nutt and P. McLennan (Eds), *Facility Management*. London: Blackwell Science.

CHAPTER 4

1 J. Connor (1997) Outsourcing facilities management. In J. Worthington (Ed), *Reinventing the Workplace*. Oxford: Architectural Press.
2 N. Gillen (2003) Future sustainable city forms: two profiles of emerging work patterns and their implication on the strategy and planning of work environments, *5th International Symposium of the International Urban Planning and Environmental Association*. Creating Sustainable Urban Environments: Oxford Brookes University.
3 W. Olins (2003) *On Brand*. London: Thames and Hudson Ltd.
4 C. Handy (1990) *The Elephant and the Flea*. London: Random House, and C. Handy (1990) *The Age of Unreason*. Boston: Harvard Business School Press.
5 Olins op.cit.
6 A. Harrison, P. Wheeler and C. Whitehead (Eds) (2004) *The Distributed Workplace: Sustainable Work Environments*. London: Spon Press.
7 R. Sennett (1998) *The Corrosion of Character*. New York: WW Norton.
8 802.11b Wireless LANs, (11 July 2004) http://www.wlana.com
9 W. J. Mitchell (2003) ME++ *The Cyborg Self and the Networked City*. Cambridge, MA: The MIT Press.
10 A. Malhotra, J. Stamps, J. Lipnack and A. Maichrzak (2004) Can absence make the team grow stronger? *Harvard Business Review.*

CHAPTER 5

1 R. K. Lewis (2003) Architecture and the global city, paper presented at: *New Global History and the City*, January 9–12. European University, St. Petersburg.
2 R. Harbour (2001) Office politics. *World Architecture*, May 2001.
3 Cited in: H. Ibelings (1998) *Supermodernism: Architecture in the Age of Globalization*. Rotterdam: Nai Publishers.
4 J. J. van Meel (2000) *The European Office*. Rotterdam: 010 Publishers.
5 D. J. M. van der Voordt, J. van Meel, F. Smulders and S. Teurlings (2003) Corporate culture and design. Theoretical reflections on case-studies in the web design industry. *Environments by Design* 4(2), 23–43.
6 T. E. Deal and A. A. Kennedy (1982) *Corporate Cultures: The Rites and Rituals of Corporate Life*. Reading, MA: Addison-Wesley.

7 G. Hofstede (1991) *Cultures and Organizations: Software of the Mind.* London: McGraw Hill.
8 R. Slavid (1998) Opel HQ in Russelheim Germany. *The Architects Journal* 13(6): 28–32.
9 E. T. Hall and M. R. Hall (1990) *Understanding Cultural Differences: Key to Success in West Germany, France and the United States.* Yarmouth: Intercultural Press.
10 Cited in: J. J. van Meel (2000) *The European Office.* Rotterdam: 010 Publishers.
11 F. Duffy (2001) On the job – design and the American office. – The European Office. *The Architectural Review,* March 1.
12 Europroperty Cross-Border Business (1995) *Europroperty* special issue.
13 P. Garforth (2004) Energy efficient buildings: uncompetitive costs or competitive prerequisite? Paper presented at *Building Performance Congress,* Frankfurt-am-Main, 19–22 April.
14 Hafeez Contractor's Interview (2004) *Times Property Bangalore* (March 12).

CHAPTER 6

1 F. Duffy (1997) *The New Office.* London: Conran Octupus.
2 A. Harrison, P. Wheeler and C. Whitehead (2004) *The Distributed Workplace.* London: Spon.

CHAPTER 7

1 G. Hamel and C. K. Pralahad (1994) *Competing for the Future.* Harvard Business School Press.

CHAPTER 8

1 F. Cairncross (1997) *The Death of Distance.* UK: Orion Publishing.
2 DEGW (2001) *The Initial Space Environment Model,* unpublished research report. SANE, The Distributed Workplace 2001.
3 F. Duffy (1997) *The New Office.* London: Conran Octopus.
4 European Commission (2000) *A European Way for the Information Society,* Luxembourg Information Society, 2000.
5 European Commission (2000) *Information Society Technologies: Case Studies of the Information Society and Sustainable Development,* IST, May 2000.
6 European Commission (2003) *ISTAG in FP6: Working Group 1 Final Report,* 16 September 2003.
7 K. Kelly (1998) *New Rules for the New Economy: 10 Ways the Network Economy is Changing Everything.* UK: Fourth Estate.
8 L. Kreitzman (1999) *The 24 Hour Society.* London: Profile Books.

9 W. J. Mitchell (1999) *E-topia: "urban life, Jim – but not as we know it".* Cambridge, Massachusetts: MIT Press.

10 F. Radermacher (1997) Building the information society: labor pressures, globalization, and political goals of sustainability as "Challenges to the Regions in Europe". Paper submitted to the conference *Regions in Touch with Tomorrow,* Tübingen, 20 February.

11 D. Rosenberg et al. (2001) *The Initial Unified Framework (D4),* SANE internal deliverable document.

12 J. Rosenoer, D. Armstrong, and R. Gates (1999) *The Clickable Corporation,* USA: Free Press.

13 J. Van Meel (1996) Workplace design: global or tribal? Address given to *Workplace Forum Conference* I, London, 9–21 June.

14 K. Williams, E. Burton and M. Jenks (2000) *Achieving Sustainable Urban Form.* London & New York: E & FN Spon.

CHAPTER 9

1 J. Myerson and P. Ross (2004) *The 21st Century Office.* London: Laurence King.

CHAPTER 11

1 F. Duffy, A. Laing and V. Crisp (1993) *The Responsible Workplace.* Butterworth Heinemann.

2 F. Duffy (1992) *The Changing Workplace.* Phaidon.

3 A. Harrison, P. Wheeler and C. Whitehead (2004) *The Distributed Workplace.* Spon Press.

CHAPTER 15

1 F. Duffy and J. Tanis (1993) *A Vision of the New Workplace,* Site Selection and Industrial Development, April 1993.

2 P. Drucker (1969) *The Age of Discontinuity.* New York: Harper and Row.

3 K. Kelly (1997) New Rules for the New Economy, twelve dependable principles for thriving in a turbulent world. *Wired,* Issue 5.09, September 1997.

4 A. Laing, F. Duffy, D. Jaunzens and S. Willis (1998) *New Environments for Working,* E&FN Spon.

5 J. Schumpeter (1975) *Capitalism, Socialism and Democracy.* New York: Harper (first published 1942).

6 F. Duffy and J. Tanis (1999) A vision of the new workplace revisited. *Site Selection Magazine,* September 1999.

7 DEGW, Ove Arup (London), RHUL (London), Telenor (Oslo), IAT (Stuttgart), Institut CERDA (Barcelona) and FAW (Ulm) (2002), *Sustainable Accommodation for the New Economy* IST-2000-25257, European Commission, Brussels.

8 A. M. Laing (2003) Re-thinking corporate real estate after September 11th. *Journal of Corporate Real estate* 5(4): 273–292.

9 Tall Buildings, The Museum of Modern Art (2004) *Preface by Terence Riley.* New York: Department of Publications, The Museum of Modern Art.

10 J. V. Lovine (2004) Building a bad reputation. *New York Times,* 8 August 2004.

11 F. Duffy, A. Laing and V. Crisp (1993) *The Responsible Workplace,* Oxford, England: Butterworth Architecture.

12 F. Duffy (1997) *The New Office,* london, England: Conran Octopus.

INDEX